Images of Desire

Images of Desire

Finding Your Natural Sensual Self
in Today's Image-Filled Society

JAQUELINE LAPA SUSSMAN

A Tom Doherty Associates Book
New York

The imaging exercises in this book were developed by Dr. Akhter Ahsen and are the
result of his work and research which spans most of the last half of the twentieth century.
The images were edited from their original versions for linguistic reasons, to meet the
needs of the present audience. The final instructions were developed in consultation with
Dr. Ahsen and meet with his approval in their present form. This also acknowledges
that Dr. Ahsen holds the copyright for the instructions and that he has extended
his kind permission to reproduce them here.

IMAGES OF DESIRE

This book is printed on acid-free paper.

A Forge Book
Published by Tom Doherty Associates, LLC
175 Fifth Avenue
New York, NY 10010

www.tor.com

Forge® is a registered trademark of Tom Doherty Associates, LLC.

Design by Jane Adele Regina

Library of Congress Cataloging-in-Publication Data

Sussman, Jacqueline Lapa.
    Images of desire : finding your natural sensual self in today's image-filled society /
Jacqueline Lapa Sussman.—1st ed.
        p. cm.
    "A Tom Doherty Associates book."
    ISBN 0-312-86911-8 (alk. paper)
    1. Sensuality. 2. Sensuality—Problems exercises, etc. 3. Eidetic imagery. I. Title.

BF575.S42 S87 2001
155.3'1—dc21

2001023182

First Edition: May 2001

Printed in the United States of America

0 9 8 7 6 5 4 3 2 1

I dedicate this book to the memory of my parents.

To Henry Lapa from Pilica, Poland. Who, when I was eleven years old, looked at me and said out of the blue, "One day you will write a book."

Whether he was peeking into my future destiny, or whether I actualized his words will always remain a mystery. This book is dedicated to the memory of a deep soul, my father, who taught me to have visions and pursue them.

To the memory of my mother, Lila Goldblum Lapa, from Kielce, Poland. Who one day looked at me when I was a teen and said, "I see you counseling people." Her prophecy also came true. This book is dedicated to the memory of a deeply courageous and passionate woman who gave me the strength to persevere and the idealism to help others.

And remembering the invocation of Odysseus, this book is especially dedicated to the memory of all the ancestors of humanity. May this work serve as a monument to all of you. It is a testament to your suffering and to the profound rising up of the human spirit. Your lives eternally run in the blood that is in me.

Contents

Acknowledgments

First and foremost I am most indebted to Dr. Akhter Ahsen, my close friend and mentor, for teaching me all I know about Eidetic Imagery and its complexities, for his encouragement on the book and for being a profound illuminator and inspiration in my life. I have been most blessed to have a friend such as he.

To my family
This book would not be possible without the help of my husband, Richard Sussman, who has been a constant support in the expression of my life purpose. He offered himself as a wise sounding board which helped expand my thinking, as well as a willing partner, taking care of the details of daily life so I could focus on the book.

Gratitude is due to my son, Zachary Sussman, for his excellent feedback on many sections of the book. But most of all for his often quiet, but palpably felt pride as I diligently worked. The depth of his belief that I should follow my passion has been immensely inspiring.

Loving thanks to my daughter, Lila Sussman, for her shining spirit which often brought joy and respite from overly concentrated working days. I am most grateful for all the help she gave me serving as my advisor for the chapter on teenage life. Her abundant light continuously enlivened my spirits.

To the wonderful people at Forge
I want to thank Linda Quinton for believing in what I have and for partaking in the quest to share it with the world.

I am indebted to my editor, Bob Gleason, for his immediate grasp of the potential of eidetic imagery for the lay public and for formulating the concept that made this book a reality.

Two people I especially want to thank are Jennifer Marcus in publicity for her enthusiasm and commitment in promoting this book and Brian Callaghan for his thorough editorial assistance.

To those who helped make this book a reality

Deep appreciation is due to my agent, Carol McCleary, who on our first meeting immediately shared my vision and joined me in a passionate and dogged pursuit to see this book come out. I am most appreciative for her relentless spirit and loving friendship.

Much gratitude is due to Junius Podrug for his help and assistance in recognizing the depth, scope and complexity of the work and in helping to translate it in simple terms so that it can be applied for use by all.

Hilda Podrug has been most gracious in transcribing hours of taped material, for opening her home and offering great hospitality and fabulous meals during work meetings.

I remain most appreciative for the support of those who generously came forward and helped me by reading sections of the manuscript, by giving me honest feedback, by sharing their expertise and experiences, and for feeding my spirit in innumerable ways. I thank you all for your nurturing, time, and love:

Nancy Bent, Robert Blasetti, Fran Brody, Frank Don, Leslie Dagnall, Howard Finkelson, Stephen Garretson, Jody Robertson Garretson, Dave Gecinces, Bob Griswold, Donna Hoffman, Judy Hockman, Barry Katz, Susan Katz, Mark Lazar, Ann Monastra, Chris McDonald, Toni Nixon, Terry Twigg, Jean Satti, Jane Slimovich, Warren Steinberg, and Veronica Willson.

A Return to *Natural* Sensuality

Sensuality is the inner warmth that radiates from some people and makes them objects of desire. Sensuality is not the sex appeal generated by the contemporary social icons of a "hot body." That is a short-term, artificial, outer image. Sensuality is a deeper, longer lasting, and richer essence that appeals to the opposite sex, a warm spirit that we carry within.

A sensuous person is a warm soul. This warm appeal is in all of us at birth, but many of us have lost it because of the layers of false images that have been instilled in us by society.

People are sensual when they feel sensual. What we feel *inside* is radiated to the world. But too many of us are sending the wrong signals because we have been brainwashed with false images of sensuality, images that have smothered our natural sexuality.

We entered this world warm, naked, and sensuous, unashamed and unencumbered by hang-ups. From that time on, our natural sensuality was altered by our parents, peers, and misdirected influences from our culture. Because we have fallen from grace from our own original sensual spirit, we carry subliminal attitudes and body language that turn off—rather than *on*—people we are attracted to. And yet it is still there, our God-given, natural capacity for pleasure in our physical body and mind.

Many men grow up to believe that a woman's sexual appeal is somehow wrapped up in the contours of her body. I have heard women in their twenties rate a man's sexiness in the same way. These individuals are out of touch with their own sensuality.

We are a civilization of people hungry for sensual love while drowning in an ocean of sexual frenzy. Never before have so many women and men been so sexually fixated and emotionally unfulfilled. What was once a good-night kiss is now expected to go much further than that, yet we are emotionally starved while being sexually saturated. The sex being marketed to us by every medium has a pornographic quality. It conflicts with the true nature of our sensuality.

Men and women have had their natural sensuality smothered by false images. Sensuality isn't a brand of perfume, silicone in breasts, penile implants, or bathing suits that let it all hang out. It's not something you pump up at the gym or buy at the lingerie counter.

Nor does beauty equate with sensuality. Physical attractiveness and sensuality are not the same, but our society has put such an emphasis on superficial outer beauty and sex has been so commercialized—and impersonalized—that most of us have been dulled emotionally. We may vary in physical appearance—few of us are the stuff of magazine covers. It's not a question of how good-looking we are; the world is full of people who have happy, passionate, sensuous sex lives but couldn't get through the door to a beauty contest.

But that natural, sensual warmth we were born with is still within us, ready to be drawn to the surface to be rediscovered and used.

People who are not sensuous have lost touch with the sensuality they were born with. It became tarnished as their sexuality was shaped by their parents and society. Few of us are aware that we are carrying this supression that causes us to feel inadequate or to freeze up, sending the wrong signals rather than expressing our honest passion.

We can reclaim our original nature through *eidetic imaging*, the science of emotions that is on the cutting edge of psychology. The process treats the brain like a computer. The brain stores and processes information in the form of "images" that commonly run through our minds like film clips. With imaging techniques, we are able to replace negative images (the baggage we carry) with positive ones that permit us to glow with our natural sensuality. The first step to reclaiming our natural sensuality lies in our desires, and imaging can help us discover them.

What are your desires? Are you looking for a permanent, loving relationship? Are you in a relationship that needs to have passion infused back into it? Do you want to make yourself more desirable? Become a better lover? Or do you want to experience the divine, the spiritual aspect of sex that most of us never achieve?

Some people just want to be ravished. Some want to be savored, their body caressed by sensitive, knowing hands. Some want a deep experience of spiritual merging with another.

What are you looking for?

Take a moment. Imagine that you are with your ideal lover. Let the scene play out in your mind like a movie.

What are you doing to each other? How do you feel?

In this image of desire, there is a key, a clue, to what you are looking for about yourself and your sensuality. But you will not find the answer to your quest, your desires, in fantasy. Fantasizing doesn't bring about the necessary insight that you need to understand why you can't achieve your desires and what you can do to obtain them.

The key to change, to achieving our desires, is found internally, in our minds, and in a form that is similar to the fantasy lover we just imagined. These images are "film clips" in our minds, but they are not scenes we invent. Instead, they are part of our memory bank.

Let's assume you want a loving relationship with someone but have not been able to achieve it. Rather than imagining a fantasy that won't help you achieve your desires, you can access your memory bank and see in your mind's eye an actual scene in which you spoke to the person. The actual scene, a visual film clip from your memory bank, is called an *eidetic image*. All of your interactions with other people and situations are filed away in the memory bank of your mind. Just as we scan a computer disk to bring up information we've registered, we are able to call forth our actual experiences from our memory and examine them. From that examination, we gain insights and new perceptions about ourselves and other people. Once we understand who we are and how our present sensuality was formed, we can make changes.

Let's do an eidetic image so you can see how simple the process is. Relax for a moment in a quiet spot. Now, keeping your eyes open or closed (obviously, you will need to open them to read these instructions), see your parents standing before you in your mind's eye.

Examine the image for a moment. Who is on the left and who is on the right side as you look at them?

Now see whether you get a feeling of personal warmth from your parents' bodies. Whose body gives you a better feeling of personal warmth? What kind of feeling does the other parent's body give?

Concentrate on your mother's body. How do you feel? Now concentrate on your father's body. How do you feel?

Images of our parents are prime images imprinted in our minds. For most people, the image of their mother has been imprinted on the right side and their father on the left.

The fact that your parents had a certain body temperature in your images of them, and a position (left or right), has significance in terms of your connection to them and to your own connectiveness to the world and your personal life force. No matter how old we are, no matter how long we have been away from them, we tend to unconsciously emulate our parents—or to react in the opposite way. As we get more involved in imaging and practice, we will discover that things as simple as the body temperature of our parents and their position in our mind's eye have influenced how we deal with the world.

We will probe ourselves and our relationship with our lovers (by *lover*, I mean spouse, significant other, or someone we desire but haven't yet connected with). We will examine how our parents, culture, and other factors shaped our sexuality. In doing these and dozens of other images, you will gain enormous insight into your own sensuality and the sensuality of those you desire.

We will know our full potential only after we peel off those negative images that get in our way.

Unfortunately, even if you had the nicest parents and most comfortable circumstances, you will have to unearth and resuscitate the marvelous person who is you, the person you were at birth before layers of fear and self-doubt coated you or left you at war with your emotions. To be the best you can, you need to rediscover yourself.

Sometimes the negative images seem subtle or too simplistic.

Let me give some examples from my own life.

When I was about four, my girlfriend and I were playing "doctor" with a friend named Tommy. Checking his body, we discovered something different, and we found it interesting because we didn't have one. So we decided to put toothpaste, the "medicine" we were using, on Tommy's special part. He was lying naked, and we were rubbing toothpaste on him when my mother came in and yelled, "What are you doing? Shame on you!"

That was the first time I felt shame about sexuality. Most of us experienced some sort of embarrassment during our sexual innocence. Usually it was triggered by a minor incident, but the parental attitude that caused the embarrassment is more subtly (and sometimes savagely) hammered into us for the first two decades of our lives. Later on, these "minor" incidents become land mines that explode in our inner mind when we deal with another person in a sexual way.

The second shame I felt was when I was five. My girlfriend Sylvia, who was a little older, had somehow watched her parents have sex, and she showed me a sexual position, simulating their movements. Of course, at that age I didn't understand what sex was. That night, when my father was putting me to bed, I said, "Look what Sylvia showed me," and rocked back and forth with my hips. I looked up at my father's face and saw shock and shame. I felt ashamed of myself, but did not know why.

That I can remember these "minor" incidents is an indication of how strongly they affected me.

Sometimes the emotional scarring is not that subtle. A woman in her thirties who consulted me was very uptight and controlled during lovemaking. She couldn't relax and was losing her lover because of it. Through imaging, she unraveled layers of her past, including many "minor" sexual incidents. She also realized the effect of a very major one.

As a girl, she was very confused about sexuality. Her parents were strict churchgoers, and she attended a religious school where girls got the impression that any sort of sexual contact was sinful. And yet she knew her parents hid pornographic magazines in their bedroom closet.

One morning, she masturbated before going to church, and so she went to Holy Communion feeling unbelievably guilty. She knew she had committed some kind of sin. She didn't know if it was a mortal sin, but she knew it was bad, that her purity was tainted, and that she didn't deserve a relationship with God.

Over twenty years later, those images of "tainted purity" were still controlling her sex life and smothering her sensuality.

THE *UN*SENSUOUS WOMAN AND MAN

During lunch in a restaurant with two associates, we quietly observed other diners.

At one table sat Ms. X, who appeared to be in her late thirties. She was well groomed in a midnight-blue business suit, and her hair had a fashionable blown-wet look. Her makeup and jewelry (a single strand of pearls) were in good taste. She wasn't the stuff of magazine covers, but she was stylish. She wore neither a wedding band nor a diamond ring, so we assumed she was single or divorced.

Ms. X struck all three of us as a woman who wouldn't have a problem attracting a man—but who probably would have a problem establishing an ongoing, romantic, fulfilling relationship. Even though she was outwardly attractive, there was a hollowness about her. She lacked sensual appeal. As we talked further about women who have "it," we acknowledged that they exude a sense of inner mystery that Ms. X did not have.

Women hold the mystery of all life. Within a woman, life springs forth, develops, grows, and emerges fully formed. The secret of this mystery is that she contains knowledge of both the masculine and feminine within her womb. Within its shape is an opening or space formed exactly in the configuration of his phallus. Thus, she contains the All, the totality of all life, by having both the male and female structures, physical and psychological, within her. She is whole and already unified. Males can only experience this wholeness by coming into her. He has knowledge of only the masculine, of himself. By coming into her, only then can he know both sides of creation and complete himself. This is the secret of her allure. This is why men desire to come home to her . . . to experience the totality of life through sexual union with her. For this reason women are held in glory and pursued to the ends of the earth. This is the secret of her power, her beauty and of her magnetic draw.

The most attractive woman is one who values and loves life first. She conveys a feeling that she has everything in her. She feels desirable. The man sees in her eyes that she "has it." When she sees in his eyes that he is attracted to her, then she gets turned on to him. She is the source of the attraction.

Women who know this are the most sensually attractive. They instinctively know their value first, and then they value the man. If they think the man is more desirable than themselves, they lose their appeal. Women have it. Most cartoons and love stories have the man chasing the woman because she is the one with the desired sensual mystery. And the secret is that she has knowledge psychically deep inside, of both her and him.

Women who are comfortable with their role as the physical and spiritual home for a man's sensuality are warm and lush within, and this warmth radiates from them. They have a knowing confidence. And men instinctively pick up on the mysterious aura around these sensuous women.

Women who are ill at ease with being home for a man's emotionality are not in harmony with their feminine sensuality. They may *think* that they are hot stuff. They may *think* that every man they meet wants to bed them—and they might be right. Many of these women have fabulous bodies, and some appear frequently on the covers of fashion magazines.

But even if they attract men, either they can't keep them or they don't want the type of man they attract. They have cold sex lives, not because they were born empty of sensuality, but because their natural feminine essence has been dispelled by life's negative events.

The male is designed by nature to unify and bond with the female physically, emotionally, and spiritually. The sexual organs—the vagina and the penis—are made for each other, but they are merely vehicles given to us to make the connection to each other's spirit. A man wants to go "home" because he wants to join with a woman and find ultimate peace and joy within himself, and he does this by resting in her.

By nature, a man is always looking to bond spiritually with a woman. And a woman is designed to be known by a man.

When a woman feels comfortable about her sensuality, she is comfortable being "home" for the male part. Because it is how nature meant her to be, a woman filled by the male essence finds the experience deeply pleasurable and satisfying. She knows that her lover is the vehicle that will take them both to the gods. A woman who enjoys being home for a man, by his presence, knows the mystery of her femininity, that she is the temple at which a man comes to worship.

What made it obvious from watching Ms. X that she would not be comfortable being "home" for a man? Sensuality is by definition a matter of the senses, and the aura surrounding her was not one that appeared inviting. She would have had this almost subliminal coolness even if we had seen her wearing a bikini on a beach in Tahiti.

We're not psychic, but we have treated so many women like Ms. X that we could draw some generalities about her that would not be too far from the mark. Watching her, her body language and her mannerisms, and hearing her voice, it struck us that despite her pleasant appearance, she was not a woman who knew how to unite spiritually with a male. She was not a warm soul or a warm bedmate, because she lacked the radiance with which women who are in tune with their sensuality glow. This woman was outwardly attractive but inwardly empty.

"My mother was slightly obese," my male associate confided, "yet she radiated a sexual warmth that attracted my father, who was a slender, well-built man. Her weight increased after my father died, but men were still attracted to her."

Ms. X was not glowing confidently because she seemed too tense and controlled rather than at ease with her spirit and body. Appearances are very important, but all the beauty money can buy won't get us true love. No matter how much a woman thinks she is comfortable about sex and her relationship with men, obvious and subliminal signals coming from her can eventually turn off most men.

Looking at Ms. X, I felt empathy for her. She was a victim of her upbringing and of society, yet *she had no clue*. Somewhere along the line, she was programmed not to expose her true heart, not to know her essence in dealing with men, but she had no idea that it had happened.

I felt that somewhere deep inside her must be frustration, anger, and even fear. Her surface persona was one of confidence, but internally she had an intuitive knowledge that something was wrong.

From working with thousands of people with intimacy issues, I could see by observing Ms. X that she seemed to have a fear of being overpowered, dominated, and controlled by a man. She reacts by being uptight and rigid rather than by expressing that confidence and inner fullness with which nature had equipped her. She *thinks* she has power in dealing with men; she probably has made more than one man jump through a hoop. But she doesn't understand that while she has the right "package" of clothes and looks, the way she uses her feminine energy ultimately turns men away.

Within her are layers of false sexuality, which smother her own innate knowing. She is a victim of the wrong messages, often subliminal, that parents send us, and on top of that of the false images of superficial sensuality that magazines and TV bombard us with. Perhaps her father was very controlling and she saw her mother dominated, or maybe her mother had inhibitions about men that she subtly passed on. Or perhaps a deep fear of sexuality came from strict shame-inducing and misdirected religious training.

Whatever the reason, Ms. X was not in touch with her own true sensuality. The fact that it is not her fault, and that she isn't even aware of it, doesn't make her pain any less. If she were to probe the images that form the basis of her present sexual attitudes, she would find that something from her upbringing has restricted her natural sexuality. And it probably not only affects her sex life, but permeates other areas of her social interaction as well.

There is a direct correlation between sexual coldness or warmth and a person's emotional disposition toward life. God and nature did not design us to be cool sexually. We are designed physically and emotionally to reach sexual highs that no drug can take us to. So when our sexual energy is being obstructed, it will usually reflect itself in other areas of our life.

A man we covertly observed in the restaurant—a slightly overweight guy with a diminishing hairline—was different. Mr. Y emanated an inviting sexual warmth. He was an example of the type of attractiveness that doesn't stem from physical appearance. He was taller than average, but he was no hunk. In fact, he had love handles, and he probably hadn't been in a gym since high school twenty years before. His companion was a well-proportioned and very attractive female. And she was enthralled by Mr. Y's every word.

While a woman coming into contact with him might not realize why she was attracted, a woman can instinctively sense that Mr. Y is a man who enjoys women—touching them, caressing them, making love to them, admiring them. Women pick up on that subconsciously, and it's a sure turn-on for them. What women feel about Mr. Y is that he is comfortable with his masculinity, comfortable with himself to the point that he can relax and truly enjoy a woman. He has nothing to prove. Sex isn't a game of conquest for him, but he savors women the way some people savor fine wines. He will celebrate a woman, will love her, will love her body, her hair, her skin.

The fact that Mr. Y couldn't win a male bathing-suit contest is not a turn-off because he oozes a warm sensuality to which women are attracted. There was an energy about him that told the woman sitting next to him that he would be comfortable coming "home" to her.

Men who are sensuous also have an inner spiritual warmth that radiates from them. The sensuous man is comfortable uniting physically and spiritually with a woman. Too many men have treated sex as part of their ego—a trophy to possess—and they act like their fast car or big bank account is an extension of their physical maleness.

We realized that Ms. X and Mr. Y reflect much of what is going on in our society. The man was in touch with his sensuality, and the woman, despite her more polished appearance, was not.

Ms. X is a victim of life's forces—parents, religion, peers, and society in general—who altered her natural knowledge of sensuality with layers of irksome baggage. She, like so many of us, ended up with a variety of unnatural mental and emotional states. Some people are promiscuous; others are frigid; more of us simply give off the wrong signals. Few people unable to establish a permanent, loving relationship realize that the problem is in themselves—and not in someone else.

The natural state of sensuality that we are born with is still there. It is just hidden under negative layers that are placed on us by parents and society.

I know few women whose introduction to womanhood—the problematic advent of their menstrual period and the development of breasts—was not without negative impact. Conversely, few men reach manhood without being falsely conditioned about "acting like a man," with all of the repression that involves.

The purpose of *Images of Desire* is to get you back to that natural, sensual state within you. It is a book for people who want to change. To change, you have take an inner journey and unlock your sensuous spirit. We will take a closer look at what sensuality is and why we are—or aren't—sensuous; how "sexy" differs from "sensuous" and how sex differs from romance. We will look at the reasons romance and sensuality are affected by modern living: the primordial roots of our sensuality, how our history has tarnished it, how to improve our sensuality, how to assess our lover's sensuality. We will also cover a number of areas of specific interest, from having a permanent loving relationship to having an affair, from mercy sex to teen sex, to the form sexuality takes as men and women grow older and women enter menopause.

In a sense, we will be making a journey, an inner one, not to foreign lands but back to our natural self. The journey will be made through the process of imaging.

While the concept of imaging may be new to you, eidetic imaging techniques are as old as the ancient Greeks and as fresh as psychology in the third millennium.

Just as many of the great movements of the science of psychology are identified with specific people (Sigmund Freud, Alfred Adler, Carl Jung, B. F. Skinner, and others), the pioneering work in imaging in the last half-century has been associated with the name of Dr. Akhter Ahsen. Today, as a result of Dr. Ahsen's seminal studies, the practitioners of imaging are associated with many of the great universities, including Harvard, Oxford, Stanford, Yale, and institutions around the world. In my own work with imaging, I have been privileged to be associated with Dr. Ahsen.

With imaging sessions, we will literally peel back layer after layer of negative aspects about ourselves and our sensuality. We will unload the baggage that has been placed upon us since birth, those negative aspects that keep us from being the warm and luscious person we want to be, and return to our natural sensuality.

2

The Looking Glass of the Mind

Seeing the Naked Truth about Our Sex Lives

To properly assess our sensuality and our love lives, we need to uncover layers of our history. But before we go back to our beginnings, I want to show you how easy and effective eidetic imaging is. This short exercise, using another person as an example and then imaging your own love life, will teach you some basic and effective imaging techniques that can be used to gain insight into any number of situations.

The techniques let you take a good look at someone—spouse, lover, a person you are attracted to—and find out what makes that person tick. The images are wonderful for learning how to approach a person you are afraid will reject you—or about whom you wonder. They let you "check the person out."

Surprisingly, while the techniques permit you to go very deeply into yourself, peeling away those layers of history, they also let you look at yourself through the eyes of this special other person to *see what he or she thinks about you.*

All of us wonder about our sensuality. How attractive are we to other people? To find out, we need to know how others see us. But how can we see someone in our own mind's eye and gain insight not only into them but into ourselves?

Let's say you're interested in dating someone at work. Can you probe yourself and discover more about the person, even to the point of gaining insight into what he or she thinks about you? One of the wonders of imaging is that this can be done as easily as assessing yourself.

It's not difficult. By seeing the image in your mind, and moving in close to it and examining and reexamining it, you can uncover tremendous information about the person that you never realized before. As will be explained, your mind not only registers the most minute details abut the person, but it also imprints the person's attitude toward you. By probing the image, you will be able to find out what the person thinks about you.

The image of the person we love or have strong feelings for is an emotionally charged, prime image. It's also a reflection of the person's own emotions, perceptions we have registered mentally but have never before analyzed with an imaging tool.

When we relax and concentrate on using an imaging tool, will see a composite of our feelings *and* the person's feelings toward us. (In this case, we will use images called "Walk-Around," "Story in the Eyes," and "Co-Consciousness.")

What these images do is break the narrow or fixed perception we have of a person. When we see a person from only one angle, when we have conceptions about a person early on that are engraved in stone in our minds, we tend to fix on only those attributes. But as we noted, our mind's eye takes in much more detail than we keep stored in our conscious mind. To really look at a person, to see him or her from all angles, we need to retrieve information from our memory bank. We do this by concentrating on an image of the person, viewing it from different perspectives, with the goal of seeing the many details we regularly miss.

From these nuggets of information, we are able to gain new insights and perceptions about the person and our relationship.

WALK-AROUND IMAGE

Walk-Around involves taking a close look at a person you want to know more about, and then going closer and closer, deeper and deeper. The technique is used to gain insight about the individual. By imaging the person, you expand your awareness about the person's motives, fears, and emotions.

By seeing your lover, spouse, etc., in your mind's eye, and then slowly walking around his or her image, you see all the subtleties that you miss in dealing with the person in the flesh.

You begin by seeing in your mind's eye a person about whom you want to gain insight. Since we are dealing with sensuality, let's direct our attention to a spouse, a lover, or someone we want to date. If you are having a stormy relationship with someone, or can't seem to click with a person you'd like to click with, this image will be a terrific source of insight for you.

Before we get into actual imaging, let's look at the example of a woman who is having trouble with her lover. Taking a quick look at how she handles the problem will give you practice with doing the images.

Lori, a 35-year-old divorced schoolteacher, wants to have a permanent relationship with her boyfriend, George, a basketball coach at her school. They have been going together for five months. Lori wants marriage and all its accoutrements, but she can't get him to make a commitment. He has been acting more and more aloof and evasive when she brings up the issue of their "future."

Lori is much like Ms. X. She gets guys because she is relatively attractive, but she isn't able to keep them. Her relationships with men follow a set formula: they date for a while, start having sex, go out for a few months, and then when Lori starts asking for a commitment, the man moves on.

Obviously, something is wrong. Lori can't put her finger on it; in her own mind, the problem is with the men she dates. She may be partly right, but even so, the fact that she consistently dates men who do not want to get involved with her raises questions—about her. George has been married once before, and Lori attributes his reluctance to marry again to being gun-shy.

She believes she knows the man. She has been out with him numerous times, been to bed with him many times, has seen him dressed and naked from all angles. But like most people dealing with significant others, Lori tends to have tunnel vision, seeing George in a narrow frame that is tainted with a lot of wishful feelings on her part.

Lori needs to step back and look at the situation—and herself—from all angles. She doesn't need any more background information about George or the situation than she currently has. She has interacted with him and stored in her brain all of the nuances, the hints and subtleties, the almost imperceptible body language.

When I was in Florence, I went to the Galleria dell'Academia museum that houses Michelangelo's masterpiece, David. The statue is in the center of a gallery so that one can walk around it, taking in every nuance. As I circled the tall, handsome figure, more and more detail came alive for me. The marble statue was a symphony of life and form that resonated with sensuality.

The process of walking around a work of art, examining it for all its wonder—and flaws—is the same process that Lori will use. She will start with the Walk-Around image that permits her to draw fresh insights about George by viewing him from several angles. We will take Lori through the image first, and then provide the instructions for you to use the image.

Lori begins by relaxing in a quiet place and seeing in her mind's eye an image of her boyfriend. The mental picture she sees of George is lifelike, three-dimensional. It is a prime image, an eidetic image—that is, it is a composite of everything she has ever learned consciously and sub-consciously about him: his attitudes, feeling states, sensitivities, vulner-abilities, strengths, weaknesses, prides, and prejudices.

Lori wants to figure out how to get George to marry her, and that question can only be answered by looking at George's whole being. She begins by looking at the image of George from the front. She sees a warm, jovial, friendly guy, the kind kids and other teachers fondly call "Coach." He's easygoing, but can be a little explosive in the heat of a game; when he's out on the court with the girls' basketball team, you'd think that millions rode on a high-school game. But around Lori, he is much more relaxed; he likes a beer, going to the movies, hanging out and watching games on TV, and having sex.

She sees his easygoing grin and friendly countenance, but in looking at the image more closely, she also notices worry lines on his forehead. She moves around the image, now seeing George from the left side. His chest is puffed up; he's a macho guy, a guy who likes to think he can handle anything. But on this side she senses something about him that she never noticed before. There's a little bravado about him, a little pos-turing, as if he has an Achilles heel that he keeps well hidden. She still gets the sense that he believes he can handle anything, but deep down he is not as sure of himself as he pretends to be.

Moving around to his back, she examines his neck and shoulders. He has an athletic neck, full and muscular—an aggressive neck; he's the kind of guy who is a little pushy and goes for what he wants. It's a very mas-culine attribute and one that she likes; his assertiveness turns her on.

Now Lori moves around to his right side. She sees his chin sticking out a little, thrust forward like he's ready for an argument, but she also senses that underneath is sweetness and tenderness. She can see that he is genuinely caring toward the teens he teaches.

Before you probe and walk around someone in your own life, I want to show you two other imaging techniques that go hand-in-hand with the Walk-Around Image. They're called the Story in the Eyes and Co-Consciousness.

STORY IN THE EYES

Our eyes are a silent organ of communication. They are truly the win-dows to the soul, not just for poets, but for those of us who want to find out more about a special person in our life.

Of the whole person, the eyes communicate the most. Yet they are the hardest to hide your thoughts behind. You can mask anger or annoyance behind a grin, but your eyes are expressive liquid pools that reveal more than we often want to reveal. Intuitively, we look at a person's eyes to see whether or not they like us. Some studies have shown that when we look at someone we don't like, our pupils contract, subtly exposing our feelings even if we control our facial muscles. But when we like the person, our eyes dilate. Perhaps this is what happens when someone says a child is the "apple of my eye," or when a character in a book says, "My eyes lit up when I saw him." A friend of mine swears that Middle Eastern rug dealers can tell which rug you prefer by watching your eyes, because the eyes dilate most when you look at the rug you like the best. When lovers who have been apart are reunited, without being conscious of it, their eyes dilate because they are happy to see each other.

Because the eyes are windows to our emotions and thoughts, by looking at a person's eyes we can gain information about how the person feels about life.

As mentioned, eye maneuvers (dilating, contracting) are so subtle that we don't realize consciously that they have occurred. *But we saw the movement* (even though we didn't pick up on it at the time) and registered it in our brain, and now we can go back and examine the eyes for those subtleties that have been communicated but never thought about.

Coming back around to the front of George, Lori looks into his eyes in the image. The feeling she gets is that George is attracted to her. But there is something missing, and she feels that he's being evasive, almost as if George doesn't want to look her straight in the eye. She asks the image a silent question: why won't you marry me? And the eyes go blank on her.

Frustrated, she knows he won't commit. She now needs to examine the image further to see why he rolls over and plays dead when she asks for a commitment.

CO-CONSCIOUSNESS

Lori has stood in her own shoes and thought about George. Now she is going to stand in George's shoes and see what George thinks about her.

"Co-Consciousness" is a technique for seeing how another person perceives us. Lori has stored in her own mind all the information she needs to find out what George really thinks of her, all of the subtleties—that squirm she didn't notice when she mentioned a forbidden subject; the eyelash that got batted when she asked for something; all the loving, angry, boring, pleasant, and unpleasant reactions that were revealed by his body language and inflections in his voice, but that she wasn't consciously aware of when they were together.

Lori again sees an image of George, and this time he is looking at her. Moving in closer to the image, she steps into his body and looks back at herself.

Looking at herself through George's eyes, she studies her image.

She sees a woman who is standing rigid and motionless. The image is rigid yet fragile, as if it could break easily. And she sees something else, something revealed by her own eyes: desperation.

She is shocked, crushed. She can't believe that George would think of her as desperate. Or that she could be coming across to someone as desperate. She sees a woman who has had many relationships, who has been able to attract men, yet who puts out an aura of being desperate for love and marriage.

Devastated, Lori calls a former boyfriend and asks him what he thought of her. He tells her truthfully that he was never completely comfortable around her, that he felt he was always walking on eggshells, because rather than relaxing and enjoying the relationship, she was demanding more and more from it.

She realizes that George is never completely relaxed around her either, that he appears to be as he drinks a beer and watches his games, but that she is frequently hovering, wanting attention. When they go out to dinner, she is never totally happy about the restaurant, the food, the service, or the ambience.

She isn't taking into consideration George's need not to be hassled. He wants to be with her, but he stops short of a full commitment because he is not 100 percent comfortable with her.

What Lori learns from the imaging is confirmation that George has his own problems and is hesitant about marriage. But more importantly, she now has insight into the fact that *she is also the problem*, that she is turning off men without even realizing it.

The insight into herself ends the cycle of frustration and despair she has felt. She decides that she is going to take charge of her life and not be desperate or critical of men.

HOW TO WALK AROUND ANOTHER PERSON

This image will break your fixed perspectives on the person you are seeing. Often we get stuck in seeing someone in a narrow way, which limits how we interact with them. For example, we may think a person is aloof. However, by seeing all sides of them, we suddenly discover that they are shy and that is why they seem distant. In changing how we perceive them, it frees us to interact with them with clarity.

The Walk-Around Image is so important that I will lead you through the image step-by-step, as well as provide numbered instructions so you can do it anytime you like. Each time you repeat seeing the image, you will gain more insight.

Again, as for any imaging, you may keep your eyes open or closed. You should be in a place where you can concentrate without being interrupted.

If you don't see the image clearly, don't worry. You will still get the information by focusing on it through the feelings and meanings the image brings to you.

Start by seeing in your mind's eye the person you want to gain insight about. Look at the person from the front. How does he or she appear? Notice the body language, the emotions you can read on the face, and anything else that strikes you.

How do you feel as you see the image? Let the information about the other person simply come to you.

Now move to the right side of the person, and look at the person from that side. Be aware of how the individual looks, his or her posture, the feelings you sense. What do you see? Let all of the impressions come forward. How do you feel now that you see the person from this side? Pleasant? Unpleasant? Neutral?

Now move to the back of the person, and observe him or her from that angle. Again, just let the information come, whatever it is. When you see the person from the back, how do you feel? Pleasant? Unpleasant? Neutral?

Now go to the left side. Again, how do you feel?

Go back to the front. How does the person appear? What are your feelings?

Do you have a different understanding of this person than when you started?

Throughout this box, the images are presented in numbered form for your convenience.

WALK-AROUND IMAGE

1. Relax, close your eyes if you like, and see an image of a person whom you want insight into. If the image is vague, just keep looking. The information will come in sense impressions or feelings.
2. Look at the person from the front. What do you see? Notice the body language, the emotions that you can read on the face, and anything else that strikes you. Let the information about the other person simply come to you.
3. How do you feel as you see the image?
4. Now move to the right side of the person, and look at the person again. Be aware of how the individual looks, his or her body posture, the emotions you sense. What do you see? Let all of the impressions come forward. How do you feel now that you see the person from this side? Pleasant? Unpleasant? Neutral?
5. Now move to the back of the person, and observe him or her from that angle. What do you see? Again, just let the information come, whatever it is. How do you feel as you see him or her from the back? Pleasant? Unpleasant? Neutral?
6. Now go to the left side. What do you see? How do you feel?
7. Go back to the front. What do you see? How do you feel?
8. Do you have a different understanding of this person than when you started?

Keep walking around the image until you are satisfied that you have obtained insight into the person. You can repeat this exercise over and over. Each time you do, you will add to your store of new perceptions.

HOW TO SEE THE STORY IN SOMEONE'S EYES

In the Story in the Eyes Image, you look into a person's eyes after you have walked around him or her, seeking out the clues and nuances you failed to notice in person.

The instructions use a lover as an example, but you can look for the story in anyone's eyes. The actual instructions follow.

STORY IN THE EYES IMAGE

1. Picture your lover's eyes.
2. Concentrate on the eyes.
3. Do his or her eyes give you any particular feeling or tell you any story?
4. Concentrate on the story in your lover's eyes.
5. Do you experience pleasant or unpleasant feelings as you see the feelings or story in the eyes?

Repeat the image until you are satisfied that you have learned what you can out of it.

CO-CONSCIOUSNESS: HOW DOES MY LOVER SEE ME?

Co-Consciousness is a technique used to see yourself through the eyes of someone you are having a problem with or who you just want to know better. You can gain insight and understanding about yourself and how others feel about you by standing in their shoes and looking back at yourself.

Because our mind registers the emotional states of the other person, through imaging we are able to gain insight about the person's feelings toward us.

You begin by seeing an image of yourself along with the other person.

As with all imaging, go through the instructions slowly, thinking about what you are observing.

CO-CONSCIOUSNESS IMAGE

1. Relax, close your eyes if you like, focus inward, and see an image of yourself in a situation with a person. Where are you? See yourself in the environment where you normally spend time with the person (home, school, work, etc.). What are you doing?

2. See the person. What is he or she doing? How do you feel when you see that image? Let the information unfold. The information will come forward. Don't worry whether the image is vague or vivid.

3. Notice that the person is either seeing you or is aware of you. Now see through his or her eyes—he or she is seeing you. Allow the image to unfold. Don't second-guess the information coming to you. Just look at yourself through the other person's eyes. Let it unfold like a movie. What does the person see? How does the person feel as he or she sees you? How do you feel as you see this image?

4. Now go back to your eyes. See that you are seeing the other person. What do you see? How do you feel as you see the image? (Let the images unfold as you go back and forth, in their own way, like a movie. Don't censor them.)

5. Once again, see that the person is seeing you. Once again, look through the person's eyes at yourself. What does the person see? Again, let the image unfold. How do you feel as you see this image?

6. Now go back to yourself. See the person from your eyes. Who do you see? How do you feel as you see the person?

You can keep going, reversing the process of seeing the person through your eyes, and then seeing yourself through the person's eyes. As you do this, more and more valuable information will be revealed.

3

Born Sensual

How Our Sex Lives Got Screwed Up

Now that you've seen how easy it is to image, we are going to go into our history and peel away layers of inhibitions put on us from the time we were born. This process will reveal to us the sources of our sensuality, what there is about us that turns people on or off, and where we got this trait.

When it comes to factors that mold our sensuality—parents, peers, religion, and society in general—our parents get the first and most enduring shot because they had exclusive control during our most impressionable years. And they are usually in control right up to our first love and first sexual experience. After that, they keep on pulling strings in our minds, even when we are gray and involved with our own children's problems.

No matter how much we think we developed our sexuality on our own, no matter how old we are, we are affected by our parents' sexual attitudes and mores.

We are not only affected by our relationship with each of our parents, but by their relationship with each other. Our parents' attitudes about their own sexuality—whether they were comfortable or uncomfortable about it, had strong sexual inhibitions or lacked them, were frightened by their parents' sexual attitudes or locked in their own fears—all come to roost with us.

Our ideas about sexuality are initially formed by what our parents expressly teach us and by what we unconsciously see about their relationship. Some things we accept; others we react against. Our peers at school come along and teach us new things, and we are influenced by radio and TV. But one way or another, we leave our parents' house with our sexual attitudes already shaped.

We don't consciously realize it, but all of us, even those of us who expressly rebelled against our parents' sexual attitudes, have deeply ingrained, knee-jerk reactions that explode in our heads like land mines when we get involved romantically. We don't realize that our parents and some misguided religious leaders are sitting in our brains, pulling the strings; none of us, no matter how we acted or reacted against them, escaped their effect on our sex lives.

A middle-aged man is still haunted by a scene from his early adolescence: he was masturbating in the bathroom when his mother walked in. She didn't say anything, but the shock and embarrassment on her face not only kept him from masturbating again, but it also put a damper on his sex life throughout his adulthood. But he didn't remember the incident until he did imaging sessions. Then he realized that while this one incident was traumatic, he had other hidden layers of negativity that he had picked up from his parents and that made him uncomfortable with romance and sex. He didn't know he was uncomfortable because his own actions to him are natural, but he signaled his discomfort to the women he pursued.

It's easy to blame our parents for everything, but it really isn't a question of blame. True, some parents are religious fanatics who think sex is evil, or they have such terrible repressions on their own sexuality that they damage the lives of their children. These people are often victims themselves, and they pass along their sexual repressions like birth defects. But most parents are just nice people trying to do the best they can in a world in which sexual attitudes went topsy-turvy when the Pill became available. Can you imagine the bewilderment of 1960s parents, raised in the solid belief that "nice girls don't," realizing that their sons and daughters were having sex with partners they never intended to marry?

A now middle-aged woman recalls that, when she was a teenager in the 1960s, her older sister became pregnant out of wedlock. Her sister was afraid to tell their mother, so the younger sister had to break the news. The mother, totally unprepared to face the sexual revolution, called the *younger* sister a whore and a slut and forbade her to date! This is just one example of how alarmed people were when the Pill and the 1960s pulled the sexual rug out from under them.

An example of the subtle way parents mold sexual attitudes concerns a woman with two children, a boy and a girl. In her younger years, the woman had had a *Playboy*-quality face and figure. She used her body a great deal for sexual power over men—with a little playfulness and a little flirtation, she soon had men lusting after her. Two children and a lot of bodily changes later, she continued to dress and act in the same manner, because she didn't know any other way to express her feminine power. Her children, seeing their mother behave this way, learned to use their sexuality in conjunction with power rather than with deeply intimate connections to the opposite sex.

Do you see how subtle the conditioning can be? This woman did nothing overtly sexual, yet her tone of voice and her body language programmed her children with deeply rooted sexual attitudes that would affect them the rest of their lives. Parents who are overly sexual confuse their children, teaching them to be uncomfortable with their own sensuality and that sexuality is a power or tool to be used in improper ways.

Even just hearing stories that reflect our parents' upbringing can affect us.

My father was a warm man and my mother a warm woman. They were comfortable with their bodies, and I know they had a good sex life, but there were things in the culture they grew up in that dampened their natural sexuality, things that I would ultimately have to deal with when the attitudes got passed on to me. I remember my mother telling me that young women in Poland, when she grew up, were not promiscuous, and that a "lady" didn't do "those things" until she was married. In his youth, my father dated many women, and was considered a playboy. He played around with women, but he would never have considered marrying one who played back. You didn't have sex with the one you loved until marriage.

Sexual attitudes were at a great moral level for them—for their time and place. But an attempt to convey these attitudes to children who had to face the radical changes of the last half of the twentieth century was doomed. In essence, my folks were raised in an atmosphere where sex was "shameful," whereas their children grew up in an environment where sex was considered a more natural state of existence. Even though my parents had an active sex life and were warm and expressive to each other, their repressions were passed on to me. Before I learned how to handle them, I grew up believing sex was partly wonderful and partly shameful.

Although I was born in the United States, my parents were Polish, and they added to my cultural confusion by moving to South America. There I was exposed to the concept that anything less than being completely virginal made you a "whore."

So much happens in our society so fast that anyone over the age of ten literally lives in a different world than the one their parents were raised in. In the 1980s, sex among teenagers was prevalent. As we entered the new millennium, teenage boys barely into puberty were demanding "oral sex" from their girlfriends along with a good-night kiss.

Our parents absorbed their sexual attitudes from their parents and the culture around them, and it got passed on, generation to generation. Rather than assessing blame, it's a matter of realizing that the sexual attitudes we were raised with are probably in conflict with the culture we currently live in. While all of us who are parents dread our children's loss of innocence, trying to pass on information that won't work for them isn't doing them or us a favor.

Not that being in harmony with "pop culture" is a good thing. The vast majority of the sexual attitudes in our culture are terrible, from preteen sex to the superficial models of what's supposed to be sexy. We are not going to single-handedly change the moral principles of society, but on an individual basis we can cleanse our systems of the false notions society has placed there and awaken the natural sensuality with which we were born.

All the information we need to uncover our inherent sensuality is within us, even though that information may have been dimmed while we were growing up. To gain that information, understand it, and change to awaken the warmth of sensuality within, we will start by accessing a series of images that are stored within us.

The images in this and later chapters will deal with you; your relationship with your parents and their relationship with each other; your relationship with your spouse, lover, or person you most desire (or your lack of relationship); and the sexual signals (and turnoffs) you convey to the opposite sex in general.

PARENTS' LEFT/RIGHT POSITION IMAGE

It was mentioned earlier that most people see their mother on the right side of the image and their father on the left, and that there was an "inversion" if this is not so. We had suggested that means a problem that needs attention.

The reason most people see mother on the right is that when a baby is nursed by mother, she holds the child so that it hears her heart beating. (Yes, mothers hold babies on either side of their chest, but the primary bonding is when the child is held so that it hears the heartbeat.)

When the baby hears the heartbeat, mother is on its right side. From the mother's point of view, she is holding her baby on the left side of her chest where the heart is. More than 67% of mothers prefer holding the baby on the left side for this reason. When father approaches the nursing scene, the baby sees him coming from the left. That combination—the heartbeat, mother on right, father on left—becomes imprinted in the child's brain.

But not everyone sees their parents this way. For example, a person whose mother was strongly domineering and did not let him or her have a strong relationship with the father may have an inversion in which mother takes over the left position. This means that mother has taken over the entire mental space, and father's images are inaccessible to the person. This can also happen in reverse, if father was domineering. Or it can also occur through the absence of one parent, such as in death or divorce.

An inversion, according to Dr. Ahsen, doesn't mean you are mentally or morally defective. It's just an indication that there is something out of the ordinary about your relationship with your parents. It means that the images of one parent are not clearly available to you because the other parent was more dominant in your psyche as you were raised. The images of the lesser known parent are stored somewhere in your brain, but you have to reverse the inversion to get this information. (Shifting an inversion needs the assistance of a trained eidetic imagery counselor for technical accuracy.) Once the inversion is shifted back to the original position with mother on the right and father on the left, new perceptions become available about both parents, revealing deeper insights into their identities. For example, one man with an inversion saw his mother as extremely domineering and his father as passive. He stayed away from women fearing they would all be like his mother. However, when the inversion was shifted, he saw that his mother was full of fear and emptiness and her controlling behavior covered her insecurities. He saw her weakness for the very first time and it amazed him. The strong, tough mother that had ruled his life was really a weak and scared little girl! He saw his father as having the inner strength to endure and keep the family together in spite of his wife's problems. This shift allowed him to relax and the tension of his mother's control over him dissolved. He now felt free to get closer to a woman.

Eidetic images reveal accurate truths about our relationships with our parents and theirs to each other. If you were raised mostly by your father, or feel very distant emotionally from your mother, you may have a difficult time imaging the two together and may find that your mother is absent in the image or that her image is dimmer.

Your feeling of unity and connection with each parent is revealed by the image. Thus, your connectiveness to the world in general is revealed: not being on a solid footing with your parents can dog you for your entire life, making you feel less secure.

So, a simple image of your parents standing before you can show you information that tells you not only about them, but about you, your relationship with each of them, and their relationship with each other.

PARENTS' LEFT/RIGHT POSITION IMAGE

1. Picture your parents standing directly in front of you.
2. As you look at them, who is standing on your left and who is standing on your right?
3. Now, try to switch their positions. Are you able to switch them?
4. Notice any difficulty you experience when you switch them.
5. See your parents standing in front of you again.
6. Who is standing on the left now? Who is standing on the right?
7. Switch your parents' position again.
8. Do you experience a problem when you switch them?
9. Notice two different feelings: spontaneous and forced.
10. Notice that you have no control over your parents' spontaneous images.

As we do more images of our parents and other people prominent in our life, as more and more layers of our history unfold before our eyes, the emotional reactions we experience and the insights we gain about ourselves and our sexuality will intensify. Although you will obtain from these images a great deal of information about yourself that goes beyond your sex life, we will be focusing on the roots of your sensuality in our discussions. What other insights you gain—for example, your connectiveness to your parents, spouse, or lover in general—are bonuses.

Uncovering the Layers of Your History
with Imaging

We will now do actual imaging. You will see an image and gauge your own feelings. Afterward, a detailed explanation concerning responses to the image will be provided.

When you see the image, there are a few basic things you need to know.

First, you may close your eyes when you see the image in your mind's eye, or you can leave them open. It doesn't matter which method you use. Second, while you can see an image almost anywhere at any time, for the best results you should be in a quiet, comfortable place where you feel relaxed. And third, you don't have to memorize the instructions. Some images have only a few instructions; others have a dozen or more. Simply read the instructions one at a time, and follow them.

So, if you're in a quiet place and feel relaxed, let's move on to seeing an image.

HOME IMAGE

The first image is that of the home you shared with your parents. If you lived in more than one home during your youth, the "home" that is pertinent is the one that comes to mind most strongly.

Optimally, the image of the home should evoke warm and harmonious family feelings and relationships. In the home setting appear the principal family figures: the parents and siblings. As you concentrate on these figures, the feelings attached to them will become clear, and early childhood memories connected with them will surface.

Here are the instructions for the "Home Image."

HOME IMAGE

Picture your parents in the house (or apartment) where you lived most of the time with them, the place that gives you the feeling of home.

1. Picture your parents in the house. Where do you see them? What are they doing?
2. How do you feel as you see the house?
3. See your father. Where is he? What is he doing?
4. Do you experience pleasant or unpleasant feelings when you see him?
5. Relax and recall memories about the place where your father appears.
6. Now, see your mother. What is she doing?
7. Do you experience pleasant or unpleasant feelings when you see her?
8. Relax and recall memories about the place where your mother appears.
9. If you had siblings, where are they? What are they doing? How do you feel as you see them?
10. Now see yourself in the picture. What are you doing?
11. Does the place give you the feeling of home?

A relaxed and comfortable home, where there are good feelings with mother and father, is usually a warm environment. It leads to good feelings of pleasure and comfort that we carry throughout our lives, the opposite of tension and stress. Disturbance is indicated if the house is not experienced as a "home," if there was some dysfunction in the family that might have affected our ability to feel confident and secure with other people in our life. If a parent is absent or extremely vague in the image, it may indicate a physical or emotional absence from, or a hostile relationship with, that parent.

However you feel toward your parents, the feelings you have when you see them are often feelings that you have toward your mate. This is important. *The way you feel toward your parents will very much describe the feelings you have toward the special person in your life.* You're still carrying those feelings from childhood.

Because we carry these parental images to our bedrooms, we need to continue to probe our relationships with our parents.

WARMTH OF PARENTS' BODIES IMAGE

The next image is "Warmth of Parents' Bodies." We did this image briefly in Chapter One.

WARMTH OF PARENTS' BODIES IMAGE

1. Picture your parents standing directly in front of you.
2. Which parent's body has more warmth?
3. How warm is the other parent's body in comparison?
4. Concentrate on your feelings concerning father's body.
5. How do you feel as you see his body?
6. Relax and recall memories as you concentrate on your father's body.
7. Concentrate on your feelings concerning mother's body.
8. How do you feel when you see her body?
9. Relax and recall memories as you concentrate on your mother's body.
10. Which parent's body do you wish to know more? Why?

During our childhood, our parents look after our physical needs. As a result, our parents' bodies should appear affectionate to us and impart a feeling of warmth. Seeing this image reveals whether our parents were able to express love in a tender and personal manner.

If our parents are warm toward us, we feel warm in return, and we learn to be warm, tender, and close with others. But if our parents are cold, we tend to become cold ourselves, or carry a tension because our needs weren't met.

If one parent is warm and the other cold, we may be warm at certain times and cold at others, or we may be more like one parent than the other. How you see your parents in the image should reveal whether you're more like one or the other in your warmth toward your partner.

Also, if your parents were colder toward you and you yourself feel cold, it will be harder for you to express warmth to your mate.

For example, one man said: "My father has a lot of warmth, and it feels freeing and liberating to me. My mother gives me feelings of being suffocated, and it feels cold and dead. I feel depressed with her. I'd rather look at my father's image because it stirs a feeling of life inside me."

This man's relationship with his mother made him feel cold, dead, and depressed. He felt this way sometimes in his relationship with his wife. Other times, he would feel warm and full of life; then he would crash and get cold again, imitating both his parents, going back and forth in the relationship. His wife was often bewildered, never knowing what his mood would be.

I worked with a woman who had a cold father and a cold mother, and thus she only attracted cold people. She once dated a warm man, and it terrified her. Used to coldness and distance, she didn't know how to act in the relationship.

From the warmth and feeling we get from our parents' bodies, we can gauge our parents' attitudes concerning sexuality. Why should we care about our parents' sexuality? Because one of the main ways our personality forms is in acting like—or reacting against—our parents' attitudes. While we tend to think of our parents in nonsexual terms, almost as if they were asexual, we have to understand their depth of sensuality in order to see how it affected us.

When we "touch" our parents' bodies in the image, a warm disposition should surface and convey feelings of acceptance and benevolence. To get back to our primal sexuality, we need to feel acceptance, warmth and pleasure towards our own sexual organs.

Obviously, there is a difference between the warm comfort we might feel for a loving parent (let's call it the "cookies-and-milk reaction") and what we sense about their sensuality. When we sense that our parents, no matter how they treated us personally, were repressed in terms of expressing their sexuality—or were inappropriate in the way they expressed themselves—we delve into the roots of our own expressions and repressions.

Do the Warmth of Parents' Bodies Image again. Only this time, ask yourself, what was your father's attitude toward sex? Your mother's attitude toward sex?

Does the temperature change? Get colder or warmer? What does the image tell you about your parents' attitudes toward sex? What does it tell you about your own?

The next image is that of "Parents' Brains."

PARENTS' BRAINS IMAGE

Picture your parents' brains.
1. Touch each parent's brain, and feel the temperature there. Is it cold, warm, or hot?
2. Now, touch your father's brain. What is the temperature?
3. Is touching your father's brain pleasant or unpleasant?
4. Now, touch your mother's brain. What is the temperature?
5. Is touching your mother's brain pleasant or unpleasant?
6. What does hot temperature of a brain mean to you?
7. What does cold temperature of a brain mean to you?
8. What does neutral temperature of a brain mean to you?
9. Which parent's brain do you tend to avoid touching?

The brain reflects how you think about things, your attitude toward things, your mental state about things. It's a very important organ for sexuality because sensuality starts in the brain. The brain, like the rest of the body's organs, displays a temperature. A parent's thought processes are reflected in the thermal images of the brain, the normal temperature representing normal activity, and abnormal temperature representing abnormal activity. Optimally, our parents' brains should appear slightly warm and pleasurable to the touch.

If a parent's brain is absent in the image, the feelings connected with the absence could have a special meaning for you. If you touch the brain and some brain matter comes off onto your fingers, the feeling connected with the sticky aspect of the brain should be explored. Notice if you have disgust or fear or dependence (i.e., unfavorable mutual dependence) connected with the images of the brain. It often means you were traumatized in some way.

As you see the images, you will realize what the hot or cold temperatures of your parents' brains mean. Usually, if you see a parent's brain sizzling hot, there's a problem, because a very hot brain generally indicates negative mental activity. If children have a parent with negative mental activity, they will not feel positively because they constantly have negative attitudes thrown at them.

Sometimes a very hot brain also indicates that the parent had a lot of rage and was explosive. That can be very scary, and it doesn't promote a feeling of closeness and intimacy with that parent.

A very cold brain may mean the parent was severely withdrawn, and a lukewarm brain indicates indifferent mental activity. This can lead to a feeling of detachment from that parent.

A man reported his mother's brain was so hot he was afraid to touch it. The heat symbolized his mother's tendency toward extreme mental aggression—she would yell, bully, frighten him. He didn't feel comfortable with women, and he acted very timidly toward them. Yet he would attract assertive, angry women, just like his mother.

Another fellow said, "My father's brain is warm, and a mild vapor is coming out of it; its color is pink, and it has a white illumination that is pleasing to me. My mother's brain is cold, not freezing, and gray, somewhat putrid, although there's not much light there." So the positive attitudes he received about life and sex came from this father. He could relax around his father and felt free to be himself. His mother made him close up, and feel distant and self-protective.

PARENTS' HEARTBEAT IMAGE

The next image is "Parents' Heartbeat."

PARENTS' HEARTBEAT IMAGE

1. Picture your parents standing in front of you.
2. Image a window opening in each parent's chest so you can see their hearts beating there.
3. See your father's heart beating. Describe its beat and its appearance.
4. Is there any sign of anxiety in your father's heartbeat?
5. See your mother's heart beating. Describe its beat and its appearance.

6. Is there any sign of anxiety in your mother's heartbeat?
7. Do you wish your father's heart to appear different in any way?
8. Do you wish your mother's heart to appear different in any way?

Optimally, your parent's heart should appear warm and affectionate and have a regular beat. The heart is our cultural symbol of love and connotes feelings of passion and compassion. The love contained within the parents' hearts is for their children.

What are your feelings on seeing each heart? Comfort? Security? Warmth? Anxiety?

The image reveals whether your parents were tender in their expression of love. A severe disturbance is indicated when the heart appears absent or cold. Fast or irregular heartbeats indicate anxiety in your parents. No heartbeat reveals an absence or regression of emotions. A small heart indicates a limited emotional capacity or stinginess. An extremely tense heart reveals a fear or inability to express emotions. A floppy heart indicates failure in the expression of emotions.

There can be sex and marriage and children without deep love. But without that depth of love, there is little chance of lush sensuality surfacing.

This image reveals your own ability to express love. When you see negative aspects of your parents' hearts, you have to ask yourself, did they fail to express their love? Do you have the same emotional malady? When parents don't have love in their hearts, they may not be able to pass on to us the ability to express love.

This does not mean we cannot love. Seeing the image and gaining insight into our own feelings opens up those blocked passages from our inner spirit.

A woman seeing the heartbeat image said: "When I look into my parents' hearts, my mother's heart beats very irregularly and moves around in her chest. My father's heart is big, with strong, regular beats that are steady. This image makes me think of the strength of my father and the insecurity of my mother. With my mother, I feel insecure in her love. I feel the same insecurity in my relationships, but my father's image makes me feel very secure because his heart has strong, regular beats. I know he's really there for me. Sometimes I feel secure, but it alternates; sometimes I feel insecure, like with my mother."

How does she carry this aspect into her own love life? With strong regular beats like her father, she adores her husband, but sometimes she gets insecure about whether he really loves her. Her insecurity causes conflict in their relationship. In doubting her husband's love, she repeatedly asks for reassurance, frustrating and alienating him because he can never prove to her that he truly loves her. She is constantly projecting the feelings she had with her mother onto her husband.

PARENTS SEPARATED OR UNITED IMAGE

Here is another image that relates to your parents' relationship with you and each other.

PARENTS SEPARATED OR UNITED IMAGE

1. Picture your parents standing in front of you.
2. Do they appear separated or united as a couple?
3. Describe the character of the space each occupies. Do the spaces differ in temperature and illumination?
4. Describe your father's space with regard to warmth and light as he appears alongside your mother.
5. Describe your mother's space with regard to warmth and light as she appears alongside your father.
6. Do father's and mother's spaces appear friendly or clashing?
7. Which space appears stronger, mother's or father's?
8. Does friendliness between your parents' spaces make you feel secure?
9. Does conflict between your parents' spaces create conflict in you?

In this image, you can see whether your parents have unity or disunity between them, as the spaces they occupy reflect their feelings of harmony or conflict. The personality of each parent is infused into the space he or she occupies. Optimally, the two should interact, with a basic harmony and a feeling of unity and friendliness between them, and each should show some affection toward the other. Do your mother's and father's spaces appear friendly or clashing? This tells if there's unity, disunity, or neutrality between them.

The differences in temperature and illumination are also significant. The meanings are found in whether the parent occupies a warm or a cold space. If there's light, it may be positive; if it's dark, it may mean depression or a feeling of unavailability of that parent for you.

The obvious qualities of the image, such as light, dark, dim, mellow, powerful, and hot or cold, tell how we experience our mother and father. The temperatures are important because very hot can mean the parent was overly angry or critical, warm that they were loving parents, and cold that the parent was overly distant. The feeling of disunity or harmony between parents is important; if there's disunity between them, it will be harder for you to create unity in your personal relationships. Because the pattern inside you came from your parents, there may be a sense of disunity within your own self that you have to deal with before finding unity with another person.

For example, if our parents weren't unified, we will recreate the disunity (or insecure feeling) in our relationships. Conversely, if we see them united, it will be easy for us to move into a relationship that feels unified. Or if our parents were overly unified, perhaps too close together, it may seem that there's no space between them. If your parents couldn't be their own separate people, you may be overly dependent on your partner in your relationship.

PARENTS' ACCEPTANCE OF YOU IMAGE

The next image deals with acceptance.

PARENTS' ACCEPTANCE OF YOU IMAGE

1. Picture your parents standing in front of you.
2. Look at your parents' skin, and concentrate on it for a while.
3. Does it seem to accept you or reject you?

4. How do you feel as you look at their skin?
5. Whose skin gives you the feeling of acceptance? To what degree?
6. Whose skin gives the feeling of rejection? To what degree?
7. Concentrate on your feelings about your father's skin.
8. How do you feel as you experience his skin?
9. Concentrate on your feelings about your mother's skin.
10. How do you feel as you experience your mother's skin?
11. Which parent usually touches you more?
12. Which parent do you usually touch more?

The feelings of acceptance convey warmth and security. The care given by parents is reflected in the positive feelings that their skin generates when they come into contact with their child's body. The contact results in the experience of acceptance and physical relief in the child. Optimally, the parents should appear warm and accepting.

When you have a feeling of self-acceptance, you naturally assume that other people will be accepting toward you, and having that attitude makes people accept you. This image reveals whether your parents were accepting or rejecting toward you. If they were rejecting, you might not feel good enough. You might feel that you're not worthy of being accepted; you may feel isolated or alienated, and you bring those negative feelings into relationships. Or you might identify with a rejecting parent and reject your partner, or identify with an accepting partner and be naturally warm and accepting toward him or her.

With this image, you can explore the issue of rejection from your parents, and its effect on you. For example, if your parents don't reject you but instead appear self-centered (which is a form of rejection), how do you feel in their presence? Are you also self-centered? If that's true, you can see the similarity between yourself and your parents, and you can understand the emotional significance of being self-centered, rejecting, or accepting.

A woman reported: "My mother's skin gives me a feeling of rejection and suffocation. It makes me feel sick inside. I feel unworthy. However, when I look at my father's skin, I feel freely accepted by him. I feel that his presence soothes me, kindles hope in me, and encourages me to live in a strong manner."

In her sexual life, this woman would sometimes act rejecting toward her partner. But she acted very warmly and accepting of her children, the way her father treated her. So she could identify with both of these feeling states that came from her parents.

PARENTS' BRILLIANCE IN EYES IMAGE

In the next image, we'll look at the brightness in our parents' eyes to see the emotions they had toward us.

PARENTS' BRILLIANCE IN EYES IMAGE

1. Picture your parents standing in front of you.
2. Look at their eyes in the image.
3. Whose eyes appear more brilliant?
4. Are they extremely brilliant, very brilliant, or just brilliant?
5. How are the eyes of the other parent in comparison?
6. What kind of brilliance or dullness do your father's eyes have?
7. What kind of brilliance or dullness do your mother's eyes have?
8. Look at the parent with the more brilliant eyes. How do the eyes affect you?
9. Look at the parent who has duller eyes. How do the eyes affect you?
10. Relax and recall memories as you look at your father's eyes.
11. Relax and recall memories as you look at your mother's eyes.

Like their facial expressions, our parents' eyes also express emotions. When the eyes appear tender, warm, brilliant, and interested, we feel that our parents are compassionate, sensitive, and loving in a personal but releasing manner. If they are dull, we feel disinterest from them and that they are unavailable to us.

Like many of the other eidetic images developed by Dr. Ahsen, this image provides further insights into whether our relationships with our parents are based upon acceptance or rejection and reveals subtle feelings that existed between them and us.

PARENTS' ARMS GIVING IMAGE

The next image is "Parents' Arms Giving."

PARENTS' ARMS GIVING IMAGE

1. Picture your parents giving you something.
2. Which parent extends the hand more completely?
3. How far does the other parent extend the hand?
4. Concentrate on your father giving to you.
5. As he gives, do you experience pleasant or unpleasant feelings?
6. Concentrate on your mother giving to you.
7. As she gives, do you experience pleasant or unpleasant feelings?
8. What does the parent who extends the hand least have in the hand?
9. What does the parent who extends the hand most have in the hand?
10. Which gift feels more precious to you?

The parents' arms represent an intermediary function between the parent and the offspring. The arms engage in activity centering around feeding and expression of love. Their hands caress, protect, and guide. They show affection.

When the parents' hand extends fully to us, it expresses complete giving, resulting in our feeling fulfilled. Ideally, in the image, our parents should extend their hands and arms fully to us.

Don't worry about what your parents are giving you in the image; pay more attention to the act of giving. See how your parents give to you? Do you feel satisfaction and good feelings when given to? Or is there a lack of feeling deserving and a lack of satisfaction when they don't give very readily?

If the hand of your parent is absent in the image, you can explore what that absence means. They could have been selfish and didn't give much, or there might have been physical violence. Absent or withdrawing hands also suggest withholding.

Hesitancy, bashfulness, or shyness suggests difficulty in giving. Forced giving indicates violence on the part of the parent who doesn't allow freedom of choice to the offspring.

The image also reveals how you give to your lover. The way you were given to and how you feel as you're given to will be feelings that you have during the give-and-take with your lover. For example, a man's mother was withholding, and he felt unworthy when he received from her. Consequently, he felt unworthy with his lover; he felt he did not deserve pleasure and he withheld giving affection back to her.

One woman told me: "My mother's arms are outstretched in a nervous, twitchy way; she cannot give freely. My father gives to me in a hesitating way; he wants to give, but he doesn't know how. When I see his hands moving, they look pure and beautiful and have an element of lightening; even if he doesn't know how, I know he wants to give, and I feel good. With my mother and her twitchy arms, she can't give freely; it makes me feel hard inside and really sad, along with a feeling of longing. This longing comes up in my relationships all the time, and it's a real pain. I can't get over it, and I turn off people with my desperate longing. No matter how much I get, I always long for more."

PARENTS' ARMS RECEIVING IMAGE

The next image is "Parents' Arms Receiving."

PARENTS' ARMS RECEIVING IMAGE

1. Picture yourself taking something from your parents.
2. To whom do you extend your arms completely for receiving?
3. How do you extend your hands to the other parent?
4. Relax and recall memories as you extend your hands toward your parents.

5. Concentrate on how you take something from your father.
6. Describe what you see.
7. Concentrate on how you take something from your mother.
8. Describe what you see.
9. Wish for something from the parent toward whom you feel less free.
10. Wish for something from the parent toward whom you feel more free.

This image determines the way you take from others. Many people have a hard time receiving compliments, praise, affection; others crave attention and gobble it up and always seem to want.

The hands represent an intermediary function between our parents and us. The act of extending the hands to receive from our parents describes our confidence in them. The usual feelings of expectation and fulfillment are associated with this extension.

In the full extension of the hand is expressed the full confidence in our parent. Think about feelings of expectation and the ability to be fulfilled in your relationships. Do you feel fulfilled? This question can be answered in this image of arms receiving. Ideally, you should see yourself being able to extend your arms and hands fully to both parents. You should be confident about taking or receiving things like love, affection, warmth, and sensual pleasure. Some people just can't allow themselves to receive love, affection, and good feelings.

I remember a man whose mother often left him alone in the crib when he was a baby and didn't hold him very much. Consequently, he shut down his need for affection. He got married, and while he could be very sexual with his wife, he wasn't great at foreplay because he couldn't stand the touching. It brought up the pain he felt at the loss of maternal physical contact. This left his wife upset and frustrated, but he couldn't connect with her because he had suppressed his need to touch and be touched. It was very sad for both of them.

In contrast, a woman who also felt her mother had rejected her as a baby had an insatiable need to be touched and to be told over and over that she was loved. Each person is unique in how they respond to how their parents treated them.

If you notice your hand doesn't extend at all to a parent, you need to reflect on the feelings you had in relationship to that parent. The answer will be in the image. How does your parent behave as you approach with your hands extended to receive? How do you feel as you take from your parent?

If you are unable to extend your hands to receive from a parent, that lack will be found in your relationships with others. You will be uncomfortable receiving from others. If you don't extend both your arms to your parents in the image, it is an indication of how you take and receive love, affection, and even material gifts from others.

If you're hesitant to receive from a parent, it can show that you're unsure of that parent. If the image of one parent or both is very vague, it may mean you're not expected to ask for things from your parents, but only to receive them when they're offered.

If you see mutilated hands or arms, it could indicate severe trauma connected with approaching your parents. Here's what one person said: "I have no hands or arms to reach my father or to receive from him, and my father holds my disembodied arms in his hands. He never gave me anything, and I feel as though I have nothing to give."

A man said: "I don't extend my hands to my father, but to my mother, but she doesn't seem to give anything to me. Instead, I have to snatch things from her. Occasionally, her hands move toward me, but I feel I've got nothing from her. Although I don't extend my hands to my father, things continue to flow from him to me."

For this man, there was a positive connection between his father and him. However, the interaction with his mother left him feeling that in romantic relationships he had to snatch love where he could; he couldn't just have love come to him. Although he experienced himself being able to give love like his father did, when it came his way, he felt a need to grab it before it went away. He could not relax enough to receive permanent love from another.

For people who see a positive image of receiving from their parents, there is a feeling of fulfillment. Look at what one woman said: "I see that I take from my father's hands; one arm is extended completely toward me, and he has a precious gift for me in his hand. I feel love coming from him as I take it. I put the gift in my pocket and feel warm inside. This good feeling is how I feel when I'm with my lover and he gives me gifts or is sweet to me. I feel worthy and cherished. I reflect that good feeling by being affectionate toward him. Now I see my mother, and my mother gives with both hands and arms extended. She puts the gift on the table and pushes it further toward me and says, 'Take it.' I can feel she has so much to give, and she wants me to have it. When I see this image, it makes me feel special and almost blessed, that I'm worthy, I'm good, that I deserve to have good things happen to me."

This woman searched until she found a man who was her "true love," because she knew deep inside that she deserved it. Her attitude came from her relationship with her parents. In fact, her true love lasted a lifetime.

5

Summing Up the Sources of Our History

How was our sexual identity, our sensuality, molded after we were born? Answering this question will help bring together the insights we obtained from the imaging sessions.

There are six ways our interaction with our parents shapes us.

The first is through our *attachment* to them. Attachment is not becoming emotionally independent. I once worked with a woman whose parents never let her grow up. They coddled and cuddled her and ran interference in almost all aspects of her life. This resulted in her having a very dependent relationship with them. It affected her ability to have a close relationship with a man, because she was not independent and could not make decisions for herself. She carried over her need to be coddled and cuddled to her relationships with men. She had unrealistic expectations and believed that a man should take care of her, stroke and pet her, completely focus on her, and baby her. This got in the way of her sex life because she wasn't acting like an adult woman but like a baby needing a daddy.

While attachment and reliance are both necessary ingredients in a loving relationship, this woman's needs overpowered the warmth she could have contributed to a relationship and turned off the men around her. Some men found the woman's need to be petted attractive—but only in the short run.

Being deprived of a parent's warmth can have the same effect. A man who had been denied closeness with his mother as a child craved that sort of intimacy. As an adult, he couldn't get enough attention, and he was constantly demanding the intimacy of sex and touching. But his girlfriends wanted something more intellectually stimulating than hopping into bed several times a day. Naturally, he ended up turning off the women around him.

The second way our sexual personality forms is through *imitation*. Imitation is duplicating our parents' behavior without conscious intent.

Unfortunately, some of this behavior can be extremely negative. Our parents' embarrassment about sex and their bodies is passed on to us. A great many people simply imitate their parents' sexual attitudes without ever knowing they are doing so. If our parents had a perfect storybook relationship, that would be fine, but unfortunately, as wise and loving as our parents might have been, their own sexual attitudes were formed many decades ago and offer little guidance for the world we live in today.

The third way is in *reaction* to our parents. That's doing something in response to some parental behavior that we don't like or don't agree with. So we do the opposite. For most of us, doing the opposite of our parents is a common reaction when we are young and feel tied down by ideas we consider old-fashioned or hypocritical. While we all do this to some extent as a part of carving out some individuality for ourselves, the extreme example is the "preacher's daughter syndrome," in which a child rebels against a parent's teachings to the point that the child suffers emotional harm.

As a therapist, I have often dealt with people young and old who damaged their own sense of identity because they recoiled from their parents' ideals to the point of self-damage. People who rebel against their parents' negative aspects fail to realize that their parents are still controlling them—they fool themselves into thinking they're free of parental control, but you're not free when someone else is pushing your buttons.

The fourth way sensuality is molded is when our *childhood biological needs* have been denied, and the consequences are dramatized. If our parents are overly fearful of sexuality, they may have a difficult time being natural with their bodies and bodily functions. They may have strong inhibitions about nudity, and they may thwart curiosity or questions a child asks about sexual organs, or they may show discomfort during toilet training. As children, we pick up on these subtleties through our parents' body language, the comfort toward their own bodies, whether their bodies seem to accept or reject us, and if they can fully give and receive physical affection. If warmth and acceptance come from them, it spreads to us, and we grow up comfortable with our own bodies and in tune with our biological selves.

When our parents are overly rigid and suppressed and don't impart good feelings to us, a loss occurs. We are denied a real biological need—that of being held, experiencing the warmth and comfort that our parents' bodies and emotions can provide. I have seen people who are tense and uncomfortable around their own parents and who go through life being tense and uncomfortable with everyone around them. When they get into a relationship, they can't relax and flow with the rich physical intimacy a relationship needs in order to be nurtured.

When my mother yelled at me for putting toothpaste on my little playmate Tommy's penis, a subtle conflict occurred within me. The message from my mother was that it was not all right to be curious, to have sexual feelings, to want to know more about the nature of sexuality. Optimally, she could have dealt with the situation in a more positive manner, letting me know that my actions were inappropriate and at the same time satisfying my natural sexual curiosity, and not making it seem "dirty." When parents are too uptight to explain what a penis is, there is a loss for the child.

Another way we develop sexually is through *identification*, the close sharing of views and feelings with a parent to the point that the feelings become identical with the parent's. It often means that the individual rejects one parent and totally identifies with the other. A classic example is the moralistic parent who believes sex is bad and is connected to hell and damnation. When children accept these attitudes and imitate that parent, they suffer a loss of their own individuality. They are forever hampered because they can relate only to people who have the exact same attitudes as their parent. They fail to realize who their own genuine self is.

The hell-and-damnation parent is an extreme example used for purposes of illustration, but overly rigid parents who have never come to grips with their own sensuality and view sex fearfully are not uncommon.

The final way our interaction with our parents affects us is through *neurotic projection*, the process of attributing one's own inaccurate thoughts to others. For example, a girl had her first menstrual period at the age of twelve. She was very excited, believing it was a wonderful step into womanhood. In her excitement, she ran and told her father, expecting him to say, 'Great, you're a woman now just like your mother.' Instead, he was embarrassed about the disclosure and went back to reading his paper as if nothing had happened. Because he treated it so casually, she took it as a put-down. She imagined that her coming into womanhood was not significant, and from this she built a mental framework that affected her feelings about her own sensuality.

Of course, her father wasn't putting her down; he was simply a little embarrassed by a subject that he himself had been raised to believe was not to be talked about. Because he froze up and pretended not to be interested, his daughter attributed feelings to him that were not true. As a result, the young woman suffered a loss of her own sexual self-esteem, which she carried into her adult relationships.

6

Sexual Signals

The Turn-ons and Turnoffs

BOLD AND BEAUTIFUL, THIS SF, 35, SEEKS EQUAL MALE, FOR LTR. I AM STRONG, ACCOMPLISHED, DIVINE, CULTURED, CRUNCHY, AND AFFECTIONATE.

VERY ATTRACTIVE, FIT, EASYGOING, SM, 43, BLONDE/BLUE, LIKES SPORTS, DANCING, DINING OUT, AND QUIET EVENINGS. CARING, INTELLIGENT, HONEST, FINANCIALLY INDEPENDENT.

LOVE IS A LONELY BUSINESS

Personal ads always make me sad. It seems to defy logic that so many people need to advertise for love in a society where it seems so free and easy to acquire—not to mention that the world is nicely divided almost equally not only between the sexes but in terms of age, size, shape, and everything else that counts.

So why do so many of us look for love in the personals, dating services, and gyms? Why are so many of us so lonely in a world saturated with sex?

There is nothing wrong with personal ads or the people who use them. However, reading the ads, it becomes evident that the emphasis is on promoting oneself with false images and shallow impressions that our oversexed, undersensuous society has placed there. The emphasis in most personal ads is on physical attractiveness.

Love is a lonely business, not because there aren't enough available people to go around, but because most of us are radiating the wrong signals. We're so caught up with surface qualities and false images of sexuality and sensuality that we don't radiate a natural, sensuous warmth from our inner beings.

Mere mortals cannot live up to the media idols that we have been given to worship and emulate. Because society is permeated by these false images, we need to take a close look at the sexual signals we are sending to others.

The natural signals of attraction between men and women can be initiated on either side. A man may see something about a woman that he likes and feel attracted to her. The woman can sense his interest and send him an inviting signal back. At times, the woman initiates the interest and waits to see if she gets a signal back. Whether he initiates or she does, the woman usually waits for a signal from the man before further courtship proceeds.

When men do imaging sessions to discover what attracts them to women, they don't usually find it's buttocks or breasts or legs. Rather, they are more likely to be drawn to an inviting essence about the woman. A man can sense a mysterious "something" in a woman, and she responds to that by sending back a signal of availability, an invitation to come toward her. Sometimes, the woman sees someone who appeals to her. She sends him a signal of interest, and he responds by sensing the mystery in her. Yes, the outer package needs to appeal to him, but her essence is the true drawing factor. He approaches her, and if she welcomes him further, the mating can continue.

Traditionally, men have been the initiators of sexual contact. But a lot of men say they like it when women initiate contact; then they don't have to worry about rejection. It gives a man permission to relax and further pursue her.

What in a woman turns a man off? When she doesn't give him a signal at all. He might like her, but she doesn't send an inviting signal to him or she rejects the signal by looking away, telling him "no."

Someone asked me, aren't there guys who chase women, who love the chase because of the challenge to get her, no matter what? Yes, but they are rare. Most men are very sensitive, and they wait for a signal of approval from a woman. Even a man who chases a woman until he gets her (that's even rarer) continues chasing only because the woman is giving him mixed signals. If a woman gives a clear "no" signal, it's over.

What in a man turns a woman off? Sometimes a man goes his own way and doesn't respond to a woman's signal of interest. However, sometimes a woman may be tempted to try again get his attention. If he responds to her pursuit and then sees something in her which draws him—that mystery—then the play begins. But he needs to respond to the mystery in her, or it goes no further.

Another turnoff is aggressiveness. Men have been conditioned in our society to be more aggressive than women, so aggression in a male is usually more tolerated than aggression in a woman. Men, in general, are not comfortable with women they find aggressive. By *aggressive*, I don't mean confident or assertive. Many men love, admire, and respect confident women. However, they find a woman's aggressiveness can be a turnoff, especially if it erupts into competition that is combative. Men have a hard time tolerating combative signals from a woman. It sends conflicting signals to them and kills their passion.

This is a sensitive area because many women today believe they have the right to be as aggressive as men. While they may be morally and logically correct, the state of affairs in the animal kingdom is that the male still struts and paws and grunts and shows off, while the female watches and selects the best strutter. And we, being part of the animal kingdom, respond to subtle genetic mating signals.

There is a difference between competing to be the best you can and being aggressive and combative. Being one up on someone puts the other person down. It is this latter form of behavior that turns men off.

Beauty is very compelling, and beauty of many kinds naturally draws people. There's outer beauty, which has magnetic power and can draw a person sexually. But for women to worry so much about hair and makeup and nails, and to struggle so hard to be beautiful, and for men to focus on being buff and handsome, implies an empty feeling inside that only physical beauty is sexual.

Emptiness is completely unattractive. People who are sexually attractive to each other sense in the other person some quality, some essence, that in one way or another is beautiful, whether it's a sparkle in the eye, a loving manner, or a sense that the person is connected to their inner sensuality. The thing that attracts someone to another person is a quality that emanates from inside. And it makes the person feel good to be with the one they admire.

Women looking at a man they like described warmth, strength, humor, lovingness, and a sense of inner security as the things they were attracted to. Those qualities made them feel good and drew them to the man.

Conversely, the men said that the woman who attracted them had an inner sensuality, that she was connected to her own essence. They felt an openness from her, which means they felt the woman would receive them. They sensed a friendliness, and they experienced beauty in some aspect of her—her skin, color of her hair and eyes. It wasn't necessarily classic beauty, yet some physical aspect appealed to them. But more compelling was an essence that drew them in.

The things that sexually draw a person to you are qualities of the soul, qualities of the innermost self, be it lovingness, warmth, openness, sweetness, a feeling of deep comfort with oneself, integrity, or strength.

That inside thing, the most compelling sexual thing, is intangible. It is our own true nature that is sexy, not the outer veneer. The toys we have acquired, the power symbols—cars, houses, high-powered jobs, proportions of our bodies—these are not ultimately compelling. It is the intangible, which many of us have lost along the way while trying to have perfect bodies or to be successful, that is our real nature. Sexual appeal has to do with self-love, self-worth, self knowledge. If we look just for success and power or to our own outer beauty, we are left alone and empty. When we look inside, we see nothing. It leaves us conflicted, and we feel lonely and in exile from our innermost self. People who are conflicted, alone, and empty inside, no matter what they have on the outside, are truly not attractive. They cannot attract others to them in an enduring way.

Living in compliance, compromise, or compensation to other people also diminishes our inner sense of self. If we live compromised, we lose the central ability to live in harmony with ourselves, with others, and with our environment. And that is the loss of self. When we find our true selves again, that energy emanates to others, and it is extremely sexy.

The most compelling attractive quality is not beauty or physical perfection but the sweet offer of true love. And everyone is drawn to that.

If you look to advertisements for what is sexy, you see women selling clothing, perfume, deodorants, entertainment, makeup, and so on. Yes, the models are pretty on the outside, but they also exude some internal quality, be it a playfulness or warmth, which is their most compelling draw. They look confident, they're enjoying themselves, they're happy. They don't look like they're insecure or conflicted within. They're connected to some inner spark. That's the ingredient that makes them appealing.

Sensuality is within us. It is the feeling of almost touching a paradise that exists inside us, a place of voluptuous beauty, innocence, and camaraderie with all living things. In the fullness of this feeling state, nature outside blends with our nature within, and we can feel at peace and in harmony with ourselves and others. And that paradisiacal feeling is the essence that other people pick up on; it's the strongest sexual and sensual signal to others. It can truly be released only when we're comfortable with ourselves.

Awareness of the differences between the sexes is a fulfilling feeling. For example, it's very pleasurable to be a woman and sense the difference in a man. It is this perception of the differences, from a personal and universal perspective, that is the most erotic. The difference feels like a sweet harmony that evokes passion and a desire to explore and commune with the difference of the other sex.

Women are turned off by a man who isn't in touch with his own essence. Such a man tends to be self-centered. He is one who can't surrender to the lush fullness of the woman. No matter how powerful a man is, in his heart he must surrender to the woman in order for his passion and love for her to erupt.

A domineering man, the kind who feels he is going to take care of the "little woman" and in that way demean her, the power-monger kind of man who doesn't know how to respect, value, and meet her in honest openness and vulnerability, is a real turnoff to a woman. And a cheap man who won't be generous with her and won't affirm her value and worth is a turnoff to a woman too.

Conversely, women who are critical, combative, and hostile and who don't have a feeling of love for men or an appreciation for and understanding of who they are, are a real turnoff to men.

Men and women are obviously different, but the difference, as mentioned earlier, is extremely pleasurable and sensual. When a man and a woman are equal and when both are full in their own essences, it makes for a very attractive dynamic, of polar opposites coming to unite. It is deeply pleasurable and extremely fulfilling.

Think about when you're attracted to somebody who is attracted to you—all of a sudden, sparks fly, and there is a flowing feeling. Your brain sends chemicals to the body that cause heightened excitement, relaxation, and sensuous melting. It releases a chemistry that is the exact opposite of stress. It is the play of opposites in nature coming together. It is true sexuality.

The most important things to remember about sexual signals are:

- They are initiated on either side, but neither side likes overt, combative aggressiveness.
- They are very subtle. Unless you're selling your body for money, overt signals send the wrong message. The other person just needs to know whether you are interested. Overdoing it leaves the impression you are overeager or desperate. Underplaying says you're not available, so the chase stops. Overt signals are usually a complete turnoff. They may attract someone who wants sex, but they are not the stuff of long-term, loving relationships.

- They are sent through *natural* body language, using eyes, lips, facial expressions. If you are afraid you're turning other people off, you'd be better off doing almost nothing rather than trying to act. Smile a friendly smile, and leave it at that. The worst thing you can do is to *try* to give a signal. It has to come naturally, from within, and emanate from your smile, eyes, and body language. When you are confident with your sensuality, you'll give the right signal.

SEXUAL ATTRACTION IMAGE

Let's do an image that will clue us in on what the *sexual attraction* is between men and women. It will tell you not only a great deal about your lover but about yourself.

And it will give you insight into what attracts or repels you about the opposite sex.

SEXUAL ATTRACTION IMAGE

1. See an image of a person you are sexually attracted to.
2. What do you see?
3. What attracts you to the person?
4. How do you feel as you see the image?
5. See the person going away. What happens in the image? How do you feel as the person leaves?
6. See the person staying around you. What do you see? How do you feel?
7. See the person come toward you. What do you see in the image? How do you feel?
8. What do you spontaneously want to do with the person?

A woman who imaged a man she felt attracted to said: "I'm attracted to his eyes. In the image, he has very deep eyes that I can just melt into. There's a feeling of solidity and strength and warmth that comes from him that deeply attracts me. I feel like I can relax and be myself, my full sensual self, with him. There's something about his strength that makes me feel feminine. I want to be playful with him, flirtatious, and move all around him, teasing him, drawing him toward me, and eventually I want to have him melt with me. I see that means I am really turned on to him and want a sexual encounter."

On the other hand, here's a woman who saw the man in her life, her husband, in a slightly different light: "When I see him in front of me, he appears irritated. I feel irritated by him. There's a place when I look at his face in the image where he looks very sweet in the way he did when I fell in love with him. Yet there's also a feeling of irritation coming from him because he's really a moody person. I'm not drawn to the irritation; I'm drawn to the sweetness in his face, so it's a mixed feeling.

"At times I want to go closer to him and at times back away, and that's how I engage sexually with him. I just realized that. Sometimes I want to be sexual with him, and sometimes I want to move far away.

"I see him going away, and I feel a sense of peace and relief that I don't have to deal with the irritation, but I also miss him; after a while, I begin to miss him if he is gone too long.

"I see him staying around, and I'm happy he's around, but I feel kind of irritated. He's not an easy guy to be around. I am kind of ambivalent being with him. It isn't an easy peacefulness, due to his moodiness; it's just a rocky kind of feeling to be with him; it's not smooth and peaceful.

"This has given me a lot of clarity about the subtle feeling states I go through with him and why I don't feel really sexual toward him a lot of the time."

You can see how two women reacted differently to the men in their lives. For the first one, there was a lot more feeling of sexuality, flirtatiousness, and playfulness. She felt more longing and desire to merge with the man. She could be more relaxed and more feminine than usual around him. She felt like enticing him toward her.

The second woman experienced a much more problematic relationship in which her sexuality could not come forth fully. The first man had strength, solidity, and warmth that fully brought the woman's desire out. The second man was moody and irritable so his wife's desire for him was compromised.

A husband who saw an image of his wife said: "I see her and I like her, and there's also a feeling of difficulty. She's very critical and judgmental, and she's not as open as I'd like her to be.

"When I see her go away, I like it. I get the house to myself; I get space; I'm on my own. When she is around, it's annoying. I really like my space without her. I love her and don't want her to leave for good, but I like being without her for the peace I get.

"You know, after twenty-three years of marriage, personal space is so hard to come by that the space becomes delicious. After twenty-three years, she bitches a lot, so the criticism and judgments from her really have turned me off."

Another man said: "It's really important to me that a woman is open and that she comes toward me. Then I feel that there's a possibility for intimacy and that I won't be rejected, and I don't have to work so hard. I see an image of a woman who comes toward me, and she's open and smiling. There's a brightness in her eyes, and she doesn't give me a hard time. Those are the women that I get turned on to."

Some other men who did the image reported that the feeling of openness, availability, lack of criticalness, and noncombative signals were what drew them to women. They liked women who were forward enough to signal that they would be receptive to their approach.

Some middle-aged men were gun-shy about approaching women because they might get "slammed." One man, who described himself as a veteran of the sexual revolution, claimed he used to be afraid to open a door for a woman he didn't know for fear she might snap at him.

Reading some of these reactions, one might wonder where good old-fashioned romance has gone. But it's not dead, as this young woman's experience shows. "His smile attracts me, his eyes are warm and friendly; they sparkle, and there's life in them. I feel warm and cozy and love being with him. There's a communion between us, and we embrace and kiss and move toward sex. I feel warm and safe."

The preceding examples have several things in common. One woman desired to move around the man she was attracted to, flirtatiously playing with him as if she were the sea and he was a steady rock at the center. What she likes about him is his warmth, his steady strength. There's an oceanic fluid feeling, highly sensual, that envelops her when she is with him.

Most of the men talked about an "essence." They said it doesn't matter what a woman looks like; it's that essence, that thing that comes from inside her, that attracts them. They also liked women who did not hassle them and who initiated contact with an open, friendly, straightforward invitation—not with conflict. This was a turn-on for the men.

The women liked warmth, and they said a lot about the eyes—what's reflected in the eyes is the soul of the man. None of the women mentioned looks. They all mentioned the man's energy, warmth, eyes, openness, the way they felt around him. One woman talked about "taking him into her," which is her intuitive knowledge of being home for his essence. And there was that whole "melting," where everyone wanted to go.

Many men don't like passive women who make them responsible for the whole chase. They like a woman who is forthcoming, letting them know she is interested. They like to sense strength in the woman, too. And they don't care so much what a woman looks like—it is the essence of her that makes her beautiful.

Beauty is very subjective. Of course, there are some women who are knockout gorgeous. Everyone agrees they are beautiful, but the magnetic quality has more to do with their essence than with the shape of their breasts or buttocks. That stuff doesn't have any lasting value. In fact, none of the men mentioned it, and none of the women did.

7

Releasing Repression

Repression (or suppression) of our natural state of sensuality is the end result of how our history affects us. Things our parents said, things we heard in church, and even remarks from our peers can sit in the back of our heads, waiting like time bombs to explode when we are trying to be our best with someone we are interested in.

Any inability to fully engage in free, natural expression of our sexuality, whether it's a minor shameful feeling or a major sexual dysfunction, is rooted in the subtle and overt events of our past. Sometimes the history is so overwhelming that we become dysfunctional on many levels. A woman not able to achieve orgasm may feel shame about it and not be able to freely express her sexual needs to her lover. A man who turns off most of the women he approaches might feel insecure and overcompensate by having to boast about his other accomplishments.

People with repressed sexuality are victims of parents and a society that failed them. Sometimes that failure only affects the sexual aspect of their lives, and they may be successful in everything else they do.

But the bottom line is that if you are unable to have the kind of relationship you want with another person, it is probably due to repressive control of your sexuality that keeps you from dealing with the opposite sex in a spontaneous and enjoyable manner.

Sometimes the roots are terribly subtle, and the person suffering the repression, while knowing something is wrong, never faces up to it and so continues having the land mines explode.

In her images, a woman with boyfriend trouble saw her father always looking at her breasts. Her subconscious reaction was to be embarrassed about her breasts. When her boyfriend wanted to appreciate them, she would tense up. But she couldn't deal with the problem until she realized that incidents from her past were causing it.

A man raised by a cold, asexual mother got the message from her that his natural sexual warmth was not acceptable. As a result, he would freeze up when a situation with a warm, affectionate woman became sexual. His mother never sat him down and said, "Look, Johnny, I'm going to screw up your sex life." Instead, like most of us, he was subtly damaged over a couple of decades.

In this chapter, we'll be using several interesting imaging techniques to help us identify and release repression. One of them, called "Imaging with Filters," permits us to quickly identify how our parents and others repressed our sexuality. "Hot and Cold" quickly gets into the root problems between us and our lovers. And the third one, the "Ravisher Image," might sound like an unlikely subject matter for releasing sexual repression, but most people find the image to be fun and informative.

FILTERS: FINDING THE GHOSTS IN OUR SEX LIVES

Filters reveal to us how our brain got programmed by our parents. The technique pinpoints exactly where our repression is and how to release it. Filters can also be used to analyze the effect on us of other people.

Even though we are born whole and complete, we are programmed by our parents. This programming translates into automatic behavior, and to the end of our lives we act out what our parents subtly and overtly taught us. For some of us, this programming pops up like a ghost in the machine when it is triggered. We are in bed with our lover, whispering sweet nothings, caressing and touching and feeling and . . . you get the idea. We start to heat up, get ready to climax, and . . . oops! We don't have an orgasm, or we can't get an erection, or we tense up and say or do something stupid, because the "ghost" of our mother or father is in bed with us.

It's a knee-jerk reaction. We don't know that the ghost is there. We react to the programming without realizing that it's a result of how our parents have affected us.

We pinpoint the exact problem and its source by using what we call an imaging "filter." It's not unlike putting a filter over the lens of a camera to see how it affects the picture. We do this by imaging ourselves in a situation where we falter (e.g., tensing up during sex or on a date). While imaging the situation, we keep our father in mind, then we do the image again, this time keeping our mother in mind. By injecting our parents into the image we can isolate and identify the parental programming that has short-circuited our sex life.

The influence of a parent may be negative or positive. A mother might have been a very sensual woman, comfortable with her body and her sensuality, very warm and affectionate, the kind who kissed and hugged people. Her behaviors translate into programming in the brains of her children. So when her children experience sex, they'll probably be comfortable with their bodies, too.

Sometimes one parent is warm, and the other is cool. Let's say that the warm, sensuous woman above was married to a successful businessman who tended to be moralistic at home, a perfectionist who was rigid in his dealings with his family. A son raised by this father is likely to also be moralistic and overly rigid in dealing with the opposite sex. Part of his brain is telling him don't touch, don't hug, don't have too many feelings, take control, and keep a tight rein. That uncomfortable feeling is the ghost of the father.

However, doing the image keeping his mother in mind, the same man will feel relaxed and be comfortable in the sexual situation, drawing on the influence of his mother's sensual warmth.

In this case, the man will want to "change the programming" so that his father doesn't negatively affect his sex life. Once there is an awareness that, "Hey, I'm okay; I just have two contradictory brain programmings," people choose the programming they want.

IMAGING WITH FILTERS

The Imaging with Filters instructions follow. The problem or situation is the issue you are having difficulty with, such as getting uptight during sex or on a date.

IMAGING WITH FILTERS

1. See a problem or difficult situation in your mind's eye.
2. What do you see?
3. How do you feel as you see it?
4. Keep your mother in mind, and see the problem or situation.
5. What happens in the image while you keep your mother in mind? Let the image unfold on its own.

6. Now, keep your father in mind, and see the problem or situation.
7. What happens in the image when you keep your father in mind?

A woman who had problems relaxing and felt uptight about having sex used Imaging with Filters. She said. "I have an image of having sex with my boyfriend. I'm in my forties, have been through a divorce, my boyfriend and I are planning to get married, and I'm very happy. I see we're in bed having sex; he has this otherworldly, abandoned, full-of-pleasure look in his eyes; he's inside me; I'm enjoying watching his face, his pleasure. I'm losing awareness of his face, and I'm aware of a growing pleasurable sensation in my breasts, my inner thighs and genitals. This sensation is intensifying, I let go, and I'm moving toward orgasm. It's a very pleasurable image. Then something happens. My mind wanders, and I shut down the growing excitement."

Keeping her mother in mind, she saw this image of having sex. "A wall comes down right in the middle of my body and stops me cold in my tracks; I can't continue the sex. I have a memory of my mother yelling at me and calling me a whore after she found out I had sex for the first time. I was a senior in high school and had just started having sex with my boyfriend. She found birth-control pills, which I had hidden in my pajamas in a drawer. I see her enraged and yelling and calling me a whore; I felt humiliated and ashamed, and my privacy had been invaded. She told my father, which embarrassed me more, and her best friends. It's taken a long time to get free of the humiliation of that experience. I've just begun to really enjoy sex."

Then she saw an image of having sex and kept her father in mind. "There's a slight tinge of shame over the image. My father was shamed by sex, although he was a warm and passionate man. I can see and sense he was shamed in childhood and that carried over to me. I have a feeling of embarrassment about being so free and abandoned. In the image, I don't let go as much sexually with my father in mind. I can't surrender; I hold back and feel shyer. I've been shy about letting go in sex for many years. With my father in mind, I have a feeling of shyness."

The wonderful thing about using filters is that they help identify not only where we are blocked but where we can find a source of strength and encouragement. We do this by using as a filter a parent or other person who has been a source of inspiration to us.

One man was able to work around negative blocks by keeping his father in mind. He said, "My father had always been a strong source of encouragement and motivation in terms of my schooling, athletic activity, and career. It had a very positive effect on my attitude. He was a warm and affectionate man. With him in mind, the intensity of love for my wife deepens as we have sex."

HOT AND COLD IMAGES: RELEASING YOUR PASSIONS

Hot and Cold Images are used when you are feeling stuck or when the person you are involved with is stuck or repressed in some manner. The image releases repression.

You know from past images that the people we see in them have body temperatures. These temperatures reveal information about the personality and temperament of the person. We previously used the temperature of images to examine our relationship with our parents and their relationship with each other.

In any relationship, one partner will be hotter and the other colder. By *hot*, we mean more passionate, energetic, and warm. *Hot* can mean all of those things, and in the extreme it can mean anger. The other partner can be a little more passive, cooler, and not as sexually active. By *cold*, we mean passive, withdrawn, frozen, or unable to respond. In the extreme, it can mean frigid. These are generalities, and as you see your own images the meanings will be evident to you.

You might want to heat up if you're the colder person. For instance, a woman asked, "How can I get hot or hotter than the person I'm with and become more passionate and sensual?" Her partner said, "I'm the person who's hotter in the relationship; maybe my being hot makes my partner freeze up. Let me see what would happen if I chill out a bit and let her heat up."

Because images have temperatures to them, when we see an image of a lover or of ourselves with a lover, we can tell who is hotter and who is colder. So the temperature of the image is a great indicator of sexual energy and passion between two people. It's a very good technique to use, not only to see who's hotter or colder, but also to change the temperatures.

Even if you appear cold in the image, there's a hot individual underneath that cold person. What you want to do is bring out the heat of your sexual passion and desire. Even though you're stuck in coldness, which may indicate repression or holding back, you can warm up. How do you do this? You can work with the temperature in images.

What do the temperatures in the image tell us? Coolness means we might be acting coldly in bed, that we can't let go and allow flowing sexual abandon. We're cold and uptight. Even though we're acting out of the cold image, somewhere stored in a separate compartment are hot images of ourselves—the warmth we were born with. The Hot and Cold Images let us open up our cerebral filing system to retrieve our natural warmth and open up the part of us that is hot, passionate, and free.

Sometimes a very hot partner can inhibit a cold partner because he or she is overly excited, overly eager. So what is the solution? To do the opposite. How do you get a hot person to cool down, perhaps to meet your own sexual tempo? You use images of coldness when you practice doing Hot and Cold Images.

First, you see an image of yourself in bed with your lover. You then examine the image to see who is hotter and who is colder. This will reveal what's going on between the two of you. Then you can go back and forth, making the hot person cold, and the cold person hot, and reversing the temperature again and again, to bring out different information in the files stored in your brain.

The technique shows where you became repressed, where you are cold, and how you can bring yourself back to your natural hot sensuality. When you switch the temperatures back and forth, you will see if there is repressed sexuality in your lover or in yourself. As you switch back and forth, you'll have a somatic response of being more open, of being more sexual if you are cold, or of cooling down if your image is too hot.

Alternating between hot and cold helps in two ways:

1. It reveals the sexual dynamics between you and the other person, and it indicates who is hotter, colder, more suppressed.

2. It allows you to see the stuck sexuality shift as it begins to unfold, and to see the true nature of your sexual self, thus helping you to change in real life.

HOT AND COLD IMAGES

1. See yourself in a sexual situation with another person.
2. What do you see?
3. Who is hot? Who is cold?

4. See that the person who is hot becomes cold and that the one who is cold becomes hot.
5. Let the interactions in the image unfold like a movie.
6. Now switch the temperatures again so that the one who was cold is now hot, and vice versa. Let the interaction unfold like a movie.
7. Keep going back and forth until you come to a resolution or new awareness.

By switching the temperature back and forth, more and more information about the people and the situation is revealed.

A young woman named Elena who did the image provides us with useful feedback. Elena was embarrassed by sex because she grew up in a culture that had the virgin-whore complex. Girls were either pure like the Virgin Mary, or they were whores. They could flirt, but if they went all the way and had sex, they would be criticized and judged for their passions.

Elena was a bit shy and very attracted to a man. She thought that if she came out and expressed her full sexual passion while making love with him, becoming very active and aggressive, he would look at her with condemnation and contempt. She feared that he would think she was a whore and reject her. She had a lot of culture-induced shame about her sexuality.

Elena started her imaging session by seeing herself having sex with her boyfriend. She saw that they were both naked in her bedroom, and the nakedness was a little too much for her. She saw herself as cool in the image, and there was heat coming from her boyfriend's body. She felt withdrawn and shut down.

She switched temperatures, seeing herself as hot and her boyfriend as cool, and let the image unfold like a movie. When she did this, she felt sexual longing in her body, and she loosened up and started to kiss him and caress his body. In the image, he became more passive, letting her do what she wanted to him. It felt good to her to be more aggressive in the image. It felt like a release for her.

Elena switched again, now seeing herself as cold and her lover as hot. In the image, she saw him responding to her advances, taking hold of her and kissing her on the lips, feeling warmer despite the previous switch in temperatures. She was now feeling warm, while he was hot.

She switched again, and now she was hot and he was cold. As the image unfolded, she saw herself rubbing against his body, and she experienced a very deep sexual feeling in her genitals. She saw herself lie on top of him and move her body freely against his. He watched her and had a big erection.

Elena loved the "hot" images of herself because they brought out her sexuality.

Elena's cold images revealed her feelings of inhibition while being sexual. When you see an image in your mind—whether it's hot or cold—it will reveal the mental or emotional state of the person you are with, or of yourself. Elena was initially cold when she interacted with her boyfriend, and he looked much hotter. That's how she would approach sex, more shy and withholding because of what she had learned about sex growing up.

What she saw in the image was the way it really was. In seeing that she was cooler and he was hotter, she realized that he was the one who initiated everything in their sexual relationship. When she saw herself as hot and him as cool, the heat in the image brought out her natural sexuality that was hidden away, and she started to caress him and kiss him; her own passion was able to come forward. She saw him as cooler, which made him a little more laid-back and receptive to her advances. As she went back and forth several times, she realized that the more active she was, the more her boyfriend would cool down to receive her heat. This, in turn, made him hotter. She saw that he really liked her being more forthcoming sexually.

In the images, when you see how your lover is reacting to you, it's a very good indicator of how he or she will react in real life. This is because the images are based upon a real-life storehouse of information about yourself and the other person.

In an image of having sex with your lover, you see how your lover will react as you become more aggressive or more passive. You can see how he or she will respond in the image before you try it out in real life. It's almost like you have a movie of all of your lover's behaviors, attitudes, and reactions inside your head, and you can push a button with an image to see it play before you in your mind's eye.

The interesting part is that the image is the same as a perception that we live with. When Elena saw her boyfriend as hot, that was her perception of him. She was stuck being cold and saw herself as shy; he was hot and always initiating. She couldn't break through that. She could have walked away, saying, "Yeah, he always initiates, and I don't get a chance to," or thinking, "I'm shy, or I'm shut down, or I'm cold, or I'm scared, and that's never going to change."

When we change the temperature, our stuck perceptions change and get freed up as well. Heat in the images is part of our emotions. The perception that we're stuck with our being cold and their being hot, or our being hot and their being cold, can change so that we're no longer stuck in the same old way of interacting with each other. We can free ourselves to be any way we choose.

Elena had developed a cold image that hid her hot image underneath. The cold image was part of what history, her parents, and society did to her to shut her down, freeze her up, and hide the hot, passionate woman she really was.

The two temperatures are usually kept separate in how they are stored in the brain. So all Elena knew was that she was cold and shy, and she believed that she couldn't get to that passionate self within. She didn't even know there was heat in her.

The purpose of the images is to get back to the original sexuality that is our birthright. It is our spark, our life force. Hot and Cold Images are a great tool for overcoming inhibitions and for seeing where a problem is with a spouse or lover and what we can do about it.

If we are stuck in a sexual relationship, unable to move through frozen emotions because of fear or inhibition, we can change the temperature in the image. Different neurological impulses and chemicals will then be sent from the brain into our body. The chemicals induce warm feelings, and the neurological signals create feelings of eroticism, breaking through the frozen parts of ourselves and making a dramatic change.

There is a connection between temperature in the images and the many emotions that occur in love relationships. The temperature of our emotions can vary, and imaging is a good way to shift negative emotions to positive ones. The images will reveal and illuminate the problem, and the temperature will help heal those stuck in emotions that are too hot or too cold.

RAVISHER IMAGE

One definition of *ravish* is: "to be filled with joy or delight; to enrapture." The Ravisher Image allows a woman to rediscover her own erotic needs by imaging that she is being "ravished."

Historically women have been more socially repressed than men in being free to express their deep sexuality. A great double standard has always existed. It's okay for men to have carnal lust and a voracious appetite for sex, but it's not okay for women.

Women were supposed to be "nice girls." Before the sexual revolution exploded in the 1960s, they were supposed to be virgins until they got married. They were always to be chased and never to do the chasing. If a woman had sex before marriage, she was considered used goods. In Italy, they used to hang out the bloody sheets after the wedding night to show that the bride was a virgin.

A typical date in the late 1950s and early 1960s entailed a girl "making out" with a guy in a parked car. Kissing was okay, but sticking tongues in each others mouths was a major deal. He'd try to touch her beasts, and she'd say "no," even though she really wanted him to. He'd keep pressuring her, and she'd still say "no," but she was as turned on as he was. The boy's goal was to have intercourse or at least touch her genitals, but she was supposed to keep saying "no."

A woman's desire, passion, and lust were considered unladylike. Women were supposed to be chaste, the holders of chastity. Women were brought up to be passive in sex, not to be aggressive, not to admit their desires. To admit sexual desire was shameful.

As a result, women's natural desire was suppressed. So women had to create a double image—on the one hand, they were attractive and seductive and had guys come on to them, but on the other hand, they were supposed to say, "No, we don't want to."

Suppression comes out of shame and humiliation, out of being told you're bad to have sexual desire. Suppression means a whole part of you is labeled "not okay." You suppress natural emotions, feelings, and sensations in your body, and you're told that part of your basic nature, part of the way you were made—which is sexual—is not right. A great deal of psychic energy goes into halting those passions because someone or something in your environment—be it your parents, religion, peers, or social mores—taught you that who you are naturally, a person of deep passions, is not acceptable.

When people hide their sexuality, parts of their soul's expression, such as joy and freedom, go with it. Sexual feelings are sensations in the body, and when we deny those sensations, other sensations get locked up too.

The ravisher is not only that part of your sensuality that you don't allow out, but it is also connected to other parts of you, to facets of your spirituality, such as giving, loving, and being fully radiant. Sexuality is connected to spirituality. It is a product of the body/mind/soul trinity. When our sexuality is suppressed, our spirit is not bright.

What we do with sexual desire when society says it's not okay for us to have it is to park it somewhere deep in our mind. With eidetic imaging techniques, however, we can release it. Like the Hot and Cold Images, the Ravisher Image is designed to release our repressed sexual desires.

Working with this image, in our mind's eye we see a ravisher who comes into our bedroom. The person is someone we desire—a real person or an imagined one.

The ravisher seduces us over our objections. We get to be the good girls we were raised to be, we're not the ones who want sex; it's the ravisher forcing us to do it. Of course, the ravisher is *us* as well. When he forces himself on us, and begins to touch us, we resist, saying, "That's not me." But as women go through seeing the image of the ravisher in their minds, they begin to feel very erotic, and as their erotic feelings emerge, they recognize *they are the ravisher*. It allows all of their deep sexuality that was not allowed to be expressed to come out. It is very empowering to own one's full sexuality.

Every woman who has done this image has told me that she feels deeply turned on as she goes through it. As the image unfolds in the woman's mind, she realizes her sexuality has been hidden in the dark, just as this ravisher is. When her sexuality starts to emerge, she realizes what a beautiful role it plays in her life. When a woman's sexuality fully comes out without any inhibitions, it is a spiritual experience. She can be one with herself. She doesn't have to split off, deny, or suppress her own sexuality.

One woman who did this image experienced a flowering in her body, as all of her restrained, denied sexuality began to emerge in the image. She said, "I was raised in a Latin country in the late 1950s. We had a fixed double standard. Women were supposed to look beautiful and sexual to attract men. That was our power. It was understood that men had all the political and social power, but we had the power to make them desire us. Even though appearing sensual was valued, we were not allowed to 'feel' our sexuality. That was looked down upon and women who were free sexually were called 'putas,' meaning whores. That was the worst . . . to be considered a 'puta.' It created a strange dichotomy in me. When I did the ravisher I was surprised at how much I had suppressed my passions. At first I thought of him as "bad", then felt liberated as I realized it was a wonderful voluptuous part of me."

Here is the Ravisher Image.

RAVISHER IMAGE

1. Do you know there's such a word as *ravisher*?
2. What does the word *ravisher* mean to you?
3. Can you formulate an image of this ravisher in your own mind?
4. What happens?
5. What do you see?
6. What does the ravisher do to you?
7. Do you remember any such person doing this to you?
8. If not, this ravisher image is from your own mind, so part of your mind is doing this to you.
9. What does this part of your mind signify?
10. How do you feel toward this ravisher, which is part of your own mind?
11. See that it is a being. What qualities are coming out of it?
12. What other qualities does he have?
13. He's turning out to be different than what you thought at the first encounter.
14. See that this is your own mind. How do you feel toward him?
15. All of this is in your own mind. As you come closer to him, you see more about yourself.
16. The ravisher part is a deeper part of you, and there's more desire on your part.
17. Is there a spiritual side to him?
18. He is the spiritual side of your mind, which gets alienated. Most people see him visiting as a ravisher.
19. This is a reflection on your own soul.

A woman who did the image thought of a ravisher as an attractive stranger who sneaked into her room to have sex with her. "In the image, he does all kinds of perverse things to my body. He's touching me all over, touching my breasts, spreading my legs, exploring my genitals, and then he makes love to me."

She describes the sensation as an erotic experience, even though she's thinking of it as a seduction. She understands that she is really unleashing a part of herself and not a stranger. "I can see that it has my real erotic self locked inside of it. I tend to hide my real sexuality or sexual feelings. I've always done that. This ravisher has inside of him my real passion and my ability to completely let go sexually. I don't feel negative toward it."

As she did the imaging, she felt herself rouse her erotic spirit.

8

Back to the First Awakening of Our Sexuality
Hand-on-Pubis Image

We start out as children by being sexually naive and innocent. Then our hand accidentally falls on our pubis. It's a surprise: it feels good to touch yourself "down there."

If we could look at a filmstrip of the images of our sexual experiences, there would be one frame that shows the experience of the discovery of our genitalia. That first discovery is very innocent.

When we are young, the realization that our bodies have incredibly strong sexual feelings comes as a surprise. It's accompanied by not only surprise but curiosity. There's also innocence attached to it, because we haven't been aware of it before.

God, or nature, or whatever you want to call it, has given us these good feelings in our body, these erotic sensations. The natural tendency is to want to feel more of them. But very shortly after discovering them, most people receive some message from their parents or society that it's not all right to experience this pleasure. The experience of that first innocent awareness of sexual feelings gets overlaid with taboos. So we become conflicted. Some people shut the feelings down, never to feel them again. Some people hide them and feel them privately, experiencing shame; others sneak and do it anyway, feeling defiant; and some people are in conflict because it's bad but it feels good.

This image is important because it brings us back to our essential masculine and feminine knowledge. Feminine knowledge is one of softness, sensuality, and mystery, whereas male knowledge is of strength, firmness, and exploration. We can recapture our sexual feelings in their masculine or feminine purity. This image brings very basic and important knowledge to us, which comes right from the depths of our cellular beings.

All of the sexual experiences that we have from the very beginning to the very end of our lives, including our genetic imprints to our particular social environment, form our sexual identity. First, there's our basic genetics, the way nature intended us to be. Layered on top of this are all the sociological and historical messages that hit us once we are born into this world with all of its conventions, restrictions, prohibitions, unique cultural and religious programming. Then there are all the personal experiences we have—some wonderful, some humiliating—which further affect our sexual self. Finally, there are all the stereotypical messages we get from the culture about how women and men should or shouldn't be. Is it any wonder we forget our primal sexuality?

HAND-ON-PUBIS IMAGE

As you see this primal image, let the feeling that starts in the pubic area grow and spread throughout your whole body. Just let it come up. The feeling is an experience of the feminine self. It grows beyond just the pubic area into a feeling of softness, love, and femininity throughout the entire body, throughout the whole self.

HAND-ON-PUBIS IMAGE: FOR WOMEN

1. See yourself at a much younger age. You are lying naked on your back. Your hand accidentally falls on your pubis. See that you feel pleasure and surprise.
2. There's a special sensation like a spark, a warmth.
3. The hands go down; there's a softness and wetness of the lips.
4. The hands go further down. There is an opening.
5. As the hand touches that area, what is the feeling?
6. Let this soft pubis feeling become a feeling of the whole feminine self.

HAND-ON-PUBIS IMAGE: FOR MEN TO KNOW WOMEN

1. See yourself at your current age or much younger. You are lying on your back. You have a pubis superimposed on your genital area. Your hand accidentally falls on your pubis. See that you feel pleasure and surprise.

2. There's a special sensation like a spark, a warmth.
3. The hands go down, there's a softness and wetness of the lips.
4. The hands go down, and there is a feeling of excitement.
5. Then further down. There is a mystery opening.
6. Let your hand explore the mystery of it.
7. How do you feel?
8. Let the soft pubis feeling become a feeling of the whole feminine self.

When you first saw this image, what did you think? Did it seem vulgar? Natural? What you thought about it is how you have been programmed to think about a very sacred part of your body.

This image goes back to the original state of sexual discovery in its purest form.

For both men and women, the vagina has a mystery to it. When the vagina is touched, it's soft and warm. When women experience this in the image, it softens them and relaxes them, allowing them to understand their feminine nature.

Most of the time, men don't understand women and consider them mysteries. But a man imaging a vagina understands what it feels like to be a woman. The image allows a man to understand femininity. He comes to know the sensibilities of the woman he's with, so that when he has sex with her, he has knowledge of how her body feels to her. Therefore it heightens his ability to give her pleasure and adds to his own eroticism. It breaks the isolation and separation that keeps a man from truly understanding a woman.

Once a man understands something that is "other than himself," and once he can empathize with her experience, he can know it in himself and therefore can honor it in her.

A middle-aged man did the image in order to connect with femininity, to empathize with a woman's experience so he could heal his troubled relationship.

He saw that he was eleven years old and lying in bed naked. He had a penis in the image but imagined that it was replaced with a vagina. He put his hand down to feel the vagina. "It feels good," he said. "It's warm, like a tingling sensation, like a warmth spread over my thighs and stomach, it's a sweet warmth and tingling. I see that my hand goes further down, to the softness of the lips. I'm exploring my vagina now. It's soft, it's moist, warm, it's smooth and silky and inviting and embracing and encompassing, surrounding.

"As my hand feels that, there's an opening. My hand goes to the opening, and it's like a mystery. It's the cave of the ancestors, the cave of spirit, like the ancients living there, in the side of the mountain, and there's carving on the wall and paintings. It glides in, and there's a smaller opening to another chamber you can only get into by squeezing down, really slither through. It's tiny; if you're too big, you can't even get in. You have to force your way in further to get in the next chamber."

What this man experienced with the vagina was a mythic sense of softness, sensuality and mystery.

Now he let the soft pubis feeling become a feeling of his whole self. He expressed how he felt: "Like a melting down into the earth, I'm on my back, but I feel the earth under me. I feel my body and the earth becoming one and connecting, and the warmth is like the sun on me. My back is on the earth, my body faces the sun, and the warmth of the sun is melting me into the earth."

He has seen the hand fall on the pubis and has experienced the feeling of melting and feminine sensuality. Now he describes how he, as a male, feels towards the vagina. "Reverence, awe, love, devotion, selflessness, a total facilitator of the process, like being a conduit of consciousness, like a priest going to worship at an altar, pure, to give a sacrifice on the altar, his semen, he places his semen on the altar, and if things are right and it's acceptable to the gods, then the mystery unfolds."

How does the vagina feel toward this erection? He said: "She (the vagina) feels like she's going to heaven, this is God who is going to take her to heaven, the sexual and spiritual are really one."

A woman seeing the image said: "There's a melting that I'm feeling. It's almost like there is an energy present, and I'm somehow in touch with that feminine energy, hooked into it. It feels like I'm being recharged, like the energy is there and I just fall into that profoundly female place. There's also that titillation quality that goes with it. So there's something very sacred about it, and at the same time it's also very alive. It's almost like neurons constantly firing off all over the body, and at the same time there's a bathing in this deep presence of ease and knowing the sacred almost, as if you were a channel and you just touched into the river of energy because you are open and channel it."

This woman is experiencing feminine energy, the primal universal feminine force. This force is feminine and basic to any other knowledge; there's softness, love, fullness, sensuality, and mystery. The woman has this first, and the man tries to find it and can only do so through her.

She said: "It feels like channeling the sacred; it feels like that hookup place to the source of creation."

As you can see, this image brings a woman back to her purity, the essence of her feminine self, to the sacredness of that connection, before the world and its impurity closed her down. It's sacred, sensual, electric, and cosmic.

This image reveals that primal sexuality is sacred, and that the connection between the sacred and the physical sensations of sexuality in the body are rooted in absolute purity. The image evokes the innocent sexuality of the first touch. The beginning is where purity was found before society dirtied us. The sacredness of our sexuality still resides untainted within us.

Some people may have difficulty going back to the beginning. For example, when one woman tried to see the image, she couldn't find a place in the house that she grew up in where she could let her hand fall on her pubis. There were too many prohibitions in the house. She had a strong feeling this was not allowed. Everywhere she went, there was some disturbance and some feeling of prohibition. All that interference is reflective of how her family and society suppressed her.

Then she said: "I'm having this meaning come to me when I do the image: 'Do not touch yourself, or you'll go to hell.' There was a very puritanical atmosphere in the house, and no one acted in the least bit sexual. Sexuality was never discussed. My mother and father were very uptight about it, and there was tremendous taboo about it. As I try to see an image of myself resting to touch myself, I feel almost gagged and like my hand is bound. The message is, 'Do not touch. Bad, bad.' "

As she continued seeing the image, these considerations kept coming up, and she just couldn't relax. That is what her history did to her purity. While the first woman doing the image went right to the source of her sensuality, this woman was suppressed, and the image gave her tremendous insight into the source of her suppression.

The "Hand-on-Pubis Image" allows the essence of femininity to be felt, experienced, and known in a woman. She has that essence, that femininity within herself, and she must know it within herself first. It is born in her and exists first in her. The man sees it in her, and desires her because he tries to find it in her. If she does not know this feminine fullness in herself, the man will not be attracted to her. First, she has it; then he comes to her to find it. He then sees it in her. Once she sees that he sees it and loves it in her, she can love him.

The feeling that first comes from the pubis when it expands to a physical feeling throughout the body is the expression of the whole feminine self that draws men to women and allows women to love them.

9

Compatibility

How Do You and Your Lover Stack Up?

Chemistry. The word brings to mind something explosive in a test tube. Perhaps that's why we use it to describe how our persona mixes with another's.

Sometimes that first charge you get when you meet someone new is delicious. You are happy and at ease, warm inside. You don't know why, but you're excited, and the world is harmonious. All is well.

Other times, someone approaches you and your nerves are a blackboard the person is scraping their nails across.

These reactions are all part of this magical, mysterious thing called chemistry. However, the problem with chemistry is that it is not always a good gauge of compatibility.

All too often, we are sexually attracted to someone who turns our lives into pure hell. The right chemistry that gets us into bed with someone is often the wrong chemistry for a lasting relationship. I can't tell you how often I've heard people say that they have terrific sex with their mate, but spend the rest of their relationship arguing over the kids, careers, money, and the whole nine yards of modern life.

There are some people who believe you don't choose who you love, that love is something that just happens. Initial attraction, of our mind and libido, does seem to strike more like lightning than a well-planned maneuver. But a long-term, great relationship does not just happen. It is the product of a great deal of work and adjustment between the two people.

The Hollywood version of love just happening is called the "cute meet": girl sees guy across a noisy, crowded room, and suddenly time stands still, gypsy violins play, and everyone in the room fades except for the lovestruck duo.

Personally, I believe that a rich, romantic, and permanent relationship is less first-sight infatuation and more the slow meshing together of two spirits. That "first hit" is, of course, wonderfully intoxicating, but not all infatuation survives the stress of modern life.

We are attracted to people on different levels. There can be a meeting of the minds, an intellectual stimulation that excites and challenges us. Or there can be a sense of mission or purpose together, like working together for a charity or starting a business. And, of course, there is only a sexual attraction. A person with a beautiful body may create a pure sexual rush in us. But enduring love is a connection that encompasses the body, mind, and soul.

There can also be neurotic chemistry between two people. In this sort of attraction, one person's hang-ups fit nicely with the other's hang-ups. This can be very problematic. A woman may attract an abusive husband because there is something in her background that allows her to take abuse, or a man may attract a cold woman because he feels he doesn't deserve more.

In general, people who are compatible as lovers have an ease of communication between them. They have common values and can live together harmoniously.

Couples who are compatible have a nonverbal, natural flow between them that permits them to relax. If someone with whom you can have great sex can't be at ease with you going out to dinner or dealing with stress from work, you are not compatible. Just having great sex does not make for compatibility in the relationship. If one of you is uptight and the other has to be on guard for fear of offending you, you are not compatible, no matter how much you love one another. If you can't relax around each other and simply be yourselves without annoying the other person, and you insist upon staying together, you are in for a stormy relationship.

To be compatible with another, you have to be comfortable with yourself. When you are comfortable with yourself, you can often extend that ease and comfort to another. People sense it when they are around someone who is comfortable with themselves. It relaxes them, and they feel at ease.

When you and your lover are each comfortable with your own sexuality, then you can relax with each other and have great sex.

You don't have to work at good sex. It's not mechanical. You don't automatically go through a list of body parts in a prescribed manner. Good sex happens when your lover touches you, and your body just feels right and relaxes. You can let go. When you touch your partner, he or she feels good. When you can relax and let go, sex stops being work, and you start soaring.

TWO HANDS TOUCHING IMAGE

There are many nuances in the nonverbal interactions between lovers. These subtle cues reveal volumes about their relationship. In order to discover them, we are going to use an image called "Two Hands Touching." For example, if a woman reaches out to touch a man and the man recoils from the touch, they are not compatible. The man is not responding to the initiation of the woman—she is warm, and he is cold.

Touching hands in the image reveals whether you are compatible with another person, and what the energies are between the two of you as you interact.

One benefit of doing this image is that you can learn about your relationship without confrontation or recrimination. You can also adjust your behavior by using the insights you gain from the imaging.

Touching is a very important human act that connects us to each other. Through touch, we fulfill our basic needs. Babies need to be touched and stroked. Children raised in orphanages are emotionally damaged if they don't get enough touch and human contact. When we put a hand on a child's shoulder, give them a hug or caress their cheek, that little touch communicates volumes of love and approval and raises the child's self-esteem.

Touching is the way we communicate love, need, and caring (not to mention emotion, rage, and anger). We need the warmth of each other's bodies and each other's touch to thrive. As we grow up, we need to keep touching and be touched. The longing for physical contact never goes away.

Touch is an important vehicle of communication between men and women. A little touch, a squeeze of the hand, a pat on the shoulder, a hug, brightens our day and opens a storehouse of good feelings. With our lover or spouse, if we stop touching each other due to conflict, it's very painful. It feels like something is missing, gone awry.

When lovers touch hands, a special communication goes on between them. The entire microcosm of their relationship is revealed. So when two hands touch, it speaks volumes about the feelings between them. The touch will convey warmth, coldness, harshness, softness, longing, desire, approval, or rejection.

From the very first touch, there's contact and communication. A man takes his girlfriend's hand. If he holds it a little hard, a little possessively, she'll react by either liking it or hating it, maybe by feeling controlled.

She may withdraw her hand. If he holds her hand more intimately, more warmly, she'll sense that, and she'll feel good. She will respond in her own way, letting him know she likes it. If he holds her hand gingerly, she'll get a feeling of rejection.

The nuances between two people touching hands are profound. Even a simple handshake tells a lot about people. Some people shake your hand and you feel their soul, while others offer a hand that feels like a limp, wet fish.

In an image of herself and her lover, a woman saw him take her hand and hold it in both of his hands. She felt a strong warmth and energy coming from him. He was communicating to her from the depths of his being, a feeling so beautiful and deep that it conveyed the love and adoration he felt for her. She reciprocated; there was no resistance taking in his love. Had there been resistance, he would have felt it, but she was completely open to him and allowed that feeling and warmth into her. She became soft and loving and surrendered to him and touched him with such purity that it made him feel very passionate toward her. Passion circulated between the two of them just by their touching hands.

When you touch another person's hands, you're connecting to the other side of creation. You're the female side of creation, he or she is the masculine side, or vice-versa. The way you touch hands says a lot about you and the other person. The reaction you get from the other person, either warm or withholding, reflects the emotional dynamics between the two of you.

TWO HANDS TOUCHING IMAGE

1. See yourself extending your hand to touch the hand of your lover. See how you extend you hand. How do you feel extending it? Is there hesitation, fear, trepidation, confidence, joy? What are your subtle emotions?
2. Now see how your lover responds to your extended hand. How do you feel as you see this image?
3. Now see your lover extending a hand to you. How does your lover extend it to you? What are your lover's feelings as he or she extends a hand? What is being communicated?
4. How do you feel as the hand is extended to you? Do you want to move closer or further apart?

In noticing all of these subtleties of emotion, you can begin to discern what the problems are between the two of you.

A man touching hands with his lover reported: "I touch around her palm and her fingers in a firm but gentle manner. Her skin is soft, and I feel the bones in her fingers and her flesh, and it's soft and a little cool. I just move my hands around in a soft massaging kind of fashion, exploring. She reacts lovingly, responding back with pressure, touching my hand too. There's a nice even pressure that we have, and there's a lot of warmth and love expressed in that touch. There's a feeling of well-being as the hands squeeze each other."

When one woman doing the image reached out to touch her lover's hand, she reached out with longing and desire to connect, yet he responded with tension, withholding, and trepidation. When she saw his reaction, it made her fearful, and she felt rejected. She then pushed more to connect with him, but he withheld and withdrew even more, and she felt even more rejected. He told her she had dry, cold hands, and this deeply hurt her feelings.

When this man did the image, he became aware that he responded to her touch with trepidation. He tried not to withdraw his hands but to be more receptive when she reached out. He tried to listen through his hands to what she was saying to him. He understood that what he was really feeling was fear of being close to her. He didn't want to reject her, but she was coming on too strong for him. She had to learn to come on more lightly, so that he could respond without feeling threatened.

There is a very subtle dance that happens in two hands touching.

WHAT THE HEART TELLS US

The "Picture in the Heart Image" reveals who someone else is most connected to in life. You can use it to see who your romantic interest is most connected to.

We saw an image of our parents' hearts earlier. The steps we followed then are similar to the ones we will be using with our lover. The image will not only reveal details of our lover's feelings, but by looking again at our relationship with our parents, it will show us how we deal with our lover.

The heart is a great symbol of love. On Valentine's Day, we give each other cards with hearts on them. Many songs have been written about hearts. When our lovers hurt us, we say we have a broken heart. When we are happy and in love, we say our hearts are fulfilled.

The heart consists of the physical organ as well as its essence, the feelings in the heart. These can expand into a great love for someone or can retract in anger or fear.

With eidetic imagery, you can actually see an image of the heart of your lover and discover fresh information about the person. You can also see the images of the hearts of your parents and get a sense of how much love was in their hearts. Was there anxiety in their hearts that made them uptight or scared? Or were their hearts relaxed and open and generous? All of this can be seen in the Picture in the Heart Image.

When we see an image of a beating heart in our parent's chest, it represents the presence of love. Similarly, when we see the image of a beating heart in our lover's chest, it symbolizes the amount of love, the presence or absence of love in their heart. When we look at the heart, we can see the fullness of existence, all of life, as deeply moving and tender. Or we can see coldness and lack of tenderness, a constricted heart.

How the heart appears in the image symbolizes that person's emotional relationship with the whole world—with people, with animals, and all of nature. The heart contains love and universal compassion for all living things.

What you see in the heart reveals the person's loving nature or the lack of it. Also, as you look more deeply, there's a picture of someone in that person's heart. It may be someone who the person is most devoted to or attached to.

Oftentimes, people will look into the heart of a parent and see the children of the family. Sometimes they'll see a spouse; sometimes they'll say, "I see my mother's mother in her heart." When people look at the heart of their lover, sometimes they can see themselves.

There are no set rules; when you image the heart, the meaning of the picture will come to you. Ideally, a heart should appear affectionate and show a regular, beating rhythm. It reveals whether the person's heart is capable of expressing tenderness and love. As you look at the image, you can tell whether feelings of comfort or anxiety are there. If there's anxiety in a father's heart, for example, probably it was difficult for him to express the love he felt. Consequently, you may have gotten a feeling that you were not worthy of love.

It's important to first look at our parental images to see whether our parents' hearts produced ease and warm feelings in us or produced anxiety. The way we feel as we see the image of their hearts will have a corresponding response in us. Whether we feel relaxed and loved or constrained and unlovable is directly related to how their hearts were.

So, if our parents' hearts were constricted and anxious, and we feel anxiety and we shut down in response, we need to ask ourselves if these feelings are being carried over into a relationship with a lover or spouse. On the other hand, if there is a feeling of ease with the parental image, do we bring this into a relationship with a lover?

In the heart are feelings of affection, affinity, attachment, attraction, compassion, concern, devotion, fondness, kinship, warmth, loyalty, and love. We can look at the important figures in our lives and discover how *their* hearts affected *our* capacity to love. The direct correlation between how we feel seeing the image of our parents' hearts and the feelings we bring to our lover's heart is one gift of this image. Another gift is to use this image to see our lover.

PARENTS' PICTURE IN THE HEART IMAGE

1. Picture your parents standing in front of you.
2. Imagine there is a window in each of their chests and that you can see their hearts beating there.
3. See their hearts beating, and describe how each parent's heart beats.
4. Is there any sign of anxiety in the heartbeats?
5. See your father's heart beating. Describe its beat and appearance.
6. Is there any sign of anxiety in your father's heartbeat?
7. Imagine a picture in your father's heart. Who do you see?
8. See your mother's heart beating. Describe its beat and appearance.
9. Is there any sign of anxiety in your mother's heartbeat?
10. Imagine a picture in your mother's heart. Who do you see?

LOVER'S PICTURE IN THE HEART IMAGE

1. See your lover standing in front of you.
2. Imagine there's a window in his or her chest and that you can see his or her heart beating there.
3. See the heart beating, and describe your lover's heartbeat.
4. Is there any sign of anxiety in the heartbeat?
5. Imagine a picture of someone in the heart. Who do you see?

You will obtain your own unique insight from the Picture in the Heart image.

A married woman who was having an affair wanted to find out why she was cheating on her husband. She pictured her husband standing in front of her, imagined a window in his chest, and saw his heart beating. She saw a red heart that looked machinelike, tight, with a constriction in the middle that emanated anxiety and tension.

This woman said, "I see my husband's heart; it's red at the edges, but there's a metal trap in the middle that makes his heart beat in a very tight manner." She realized that what she was seeing was a reflection of how she felt about him. She loved him, but she said that her own chest was always tight when she was around him. She felt she could not be at ease with him or connect with him. "I've been sad about it over the years. At times, I've thought, what's wrong, he's rejecting me. But I also knew he loved me, so I was very confused. He would keep a little distance from me, and let me in and push me out at the same time."

His heart was partly stiff and partly warm. "That's how I feel around him: stiff and open and then closed, available and not available. It drives me crazy."

She then pictured her lover in front of her, with his chest open and heart beating. The heart was a deep reddish-purple, and the meaning she got was that he was a very passionate man, a quiet, deep person who kept his strong emotions to himself.

"I can see his heart is totally unobstructed; there's no anxiety. I can see there's a tremendous depth. If I touch it, it opens more and more, as if his heart is so big it would take me forever to explore. Now I see I could take years and years to get to know him, but once I enter his life, he will be loyal and devoted forever. I feel very relaxed in the presence of his heart, which is how I always feel around him. I can be myself. He's at peace with himself, whereas my husband's not at peace."

Imaging who was in her boyfriend's heart, she saw his parents and herself.

When she imaged her mother's heart, she saw a big red heart full of anxiety. "There's love for me, but she was anxious and would get distracted and sometimes have no time for me. This is exactly the same as with my husband; it's like he can't be there fully with me. I see that's why I married my husband; I'm recreating the same feeling I had with my mother."

When she saw her father's heart, she saw a dark, deep red. "There's no anxiety. There's tremendous love, but I get a feeling of pain; he saw a lot of bad things in his life. I'm very comfortable in the presence of my father's heart. Like my lover's, I can move into his heart, and it's infinitely accepting. When I see a picture of someone in my father's heart, I just see light; he was a very spiritual man and had love for everyone. His heart is profound, like my boyfriend's."

The imaging made her realize that she had married a man who made her feel anxious like her mother had, and that she was having an affair with a man who gave her a deep sense of spiritual love as her father had.

A person will be damaged in the ability to love and be loved if the parents' hearts appear absent or extremely anxious. The woman realized that her husband's tense heart was a result of his fear of expressing his emotions or tenderness. A very floppy heart could mean a failure in the expressing of emotions. Irregular heartbeats indicate anxiety; absent heartbeat can mean an absence or repression of emotions.

If you see a small heart, it could indicate limited emotional capacity, the inability to give fully. Many women who had good relationships with their boyfriends had fathers whose hearts appeared big and full.

As you see the image of the heart, you will come to an understanding about the person's capacity to love. Trust what you get.

Often, we think there's something wrong with *us*. The meaning we get from viewing another's heart can help us discover whether we have a problem or if someone else does and we're just responding to them.

10

The Sensuous Woman

For modern women, there is a lot of pressure to be beautiful, slim, in physical shape, active. This pressure comes from the media, lovers, and peers. Women are supposed to look like movie actresses, and so they struggle with diets and the latest fashions. From the time they're little girls, women are very aware that their value resides in their appearance.

Even though girls are now encouraged to be intelligent and have college degrees and careers, they still are pressured to look a certain way. While it's great that opportunities for women have opened up in the last several decades, women still have problems as women. Society in general, and most of us in particular, are clueless about who and what we are on the inside.

Women must first connect to their unique inner sensibilities as women, in order to express their feminine inner nature fully. What is that inner nature, that unique essence that comes from within and emanates outward?

That inner essence is a *feminine* essence. The word *feminine* has been used and abused and may connote a number of things. In the past, femininity implied weakness and helplessness: in the golden age of silent movies, the heroine fainted into the hero's arms. Before that, southern belles were fragile and beautiful and needed men to open doors for them and balance their checkbooks. In the stormy 1960s, the word sometimes connoted burned bras and revolution in the home and office. Here, however, I'm using the word in a more classical, more natural sense—feminine versus masculine, not in a competitive way, but in the sense that each sex has its own unique qualities. Women's natural qualities have been lost under conventional images of what femininity should be.

Weakness has always been considered a feminine attribute. Perhaps in the days when the world was conquered by sheer brute force, that had some basis in truth. But today a woman can make strategic global decisions just as easily as a man.

As we delve deeper into the female psyche, what we find is tremendous strength. There's an enormous power that is rooted to the very fabric, the very depth of nature itself.

Women need to understand and reconnect to their inner core of knowledge, to know that it's within them and to live in tune with it. Doing so makes them so much more attractive to men. Men long to be with women who know themselves in that profound way. Men need women, and men love women who know who they are. When women know themselves, it allows men to relax, to enjoy their presence, and to have an equal partner with whom to share life.

In the model of feminine as weak, men have been overburdened, having to take charge of everything. Even though it looked like power to the male, it was really depleting for them. What has become obvious to me in working with women all these years is that the more in tune a woman is with herself—loving, strong, soft, sensuous, powerful, wise— the more adored she is.

FIRST BLUSH OF WOMANHOOD

Discovering our depths as women means stepping back and looking at the events that shape our psyches. A primary one is when a woman first develops breasts. Historically, men have often expressed a sense of wonder and warmth towards young girls who are beginning to develop, not as sex objects, but with a deeper appreciation, much as if they are seeing a flower go from a bud to full ripeness. Through the ages, male artists, writers, and poets have expressed wonder and a deep affection upon seeing their daughters and other young women turn from girls into adult women.

All girls experience the first stirring of sexuality. It begins with budding breasts and the menstrual cycle. Sadly, along with the magic of transformation comes societal damage that affects women for the rest of their lives, emotionally crippling many of them. As painful as it may seem, many women who cannot maintain a permanent, loving relationship with a man will find the seeds of their discontent in these early years.

We will examine these and other elements that injure or handicap a woman's sensuality. Both men *and* women should become familiar with the origins of sensuality of not only their own sex but the opposite one as well, because it will help them to better understand and relate to the other in romantic relationships.

As girls develop into women, there is a critical transition point that happens around the age of eleven, give or take a couple of years. It's when girls start to develop breasts and begin to menstruate. It's a very special time for young girls, a time when there's a big change in their identity. They are still innocent, and thoughts of turning into women are exciting. It's a very positive state of mind. Girls look forward to being grown-ups. They realize that they too will have the power and presence of the adult women around them. It is the springtime in a young girl's life.

In working with lots of young girls, I have witnessed the excitement that they go through. It's a very positive time of initiation into womanhood, when they formulate images in their mind of being adult women.

Then society, with all its social problems, descends upon the girls, and they begin to shut down their initial excitement about becoming women. Often boys tease them, or their parents don't know how to deal with their sexuality, so send them the wrong messages. Sometimes people treat them in ways that make them feel shame—for instance, older boys might make crude jokes. What a shock it is to a girl's hope and innocence.

I have conducted seminars for women in all walks of life in the past twenty years. The participants ranged from women executives to poor teenage girls. Ninety-nine percent of the women—regardless of class, race, stature, or upbringing—experienced some form of humiliation, embarrassment, or shame associated with their developing breasts. Something always seems to occur that shuts down a girl, hurts her, and makes her feel embarrassed. Unfortunately, because these jabs come at such a sensitive time in a girl's life, these messages affect her very deeply as she forms her identity as a sensual woman.

There are no rituals in our culture for girls passing through the transition from girlhood into womanhood. There are no teachings to help parents—or boys—understand how to treat girls during this delicate time. Girls need to be adored at this time so that they can become the full women they were meant to be.

During this transition, mothers sometimes injure their daughters through a lack of understanding, often because they themselves were mistreated during puberty. Their message to their daughters should be,

"This is so wonderful; you're becoming a woman; how exciting, how beautiful you are!"

As a matter of fact, the opposite most often happens. If you ask the women around you to talk about when they first developed breasts or got their first bra, there is usually some pain or shame associated with it. Some girls develop later than others, so they feel inferior and different, and those feelings persist into adulthood. Other girls develop early or have bigger breasts than the other girls, and they carry a complex about that.

In working with adult women, I take them back to the image of when they first developed breasts, to discover how they were treated.

One young girl began to develop breasts when she was only nine. At first she was excited about it, but by the time she turned eleven she was trying to hide her chest, walking with a little bit of a slump in her shoulders. Somebody had teased her every day at school about her breasts, which left her feeling confused and shamed about her sexuality. As a result, this girl developed mixed feelings about being a woman. She had some embarrassment and shame about being sexual mixed with the pride she originally felt.

For a moment, think about breasts. See the breasts in your mind's eye. What kind of breasts do you see? How do you feel about them? If you're a woman, think of your own breasts. How do you feel about them? If you are a man, what is your attitude toward them? Desire, lust, appreciation, reverence, or exploitation?

Breasts are a very powerful symbol of femininity. They evoke primal feeling states in everyone. Men are always looking at women's breasts. Women are constantly comparing other women's breasts to their own. They are a very important body part that defines a woman as a sensual, attractive, or sexual being, regardless of their size or shape.

Breasts are an icon of sexuality in our modern culture. Think of *Playboy* and other male magazines that emphasize breasts. Think of all the breasts hanging out from the covers and ads in *women's* magazines, supposedly illustrating what makes a woman sexy.

The size of breasts can make a woman feel bad or good about herself. Just look at all the women having breast enhancement surgery, even with the health risks involved.

There are other images of the breast, besides sexual ones. These involve nursing babies, nurturing, love, sensuality, motherhood. Is there any other body part that stirs so many primal emotions? All the psychic energy that the culture projects onto the breasts . . . well, little girls who are making that sensitive transition into womanhood walk right into it. It is a heavy load to carry.

So what happens to that innocent young girl who is going from girl-hood to womanhood? What about her sensitivities? What messages does she get about her femininity from the culture around her?

Unfortunately, she gets a lot of mixed signals. Watching television or looking at fashion magazines, she sees actresses with big, unnatural, surgically enhanced breasts. As a result, I have overhead girls as young as fourteen worrying about the size and shape of their breasts. There's such a distortion created by the media that girls don't know what's nor-mal. Thus, they have negative feelings about their natural size.

It's important for men and women to understand how women have been affected by the cultural hype about breasts and for them to learn to relate to women in a sensitive way.

I think that breasts are such a hot item in sexuality for men because they bring them back to their primal connection with their mothers— to softness, warmth, and nurturing. This is an undefiled, natural long-ing in men. Pornography is a distortion of this pure desire. Whether one was nursed or not doesn't matter—it's the profound feeling of being held against mother's bosom, which is so compelling. The breasts have those powerful feelings of nurturance attached to them, such as love, caring, and sweetness.

What men are really attracted to is the sweet, tender offer of true love, which is what we are all looking for. A lot of men may have suc-cess in the world, but what they deeply long for is the sweetness and tenderness of true love, which is contained in the essence of the breast. And that is why breasts are such powerful icons. They contain the sweetness of life.

REDISCOVERING NATURAL FEMININITY

When women image the time when they were first developing, there is an initial recognition of their feminine self that accompanies the bud-ding breasts. Yet, as they look at the entire experience in images, like frames in a movie, they find that somewhere along the line, they were damaged by the way their sexuality was treated. Thus, women forget the initial excitement of their newfound feminine identity. What remains inside of them is the feeling that there is something wrong with them.

There is an image that I love called "Visionary Start." With a visionary start, women can recall their pure beginnings prior to the social
repressions that assaulted them.

VISIONARY START IMAGE

1. See a tree blossoming in the spring.
2. See the most beautiful blossoms that stand out on the
   tree.
3. See the image of the blossoms, and experience the fragrance.
4. See that the image is like the beginning of a new vision.
5. See in your mind that you have just begun to develop
   breasts.
6. There's a new feeling and a new vision of your body. Your
   mind is open. You're excited and awakened to new things,
   but the boys your age are still unaware.
7. What kind of vision of the world do you have when you
   keep your breasts in mind?

This image takes the woman back to the beginning, when the visions
of the essence of her femininity are evoked. It takes her to a time before
the boys of her age group demean her or her parents mishandle her,
before any humiliation happens, to the first stirring of excitement.

A woman who did the image remembered how she suffered under
the crude, rude comments of boys when she was in puberty. The boys
made her perceive her breasts in a negative way. Their sarcasm brought
her a feeling of humiliation about being a woman, which she carried
into her relationship with men. She felt shame about her body.

When she saw the image, she said, "When I see that my breasts are
just beginning to bud, my state of mind is, oh cool, I'm a little girl coming into womanhood. I see images of myself flipping back and forth
from little girl to woman. I have breasts now, so I can be seen in a new
light. I'm shedding childhood. The new sensation of awareness of my
breasts is like I'm a butterfly coming out of a cocoon, like I'm emerging
into something wonderful. It's very pleasant. There's a womanly feeling
that's coming from my insides out that I've never felt before. I can't
totally describe it. I feel I have power when I think of my breasts. I

sense I have female power. I feel no shame, and I don't feel a need for excuses about my breasts. When I think of them, what comes over me is a sense of fullness. It reminds me of nurturance, the way I snuggle my puppy against my chest, and of the softness and the love I feel for my friends and family. There's a power for good in my breasts. I have images of growing up, getting to wear makeup, making myself beautiful, having a boyfriend, being a mom, doing something important in the world.

"But what comes to mind is that, when others began to notice my breasts, I remember the days of hiding them and feeling inadequate. I felt very alone. I was best friends with all the boys, and then they all started treating me differently. I once climbed trees with them, but now they made crude comments and gawked at my chest. It was an awkward feeling for me to experience my body's changes. I felt inadequate for a long time because those boys made those comments. My mother didn't seem that interested in what was going on. She dismissed my concerns and made light of them. No one understood my turmoil. I thought there was something wrong with me."

She saw an "image of the world," keeping her breasts in mind: "Now that I'm an adult, I feel like my breasts are what they are, beautiful things which distinguish me from men. When I see the world while keeping my breasts in mind, I feel I have something inside me to give the world, a great nurturance and love, and I approach life with that feeling. That's the essence of my sensuality, that feeling of love and nurturing. It's a very lush feeling. I like it."

Judging by women's magazines, it is clear that women are also obsessed with breasts. This is because they are an organ of pleasure and display. They know there's a power of attractiveness in their breasts. They express their inner beauty through their breasts. And men respond to that inner signal coming from the woman who knows her sensuality. It is the inner signal of the woman who feels good about herself that attracts a man, not the breast itself.

So the woman feeling her own inner sensuality binds the man to her, through the breasts, the same way as she is bound to her inner feelings. There is a nourishing quality to the breasts, and the notion of beauty is attached to them.

With the vagina, women intuitively know they have a mysterious temple in their pelvic area that men feel is "home." It's different with the breasts. Women first feel their sensuous fullness from their breasts, and men respond to the full sensuality that they emit. This has nothing to do with the size or shape of the breast. It is the essence that is contained within it.

Girls who have just begun to develop have a feeling of anticipation in their psyche, and all their mental and emotional processes hook into that feeling. The feeling of anticipation is very important, and it becomes a leading thrust of feelings and images to come.

So when you see the image of the budding breasts, there's an anticipation and an expectation that they will become the full breasts of a woman. All the images that go from being a little girl to a woman are contained in the feeling of anticipation. So the budding breasts are one image, with many images attached to it of what is to come. And that can be very exciting for young girls.

A successful, hard-driving businessman in his fifties who was having problems in relationships and wanted to learn more about the feminine spirit did the Visionary Start Image. The result gave him greater insight into the feminine mystery that had eluded him. This is what he reported:

"I see a connection of cycles of nature of the tree and the girl. The way I feel about the tree is how I feel about this girl. But the girl has more capabilities; what she's going to grow into is magnified. Both display the natural order of God, and I see the two as indelibly connected. The image is not overly sexual; it's a little erotic, but really mostly a sensational affirmation of nature. The erotic part of the image of seeing the girl is like the cherry on top of a whipped cream sundae. It is tantalizing, mouthwatering. As the blossoms continue to open, the breasts do also, so the promise of more exciting dimensions of the breasts occurs in my mind."

When he talks about the promise of more exciting dimensions, that's the expectation I mentioned before.

The man continued: "Breasts are the most wonderful things. I have been trying to figure my whole life why I'm so enamored of them. They captured my complete attention. I feel so blessed when I'm able to be intimate with a great set of them. I feel the gods have just blessed me. When I'm intimate with a great set of breasts, it takes my total attention; all else disappears, there's one focus, one consciousness; it's relaxing; it's such a fulfilling experience; it fills my entire awareness. It's better than drugs; it's the real thing; it's what real men live for. There's a timeless element to the experience. No peripheral awareness, just a connection to something divine.

"When I think of breasts, I can't do anything else. Nothing equates with the breast. I can't see the world. I have to have them. It is such a strong attraction for me; it is so powerful for me. Breasts rule; you get slapped in the face with a great set of them, and your day is complete. You can go home. It's just pleasurable, total pleasure."

Here are the images of a woman's experience: "I was about ten years old, and I was aware of my breasts developing and I had a feeling of pride about them, but I also wanted to hide them. I noticed some of the boys in the neighborhood were changing toward me. They were aware of my breasts and my sexuality. I liked that, but I also felt confused because I wanted to hide my breasts. It was a very conflicting experience. I both liked the changing attention and was scared by it. My first experience getting a bra left me very shamed and humiliated. I was outside playing with my friends. When I came in the house, my mother said, 'Okay, that's it, you can't be a tomboy anymore; you're going to get a bra.' She said this in front of Jimmy, my older sister's fiancé. And she said, 'Jimmy is coming with us to buy the bra.' I said, 'Mom, why are you doing this?' I was so embarrassed. She said, 'Because you're going to resist getting a bra, but if he comes you'll be too embarrassed and you'll have to get one.'

"Of course I went. I was totally embarrassed. My mother, my older sister, Jimmy, and I all went to the store. I wanted to die. There was some small part of my mind that wondered if Jimmy, since he was aware of my breasts, was a little bit attracted to me. So there was that little sexual feeling toward him covered by an immense feeling of humiliation. That was my introduction into womanhood."

She did the Visionary Start Image and said: "There's a feeling of pain like I have to hide my breasts. I don't feel good enough. My mom and my older sisters are better than I am. I am embarrassed and ashamed. Now I realize that this feeling has persisted my entire life. I'm sure it came because of the way my mother made me go buy a bra."

Often while seeing an image, other images come to mind. She continued, "Wait a minute, I'm having another image. I realize that when I first became aware of my breasts, there was a feeling of excitement. I was about eight or nine. When I go back to that image, to that time before anyone noticed, I see that I have a feeling of excitement. I will become one of the club of adult women. There's a feeling of specialness to being part of this club. I feel attractive and beautiful, and I will be noticed, and I am important. Because I'm becoming a woman, what I say and do matters to others. As a child, I'm not as important as I am as a woman. This is very exciting to look forward to. I feel a positive anticipation of growing up and becoming a woman. It feels really great. I had forgotten this first exciting feeling because of my mother, Jimmy, and the bra. That really put a damper on my good feelings."

This story is typical of what happens. There's always a feeling of anticipation of what is to come inside the psyche of a girl, which contains images of the fullness of her sexual essence. This essence is programmed by nature to emerge as the young girl's breasts begin to develop. The genetic wholeness of women can be recaptured through this image.

For men to find a woman sexually attractive, she first has to feel good about herself in order to emit the signals that reside deep within her. It's the women who have confidence in themselves as women who turn men on. Men feel the signals emanating from the woman, and that's what attracts them. The signals of confidence, of femininity, of strength, ooze from them and draw men like bees to honey.

How girls are treated when they first begin to develop either enhances or diminishes their innate feminine knowledge. But the knowledge can be recaptured when you take women back to the first inklings of the budding breasts. They can retrieve their wholeness and the fullness of their sensuality. Even though a woman has been shut down, she can overcome the social events that made her feel bad about herself by recapturing the true essence that still lives inside her. Her sensuality and attractiveness can be found right there in the images of the first budding of the breasts.

When we take women through the image of the breast, they experience both the fullness of nature emerging in them and also the suppressions that they suffered. By empowering or giving more weight to the nature part of the image, women can restore their original sensuality.

A woman in her thirties typified the many women I've taken through this image. She remembered: "I was in the fifth grade, I was ten, and I had just started developing. I was in class. We were doing a science project, and we were sitting in groups of four. One of the things we had to do was cut some foam rubber. I was showing how strong the rubber was. I was jumping up and down on it, and a boy said in a really smart-ass way, 'You know you need to wear a bra.' I was taken aback. I didn't know that I needed to wear one; I was completely unaware. I had been very tomboy-like and I was innocent. At that time, my mother was busy starting a new job, and my father was at work, and my brothers and sisters were involved with what they were doing, so they didn't notice that

I was developing. So the first time I heard that I was developing came from that boy, and it was said nastily and it was a shock. It made me feel badly about my body. I thought, oh God, I'm different.

"I came home and told my mother. I was very upset, and she said 'That's okay, we'll get you a bra.' We went out and got a stretchy thing that just covered my breasts; it was a training bra. I thought, how odd, do my breasts need to be trained? When I think of myself before getting the bra and developing, I feel like a little kid, androgynous and innocent, not aware of real differences between boys and girls. After the bra incident, I felt confused about myself. In a way, I felt bad, wondering why that boy was looking at my breasts, was there something shameful? It left me self-conscious. Why was he so aware of them? What's wrong with me? I see I have carried that feeling of shame, my entire life. All of this started when I first began to develop. I still feel the same about my body."

11

Aphrodite

The Goddess in a Woman

Myths from around the world are powerful stories that concretize human experiences. The lives of the gods and goddesses exemplify our own lives, the agonies and joys, emotions, struggles, and conflicts that we have. They are larger-than-life examples in which we can see ourselves.

Aphrodite is the mythic goddess of love and sensuality. When women see her as an image in their minds, she can help them reconnect to their own sensuality and beauty.

Of all the goddesses, Aphrodite was the most beautiful and most sensuous. She embodied a deep feminine essence of sensuality, beauty, and power. The Romans called her Venus. She was absolutely extraordinary, the ideal of feminine beauty and grace.

Aphrodite was not only beautiful; she was also intelligent. She had enormous power, and if anyone maligned or hurt or rejected her, they got her wrath. She expressed the full force of her anger; no one could mess with her. She was full of wisdom and knowledge and knew how to rule the world in her own female style. As an image, she is able to connect women to their true inner nature, which is not only sensual but also powerful, intelligent, and wise. For me, as a woman, when I think of Aphrodite, I feel both soft and strong, and I sense that I can accomplish many things with my feminine power.

Here is Aphrodite's story. In the pearly light of dawn, Aphrodite arose from the sea on a cushion of foam and floated lightly on the waves to the flowering island of Cythera, where she was attended by three Graces who dressed her in shimmering garments and sparkling jewels. They set her upon a golden chariot drawn by white doves that took her to Mount Olympus, where the gods rejoiced in her beauty and set her upon a golden throne and made her one of them.

Wherever she trod, wildflowers and grass sprouted from under her feet. The Graces bathed and anointed her, and sacred gardens were consecrated to her. Wherever she went, the birds of heaven heralded her, and the wild beasts grew tame following her.

They say that in the girdle of her bosom was carried all of her secret charm, desire, and sweet flattery, which stole the judgment of most prudent men. There was a magic about her, a constant temptation. Her essence was the celebration of spring.

Through her radiance and translucent beauty, Aphrodite is a sensuous renewal of love in the psyche. She is the return of nature and offers a vision of primeval love. She's not attracted by perfection; a man doesn't have to be perfect to be rewarded by the sweet and tender offer of true love.

This notion of sensuality in Aphrodite is seen in Madison Avenue advertisements. Her image is alive in products such as perfume, deodorants, and shampoos. But the true essence of Aphrodite has been lost and misunderstood. We need to bring her back so that we can connect to her sensuality.

She is represented as a beautiful, irresistible, Greek goddess to whom all men just succumb, and she offers the notion of sexual bliss. The implication is that we can have sexual bliss only if we can obtain or capture her physical being or essence. She is ever young, soft, curvaceous, sparkling, mischievous, charming, insatiable, desirous, and desirable.

All women have an Aphrodite within them. She is the essence of natural feminine sensuality, and all women were born with that essence. Somewhere inside us is that great energy of Aphrodite waiting to come out.

When girls first develop breasts and the rest of their body takes on a more womanly cast, they're coming into their Aphrodite nature. It's the Aphrodite in them, that natural essence of feminine sensuality, that becomes repressed when girls learn not to be comfortable with their bodies.

When women go through the "Aphrodite Image," the size, shape, quality, and condition of their breasts are not important. It's the essence that's contained in the breast of Aphrodite is important, and that essence is in every woman regardless of what her breasts are like.

To further explore the breast and natural sensuality issues, we start with an image in which a woman sees Aphrodite before a mirror, looking at herself from the top of her head to her waist. The mirror is a reflection of self-knowledge—she knows herself by the image in the mirror. The image makes her conscious of her natural beauty and sensuality.

The image of Aphrodite is presented here as a vehicle to help women come back to themselves, to their inner selves, and to put aside all that pressure from the outside to look "perfect." *Women need to come home to themselves so that men can go home to them.*

APHRODITE IMAGE

1. See an image of Aphrodite in your mind's eye. Aphrodite is full of love, warmth, sensuality, wisdom, and power.
2. Now see Aphrodite looking at herself naked in front of a mirror. Her breasts appear sensuous and proportional.
3. See her admiring her sensuous breasts. Her breasts are reflective of beauty, power, and nourishment, and of giving love.
4. There is a sensuous aroma of perfume flowing out of the mirror. Experience the perfume flowing in the image.
5. See that the perfume expands your awareness of your feminine nature.
6. See that the reflection in the mirror reveals your true feminine essence.
7. Experience the feminine essence emanating from within you.

Women discover the essence of their feminine sensuality in this image: the thing that drives men crazy and that men long for. When women can connect to the essence of their sensuality from the inside out, there's a feeling of fulfillment.

Sally, a fifty-year-old woman, is raising two teenaged children, has a full-time job, a house to keep, and no time or money for gym workouts. She sees Aphrodite before a mirror. It brings her back to being herself.

"The first thing that happens to me as I see the image of Aphrodite with her sensuous breasts is that I begin to soften and relax after a busy, hard, working day loaded with duties and responsibilities. A very loving feeling comes over me. It is a gentle feeling, a nurturing feeling, as if I want to be loving and kind to everything around me. It's a softening, and I feel a connection to my sensuality. This is when I'm at my best, when I'm feeling sensuous and loving and there's laughter in me. I'm very relaxed.

"When I see her sensuous breasts in the mirror, even though mine are not as perfect as hers, the feeling in me is very full. I am fulfilled. And those soft colors around the breasts just mellow me right out. I feel young. It's like kissing children and hugging puppy dogs and making love all come from that same core of soft sensuality that's inside me.

"This is nice. I've just totally relaxed; this is great. Maybe I can go through my day keeping Aphrodite in mind. In fact, that's a good image to do."

UNLEASHING FEMININE ANGER

Aphrodite is feminine, but she can be very angry too. When someone hurts you, the natural first response is anger. Anger is the mind's way of protecting itself. If I see a mother dog suckling her puppy, and I go to hurt the pup, you can image what she'd do. She'd snarl at me and attack me. That anger would be justified, as it is part of nature's self-preservation.

Similarly, when people hurt the innocence and beauty of women by putting them down, abusing them, or rejecting them, there are two choices. A woman can be angry and stand up for herself and not tolerate the abuse, hurt, or rejection. Or she can crumble and believe that there must be something wrong with her.

That's what happens to young girls when they first develop breasts. They're still so innocent that when others tease them or hurt them, they're too young to understand that their anger is deserved. Instead, they usually collapse emotionally, believing that there's something wrong with them. They carry that feeling into adulthood.

When the innocence and purity of the feminine is injured, anger is a natural feeling that comes from within. It is standing up for oneself.

If the feeling of anger is not allowed, a person can close down and become depressed. When one becomes angry when being injured, the remedy is justice in the psyche. When a person crumbles while being hurt and doesn't express anger over it, his or her mind can close down, and he or she can become depressed and repressed. This has happened to women for as long as we have had recorded history.

APHRODITE AND FEMININE ANGER IMAGE

To keep her self-respect, Aphrodite expresses anger when she's not fully honored. When someone hurts us and we can't stand up for ourselves, or when a situation calls for a nonconfrontational response, we can obtain justice in private with a soul-healing image about feminine anger. It goes like this:

APHRODITE AND FEMININE ANGER IMAGE

1. Aphrodite is beautiful, but she can be angry too.
2. She's absolutely beautiful, and she's also totally lovable in her anger.
3. Anyone who says to her, "I do not love you," deserves the wrath of nature. She lets loose her ferocious animals on the person.
4. The ferocious animals closely follow her wherever she goes. They are the beautiful decorations around her aura, as well as her power symbols.
5. The golden aura around beauty has both truth and power in it.
6. See Aphrodite's ferocious animals attacking someone. See the details of the attack.
7. See a rejecting individual you know receive a similar attack in the image.

Sally sees the image of feminine anger. "I see that Aphrodite is so sure of herself as a woman and so confident that if people put her down or reject her, they deserve the awesome wrath of nature; they deserve those animals tearing them apart.

"I see this nasty guy who teases her, puts her down, and tries to control her. Now I see a panther, bear, wolf, and dog; they just shred him to death. It's natural; it's absolutely the way it should be because she is so pure in her being, in her lovingness, and in her sensuality. Anyone who dares to hurt her is the kind of person who hurts or destroys nature. I have a feeling of righteous indignation when the animals attack the man. Her qualities of femininity, love, and tenderness are in me, and anyone hurting that deserves to be taught a tough lesson.

"I think the reason I feel so good about it is because I've been hurt and rejected in the past, which made me doubt my own femininity, my own self.

"The part of this image in which you see a rejecting individual you know receive a similar attack reminds me of a guy I dated in high school. I really liked him. One night we were kissing and hugging in the backseat of his car. We almost had sex, but I stopped him at the last minute. I was not ready to lose my virginity. But he told everybody in school that we had had sex, and it gave me a bad reputation. I had offered him my genuine love, my sexuality, in going as far as I did with him. He hurt me to the quick. This pain stayed with me for a long time and affected my sense of self. I had to deal with the rumors in school. I felt betrayed, and I internalized what he did to me by ending up doubting myself.

"So, I see the power animals that surround me in the image go after him and attack him. They don't kill him, but they threaten him and say, 'Don't you ever, ever, put a woman down again who has been loving to you!' They're really ferocious; a white wolf has him by the throat. And a tigress is ripping his pant leg. I can see that he's shaken and that he'll never do to anyone else what he did to me. I feel victorious. My self-respect is restored."

In developing this image, Dr. Ahsen said that when hostility or antagonism develops around us, we rise to defend ourselves, matching the weapons of our inner nature in the battle. This means that this image allows each woman to redeem herself from every situation in which she was hurt, in her own unique manner. The image brings her inner psychical weapons to the fore to undo the injustices she has suffered in the past. It restores her self-esteem, and she learns how to fight for herself, never letting anyone diminish her.

So the "Aphrodite and Feminine Anger Image" is about retribution and justice in the psyche. We can breathe free when we can express our anger at injustice, experience our power. While Aphrodite is completely beautiful, sensual, and soft, she's no wimp. She can stand up for herself. She has incredible strength, and her anger is filled with a radiance that's connected to truth.

"It's a great image for me as a woman," Sally said, "because it teaches me to stand for all that is inside me and not allow myself to be diminished."

APHRODITE AND HER TEMPLE IMAGE

The "Aphrodite and Her Temple Image" allows women to be freely themselves. This image emphasizes the union with nature, body, and love. The best gift women can give is the gift of themselves, knowing themselves as free, powerful, and loving. Knowing their true nature overcomes the insecurity many women feel about themselves.

APHRODITE AND HER TEMPLE IMAGE

1. See Aphrodite all by herself, standing in nature.
2. Aphrodite is nature itself; she is grass, trees, waterfalls, everything.
3. Where is Aphrodite's temple?
4. Her temple is found in three forms: as the ground on which you are standing, as love in your heart, and as your own body.
5. What ceremonies are performed in her temple? Loving your own true nature is the high ceremony.
6. What are the gifts she brings to her temple? There's only one gift: freedom.
7. What does she give you in return? She gives you the freedom to be yourself. She puts all her powers at your disposal.

A woman named Mary was having trouble with a new relationship. Her boyfriend Charlie played a push-pull game with her. He would spend time with her and be available, but then she wouldn't hear a word from him for two weeks. Then he'd come back, and they'd have a wonderful time. They'd make plans for dinner, but he would call at the last minute, cancel, and then not be seen for another two weeks. Whenever they would get a little closer, Charlie would react by distancing himself for a time. He was actually petrified. Yet Mary took his behavior personally, and her self-confidence began to erode. She liked Charlie a lot, and she was at a point in life where she wanted to get married.

Their on-again, off-again relationship went on for about three months. One day while Charlie was at Mary's house, another man called her for a date. This gave her the impetus to open up the subject of what was going on in their relationship. She confronted Charlie about his disappearing act. He told her, "I can't stand in the way of your happiness; if you need to date others, go ahead." Mary felt crushed because she liked Charlie and they had become sexually involved. His whole attitude hurt her and affected her self-confidence. She started to doubt herself, which is often the first thing women do when a man is not responsive, rather than think, what's his problem?

Mary began to question herself. "What's wrong with me? What did I do wrong? Was I too giving? Was I too available to him? I was much more available for his time schedule than he was for mine. Did that push him away? Was I too eager?"

Mary had been true to herself in the relationship. Her basic nature was to be sweet and generous, but Charlie's back-and-forth attitude made her doubt her own natural self.

Mary then did the Aphrodite Image and said: "I see that Aphrodite sees herself as confident, beautiful. She knows she's beautiful. She's in control and still very feminine. She's inviting. I can see why she's the goddess of love. She lures people to her. I feel like she's a role model for me. The fact that she's in control and confident and unshakable in who she is, is a real lesson to me not to doubt myself."

Next, Mary did the Aphrodite and Feminine Anger Image. When she saw the animals attacking a man who had injured Aphrodite, she said: "The animals rush toward him and hold him down. He is struggling. They don't kill him, but they hurt him. He's learning a lesson not to control or hurt or put Aphrodite down, either in subtle or overt ways. Aphrodite is looking detached."

She said: "It feels like he's getting what he deserves, that the animals are teaching him a lesson."

Mary then came to the part where she was asked to see a rejecting person in her own life. She saw Charlie. "Crows come and lift him in the air, and he's struggling and afraid that they're going to drop him. I see that he feels unsafe and insecure being dangled in the air. This is his medicine: the crows are teaching him a lesson and showing him how he made me feel. This is a very relieving sight to me, because he is learning about his actions, what he did to me. I feel restored. In being able to express my anger, I feel so much better."

Mary had been hurt. She had the feeling of being dangled in the air, with no stability, no one to rely on because of Charlie's back-and-forth behavior. He would be available and distant, and this gave her the feeling she had of no ground under her feet. Now the crows were teaching him.

Next, Mary did the Aphrodite and Her Temple Image. She said: "This is wonderful. I love the idea of being free; I haven't felt free ever in this relationship. I have been locked into this relationship, and I felt I had no control. I was locked into responding to all of Charlie's dynamics and hadn't been aware of it. Being free is a very powerful thing. I can see that from going through this image. It gives me a sense of freedom, and I don't want to lose that. I want to be myself. I want to come back to being myself." Then she started to cry. "This freedom gives me the space to come back to myself and to be free and not be enmeshed with Charlie's problems."

Mary explained the meaning she got from the images: "My boyfriend has no power over me now. I see him as a weak, scared, young boy who has been hurt. I see he's attracted to me, but he's really scared of my power. He's afraid to open his heart. He's afraid I'll become so important to him that he can't risk my rejecting him. When I keep Aphrodite in mind, I see I'm too much for Charlie, he's not up for the game. I have more to offer at this point of my life than he can either take or receive. I feel no ill will, only compassion, and I wish him well, but I see he's not for me. This is a relief. I can get on with my life, and knowing this and keeping Aphrodite in mind and working with these images, I'm sure I'll shift from emptiness to my own fullness."

Remember Sally? Now she is seeing the image of Aphrodite and Her Temple.

"When I see Aphrodite in nature itself, I have this relaxation that happens in my body and this incredible connection with the earth. I see Aphrodite standing, and she becomes united with the wind and clouds, with the storms. There are no inhibitions, no self-doubt, no questioning; she's just fully herself. If lightning strikes and the sky is rumbling, she can rumble too, or she can be calm, serene. She is free to be any way she wishes. She can run; she's free to be herself. That's an amazing realization.

"When I see her temple, it gives me a solid feeling, like my feet are connected to the ground and there's power under my feet. The love in my heart as Aphrodite walks is very full for everything around me, and my body feels very sensuous and connected to nature. It gives me a very powerful feeling in my lower back and legs and a very full feeling in my heart. I feel power and sensuality when I see this image.

"What I'm understanding from this image is that however I am is okay—all of me—not only that sweetness that's inside, but the anger, too, is really okay. I can freely be myself without self-doubt, without recrimination. I never quite realized that I can just be myself."

Going through these images, women become free and understand the beauty and power of their own essence. Knowing that they have something magnificent as women is really sexy. Remember the mystery women have? That is the sexiest thing around. No matter what they look like, women who know that they have that mystery within themselves attract men like crazy.

I was at a restaurant on a very crowded evening, and I walked across the room to go to the bathroom. No one noticed me. In the bathroom, my mind went to Aphrodite. I felt a sudden shift come over me. I experienced my own sensuality, femininity, and confidence; I felt in touch with that inner feeling that Aphrodite brings. I was experiencing something subtle, an aura of confidence. As I walked back from the bathroom to the table, every male head in the room turned to look at me. I was surprised. I realized that their reaction had little to do with my outer package because I'm fifty-something. I hadn't even put on lipstick. It was a subtle inner shift within my own psyche, within my own self, that created their reaction.

Some women have described this knowledge as similar to the way sports players are when they're "in the zone" and everything they do is magical. Women can walk down the streets of New York and nobody will look at them, but if they make that shift and connect to that knowing inside them, to their essence, there's a whole change in the atmosphere. This can't be faked. It is not an act. This is what people try to get by creating outer beauty with makeup, clothes, and hairdos, but the most powerful allure is that essential self-confidence. It's the most powerful sensual, sexual attraction. When a woman exudes this essence, she really is like Aphrodite, and she's not needing or wanting or longing for men. She is so sure of herself and so full of her own spirit that all the men want her. That's the difference between emptiness in a woman and fullness.

12

The Sensuous Man

Men have as many problems with their sexuality as do women. The core of the problem is that men have received mixed signals while developing sexually. On the one hand, they are taught that a man expresses himself through physical power—and on the other, they are supposed to be sensitive and caring in order to touch a woman's soul.

A man's natural sensuality is designed to connect physically, emotionally, and spiritually with a woman. But men are as much victims of the superficial sensuality permeating our society as are women.

For men there is a tremendous pressure to perform in all areas of their lives, competing in their careers, assuming they will be the main provider for their families, feeling they have to be leaders. They are rarely allowed to look vulnerable or in need. From the time they are little boys, they hear messages such as, "Boys don't cry, keep a stiff upper lip, toughen up, don't be a sissy." Their inner sensitivities are crushed with expectations of being tough and in control. They have been overburdened with all these expectations. This robs them of their wholeness and their ability to dip into a deeper, more essential part of themselves. They must look virile, strong, and always in control. They are taught that their sense of identity comes from their acquisitions or positions of power in the world rather than from within. These social attitudes squeeze the life force from them, making men more insecure and out of touch with their true masculine nature. They must hide parts of themselves or risk being ridiculed. The worst insult for a man is to be accused of being "feminine." Due to all of this psychological stress, is it any wonder that a man's life expectancy is at least ten years shorter than a woman's?

Since men are conditioned by society to express their masculinity in terms of power, physical or otherwise, they remain, like women, clueless as to what their inner masculinity is all about. If they can connect to their deeper inner spirit and their true genetic capacity as men, they can discover the real essence of power.

For men, the first intimations of all this begin at puberty.

THE FIRST STRING OF SEMEN

Boys in puberty sometimes wake up with a spot of wetness on their pajamas. They have no idea how it got there, and they are embarrassed to tell anyone. Semen is the embodiment of the transition of boys into men. It scares some boys, just as having their first period scares some girls. Boys usually go through this transition with no one to confide in and have to figure it out for themselves. Their voices start to change, hair grows in private places, and erections shoot up at the most embarrassing moments. Emotionally they are still kids, but there is a man inside struggling to emerge.

Like a girl's first period, this initiation into manhood is left unritualized and unattended in our culture.

There are many images that help men make the journey back to their natural sensuality. We have already used ones like Walk-Around and Co-Consciousness. In this section, we will deal with more images and take a look at some aspects of mythology that relate to male sensuality.

Men, do you remember that when you were about eleven or twelve, before you actually ejaculated, something thick and stringy, a string of semen, would flow from you? Semen has the power of creation and transcendence in it. It is the product of excitement, adventure, activity, discovery, and mystery. And it is an important part of a man's link to his masculine potency and passionate feelings.

The "First String of Semen Image" corresponds to the girl's breasts developing, indicating a change in her consciousness from young girl to woman. Similarly, the first string of semen represents the change from boyhood into manhood in the consciousness of the male. That first string of seminal fluid is a forerunner of things to come. It's the first signal of a change.

FIRST STRING OF SEMEN IMAGE

1. See yourself as a young boy of twelve or so.
2. See the first string of semen. It is a forerunner of things to come.
3. There is surprise, curiosity, fascination.
4. See colors in it. Let your imagination flow. There are rainbow colors reflected in the semen. How do you feel seeing them?
5. See these rainbow colors as a bridge to an adventurous world. You are venturing out. You are aggressive, exploring, curious.
6. The string is linked to potent and passionate feelings.
7. When the explosion occurs, it is like a being is taken out and put somewhere.

This image helps men get into their bodies, to make the connection between mind, body, and spirit that they were born with. When we have sex, we have to surrender to sensations and pleasures. We can't be stuck in our heads; rationality is as much a damper on good sex as insecurity, fear, and repression. For a man to have sexual pleasure other than a momentary "kick" from ejaculating, his heart has to be open. When his heart is closed or he's controlled by subconscious feelings that sex is dirty or sinful, then sex becomes perverse, a purely physical sensation without any true essence. To reach the divine, we have to experience love and tenderness.

A man doing the First String of Semen Image saw himself in early puberty. "I remember having nocturnal emissions, and I kind of spontaneously discharged, but it was semen. I felt surprise and fascination, curiosity and wonder. Seeing it now in the image, it kind of stimulates me; it makes me want to go and move and do something, an active thing. The movement of the semen is like a metaphor for the movement in my life. I'm hearing vapors escaping from a volcano that is about to let loose. It's a mixture of wind and the sound of vapors escaping, and it's a very activating feeling, like getting ready to explode, to let go."

The image created an exploratory feeling in him. The essence of the masculine is adventurous, exploratory, and active.

Ejaculation is such a forceful, active event. It is an energetic, spontaneous, vigorous, muscular activity; it is a metaphor for what a man's life
and consciousness are often like.

That first string of semen is a forerunner to male consciousness,
and it's linked to the passionate feelings inside of him.

Here's how one man described it: "When I ejaculate into her it feels
as if a part of me goes into her. I leave part of myself in her body. For me
this feels like love. I have the sense that she takes me with her."

When a man and a woman are linked sexually, there's some direc-
tionality to it. The male is movement and the woman is more receptive,
but when they're connected at a deeper level, the male and female per-
sonas melt together and are transcended by a different level of connectivity. They are no longer male/female. A woman who wants to be more
active and initiating extends herself to the more traditionally masculine
role. The male/female distinction is somewhat arbitrary because when
sex is good and a couple are really connected, it doesn't matter who's
initiating or receptive.

When a man offers himself sexually, women sometimes say, "What
does he want from me?" without realizing that he is giving love and giving of himself. Men often say it's like giving a part of themselves over to
the woman. The whole process is contrary to the man taking anything.
Physically and metaphorically, the woman receives something from the
man. The man should think of it as sharing part of himself rather than
as getting something. When either partner thinks that the other is taking something, the true essence of sex is being twisted. Sex becomes
misunderstood and distorted and separated from its spiritual essence.

THE MAN'S BRIDGE TO HEAVEN

There is an ancient Norse myth in which a rainbow was a bridge from
earth to the heavens, a bridge made by the Norse gods. The bridge was
the link between humans and the gods. However, the bridge became
flawed because of the "gods of history," who were not the original, pure
Norse gods. The frost giants were the initial Norse gods, and they were
pure. Out of them was born the next level, the gods of history. These
gods weren't honest, they bore false witness, and they did not fulfill
promises or contracts. They abused people, and they abused the frost
giants. Sound familiar? The new gods used their power to create their

own kingdom, from which the frost giants were isolated. From this animosity came a curse on civilization.

This myth represents what happened to humanity. We were supposed to be in the garden, pure, with God. Then the gods of history came, people who used their power to create their own kingdom out of greed, conquest, and domination. They isolated those who had the spirit of purity within them. This myth has similarities to the story of the expulsion of Adam and Eve from the Garden of Eden in the Old Testament in which we went from being pure to being tainted.

The destruction of the rainbow bridge, of the way we unite with the divine, is real. The gods of history used their powers for their own benefit, and just like the exile from the Garden of Eden, it ended up in self-destruction. Heaven is the pure realm: innocence, spirituality, love, and all of the divine things are heavenly. But our personal and cultural history destroyed our access to the divine. Thousands of years of cultural evil, greed, selfishness, domination, and control were passed on to our parents by theirs like genetic defects, and we grew up never making the connection to the divine because we had too many obstructions.

The rainbow bridge is seen in the semen. There is something about the power of semen and the way it thrusts that has the feeling of a divine connection. When a man ejaculates into a woman and his connection to the woman is pure, he can transcend the physical sensation and go right to heaven through his sexuality.

However, if a man's rainbow bridge has been damaged—tainted by negative thoughts ("masturbating is evil, and you'll go to hell for it!") or by the belief that a woman is an object to be used, or by fears or doubts about his sexuality—then the way he connects to a woman will be stilted. It won't take him to a heavenly state of union with her.

When men look at the First String of Semen Image, they have a feeling of masculinity, adventure, activity, discovery, doing things. As one man said, "There's a feeling of exploration."

Also, many men report that the ejecting semen image is a link to passionate and potent feelings, and that the explosion is a very giving feeling. Everything comes together in a man, and a whole being is taken out as he ejaculates into the woman.

The image often reveals the social injury done to men. Men get hurt because they think they have to be dominating. They are rewarded for their potency, for being macho, and for having thoughts of objectifying women, like "snatching a piece of you-know-what" from her. There are so many expectations put on men to be "a man" (whatever that is) that it injures their original feeling of exploration and their natural feelings about themselves as men.

We spoke earlier about "giving" in sex. Man's sexuality by nature is very giving. When we define the pure essence of male sexuality, it's really giving something over; it's connected with love and it's a gift the woman receives. It is as if a being is taken out of him and given to her when he ejaculates. He feels he gives of himself and leaves it with her. And she takes the gift into her own self, out of which new life is created.

Sex is an act of giving and love. Society distorts it by making it purely physical, degrading it, focusing on pieces of a body ("tits and ass"). That is not the real spirit of masculine sexuality. The true spirit of masculine sexuality is that of creativity, of exploration, of venturing out; it is also full of love, spirit, and passion in joining with a woman.

When we first have a sexual feeling, it's innocent. Then society comes along and says, bad girl, bad boy, you'll get warts for touching yourself. Or it says, there's a girl—just use her for your pleasure. We experience humiliation and domination, and we begin storing up repression when we should be soaring.

Our sexuality should be brimming with naturalness, but if you look at our cultural role models, TV, and movies, sex is completely devoid of any sacredness. It's all titillation; it's used for consumption, mass-market appeal, and unloading stress.

Many men don't have a good memory of their first string of semen, because the experience is laden with a great deal of cultural symbolism that affected their own sexual development. There's the family's personal attitudes toward sex, the culture's beliefs of what it means to be a man, and the society's attitude about sexuality. All of these affect a young boy's experience of the first string of semen, whether or not he is aware of it.

For some men, being a man means being macho, conquering and dominating women. Women are just objects to use for personal pleasure. Yet under all this arrogant behavior, there is a fear of women. This type of man wants to have sex with women, but not connect to their hearts. They are not taught that love is a high state of union.

All of these societal attitudes hurt men because they don't allow men to get to the basic essence of their male sexuality. The attitudes also do not permit men to connect to the feminine in a pure way, as though one belongs to the other.

For men, the bad experience with the first string of semen embodies cultural, sociological, and historical symbolism. The First String of Semen Image will bring a man back to a knowledge of his genetic wholeness regarding sexuality, with openness and curiosity, and with all the pure feeling states, emotions, and thoughts that are genetically in him. Connected to that image is his initial sexuality in its purest and most natural form.

A man in his fifties explored his sexuality with the image. This is what he experienced: "When I see this image of the first string of semen, I think of ejaculation, which is a very male thing. Ejaculation feels like a movement toward an explosion. It is like some kind of energy transfer. It's an energetic process. I've always seen it as an electrical connection; the current flows. There is a circuit that is established between her and me, with a charging at one end and a discharging at the other end. We are linked together with me as movement and she as receptive. But as we truly connect at a deeper level, it feels like a reverberation. The male/female stuff all melts together and is transcended by a different level of connectivity. We are no longer male/female. We don't know who is being the male or the female force at any particular time. We become one thing, one fused melting-down thing. We are not separate; we are one."

13

The Male Beauty Trap

Men, too, are victims of the superficial beauty trap, penile implants and butt tucks are right up there in popularity with shooting steroids and pumping iron.

In my work with men concerning their sensuality what I find most commonly is fear, as well as confusion about how to use masculine power. Movie/TV masculinity revolves around power—physical power over other males and physical and emotional power over females. Men are portrayed as sexually dominant, always in charge, and certain about what to do. The modern forms of this type of male are those who want control over the family's finances and lifestyle, men who make all the final decisions. Some men think that high-powered jobs and a high-powered car serve as extensions of their virility. They have lost knowledge of their true male essence.

Men who equate power and control with sexual prowess do not open themselves up to true love. Most men are not looking for a one-night stand, but for a permanent, loving, and sensuous relationship. Alas, too many of them don't find it because they don't know how to use their masculine sensual power to stoke a woman's inner fire.

Through mythic images, we can go beneath the layers of cultural and sociological tarnish that society puts on men about who they are and aren't, and enables them to find the true nature of masculinity. This nature is embodied in the Greek god, Poseidon, who is strong, yet open and innocent.

Poseidon is a mythic masculine image of sexuality. Coming slowly out of the sea, naked, water glistening on his body, he holds his trident as he moves. Waves hit against his chest as he slowly comes to shore, but he's powerful and the waves don't stop him. He comes ashore, water dripping off his body. He sees the temple of Aphrodite in the mist ahead, and he rapidly walks toward it, his body getting warmer as he feels the aura of femininity surrounding the temple. He sees the priestess of the temple and senses the nectar within. He rushes to the temple, to the nectar.

The image of Poseidon is very sensual, even though he has a sense of power about him. Poseidon knows how to use his power. He is strong yet vulnerable, and he longs for and honors the connection to the female. This desire and strength are very appealing sexually. He is pure and untainted in his desire for women and his innocent passion is very disarming and appealing to them.

At a primal level, men deeply long to immerse themselves the feminine, in exactly the same way that Poseidon goes directly for the temple, a symbol of the vaginal structure. The nectar in the temple represents feminine essence.

These images of Aphrodite and Poseidon are not fantasies but deeply ingrained imprints in the psyche of men and women. In the search for sensuality, Aphrodite is a symbol of the heroine and Poseidon of the hero. Both are wonderful images to access and use.

POSEIDON AND ZEUS

Mythology reveals our psyches to us by making conscious our inner desires, ways of acting, modes of expression, and conflicts.

The "Poseidon Image" describes male sensuality, male consciousness in its purest form as it moves toward a desired female. It allows a man to connect to his own passion, desire, and attraction toward a woman. It is the male equivalent of the Aphrodite Image.

Poseidon is the god of the sea. He is the son of Kronos and Rhea, who are brother and sister. Kronos and Rhea had three sons: Zeus, Poseidon, and Hades. They divided the world among themselves, with Poseidon receiving dominion over the sea. Poseidon was also known as the god of mariners, to whom he sent storms or fair voyages. He's the god of waters in general and of earthquakes.

Poseidon was also closely associated with horses as Hippios. The horse was sacred to him. It was said he fathered many famous horses, including the winged Pegasus, and in Corinth horse races were held in his honor. There were temples in the southernmost tip of Greece in his name, and freshwater springs were often consecrated to him.

POSEIDON IMAGE

Men can access the depths of their sensuality by seeing images of Poseidon.

POSEIDON IMAGE

1. See Poseidon coming out of the sea. He is coming ashore. He's holding a trident in his hand, the symbol of his power.
2. See his chest. It is strong and broad.
3. See that you have become Poseidon. As you move toward the shore, the waves crash against your chest, but the force of your power surging forward pushes against the waves as you move through them.
4. Feel the waves crash against your chest as you surge forward.
5. See that you have come onto the shore dripping water.
6. See that your body is hot, and the cool air dries your body as you move. Feel the coolness against your warm body.
7. See that there's a temple on a hill. It is the temple of the virgin priestesses.
8. See a priestess in the temple. Feel the heat in your body as you walk toward the temple.
9. As you move toward the temple, see that there's a warm fire in it and an intoxicating essence of perfume. Smell the perfume.
10. See that you are drawn to the nectar in the temple to the priestess.
11. Experience the sexual energy flowing through your body.

The Poseidon Image is one of being drawn toward the feminine in a very pure and direct manner. There's something beautiful about that. What Poseidon is moving to is something sacred. He represents an entry into the temple of Athena (the priestess), and he's going to have a sexual connection with her. In a sense, he overcomes the isolation of the sacred and sexuality, connecting the two.

Usually people think of sacredness in terms of celibacy, but Poseidon is divine and he takes what belongs to him, not in a chauvinistic way, but in a pure sense of the rhythm of nature. That's very powerful. When I've told women how Poseidon takes what belongs to him in a natural and pure manner, they get turned on by it. It's like being taken, being adored, being savored. So many women long for that pure passion, which is how Poseidon engages with the priestess.

Sometimes our history is revealed through seeing the images. One man who did the Poseidon Image saw that when he reached the temple, he asked the priestess what was wrong because she avoided him. He said, "I'm only taking what belongs to me, and the priestess doesn't feel that she belongs to me. But I realize she is a priestess, not a goddess. The priestess is more like some of the nuns who taught me in school, and I can see through this image that she opposes God because of her rigidity. Were she the goddess Aphrodite in her temple, then I would take what is mine, and she would completely and passionately connect with me."

When he heard the word *priestess*, the image of a nun came to him because he associated the sacred with the childhood experience that had thwarted his sexuality.

When Poseidon's chest thrashes against the waves as he's moving toward the shore, it represents the masculine forward-moving feeling of breaking through obstacles. His hot body, with the cool air drying it and his connection to the wind and its movement, gives men a sexual feeling. The combination of the air, water, and heat brings masculine sexuality to the fore.

Poseidon goes for what is his, which is *her*. He wants *her*. Many women love the feeling when a man says, "You are mine," not in a possessive sense, but with the sense that she's totally free. He desires her and claims her sexually so they can merge in ecstasy. It's a real turn-on.

A man in his forties did the Poseidon Image. He reported: "It's very frothy, you know, how the waves crash against my chest. There's all that froth. I also get the image of women's legs against my chest. When I come ashore, it feels really tingling; while I dry, there's still some residue of seawater, like the salt in my chest hair. With the sun beating down, it makes me feel really strong, really refreshed and energized. It's electrical.

"I see the temple on the hill. The temple is pointed, square, with a red stone top, a lot of white marble, and four pillars at the corners. Inside, it's round, and there's a stand with a bowl of lavender or rose, a soft scent that is enticing. I see the priestess dressed in a robe of soft white cotton, and she has these incredible legs.

"I'm coming up the steps. She's lying on a bench on her side, and there seems a natural connection drawing me to her. She's not moving, but there is an energetic level. Her energy embraces me. It's in the air current; there's a pull toward this incredible being. There's a real purity with her as well, not innocence, but certainly purity. It's interesting that I feel my strength as physical, but her strength as internal.

"When I came out of the water, her legs were spread out wide, and there was an incredible whiteness of her legs and thighs. We have great sex."

For men, the truest example of pure male sexuality is Poseidon. Poseidon brings to men a feeling of the masculine power, potency, and sexuality that exists within them. Like the Aphrodite Image, which shows women their feminine side, Poseidon evokes the masculine side. It brings out the purity of their passion, lust, and desire. The feeling of wanting to go directly for her, to partake of the nectar, is a very beautiful, innocent part of masculine energy.

The Poseidon Image is very helpful for men who are repressed or uptight sexually. Or for those who can't connect with the purity and beauty of their raw sexuality.

ZEUS IMAGE

Zeus is the supreme god, the head of the whole Greek pantheon. In addition, Zeus functions as a sky god or weather god, and as a god of justice and freedom. He's the son of Kronos and Rhea, brother of Poseidon, and the consort of Hera.

Zeus's sexual prowess was legendary. He seduced or forced himself upon numerous goddesses, nymphs, and mortal women, fathering countless children in the process and assuming many different forms in pursuit of his numerous conquests. The cult of Zeus was of universal significance in the Greek world. Greek households typically had statues of Zeus in their forecourt, and he was often associated with mountaintop shrines. He had temples in every city, with two of the more notable ones in Athens and Olympia.

The conventional Hera, his wife, is a goddess who stands for rules and regulations. Zeus represents freedom. They are married. There's conflict in their connection, because she wants to uphold the rules, while he stands for love but with freedom. Hera is rule-bound, and according to the law of marriage, Zeus belongs to her.

Part of Zeus's job as head god is to bridge the divine realm of gods with the worldly realm of humans. He is supposed to bring spirituality, or the godly realm, to human life. He does this by impregnating human damsels and nymphs so their offspring become half-human, half-god. In this manner, future generations have the godly within them.

But Hera is not happy about this. She gives Zeus a hard time for impregnating the human damsels. She wants him to just be with her, and she punishes all the human damsels who love to be around him. Zeus gets very frustrated. He doesn't know what to do because his life purpose is to bridge the godly and human realm, but Hera gets in the way.

Zeus is caught in a dilemma that afflicts many men and women. We need conventional relationships in order to have a safe place to rear children. But we are attracted to many people. We see somebody in the store, on the street, or at work; we find them sexually attractive, yet we're married. So how do we handle it?

A friend of mine, who comes from a highly educated, wealthy family and has a doctorate, gets sexually aroused at the sight of workmen jackhammering the sidewalk. But she won't marry a working-class man as she believes they would have little in common. Yet still she gets turned on by them. Sexual attraction and choice of marriage partner are not always in sync.

There is a dilemma between freedom and convention, and that's what Zeus's dilemma represents. Zeus can never resolve this conflict. He gets a massive headache trying to do so. Hera's son, Hephaestus, an artisan, smashes Zeus's head with some tools in order to relieve the headache. As he does this, thunder and lightning come, Zeus's head splits open, and out of his head is born the beautiful Athena, who is able to fulfill her father's mission where he failed.

How do we handle free-flowing sexual attraction? Some married people handle it by flirting but not crossing the line and having sex with the other person. Each person finds a way to handle this dilemma. I've known people to flirt in front of their spouse and create jealousy in an effort to create more passion in the marriage bed. This is crazy.

Other people become suppressed. Rather than accepting their sexual feelings as part of nature and making an intelligent choice on how to handle them, they completely shut down. As a result, they can't even enjoy sex with their partner. Others go ahead and act out, having sex freely, keeping it a secret. And some people act out and then torture their spouses by telling them the truth.

How this tension between freedom and convention is handled is a very individual situation, but it is part of our sexual experience. Sexual feelings are free and cannot be contained, and the best sexuality contains a sense of freedom, even in marriage.

People who marry, stay married long-term, enjoy sex with their spouse, and are monogamous—always acting out of love and freedom, as opposed to possessiveness and control—have the best relationships. They are freer than people who are married yet who feel controlled by the conventions of the institution and yearn to have sex with others.

There is no freedom in possession. People who possess each other through insecurity are not free. They are the slaves and the enslaved. In some marriages, possessiveness kills all passion and love. So emotional freedom and society's rules of marriage have to be worked out in an intelligent manner.

ZEUS IMAGE

1. See Zeus walking in green pastures.
2. See that he embodies the freedom of the green woods, of nature, of the earth, and the skies.
3. See that the maidens love to be with him. They love his strength and his power, and especially his sense of freedom.
4. The only one who doesn't like Zeus's freedom is his wife Hera. She wants to possess him. She chases all the maidens, punishes them, and makes them go away.
5. See yourself as Zeus walking freely in the green woods and pastures. How do you feel? Experience the freedom.
6. See Hera, who by law, feels she can possess you. Know that possession punishes freedom.
7. See your predicament. Make an intelligent choice.
8. Don't close down totally, or you become totally conventional.

A stockbroker in his thirties did the Zeus Image. "I feel very expansive, like I'm connected to the earth, but my head is also in the atmosphere, I feel very strong, very Zen-like, coming from essence. Women are around me, and it feels very, very, good. I see these women dancing around in the meadow, they seem to be lifelike, with no restraint and with an element of flirtatiousness. I like it a lot."

When he saw Hera, his mood changed. "It feels like something's on my chest, and it's hard to breathe. It feels like chains, and I hear that song, 'Chain of Fools.' "

Hera stands for rules, for the idea that, once married, you possess your mate. Zeus represents freedom. The man doing the image is caught between a desire for freedom and the rules of marriage.

This is a universal conflict that gets played out in many of our relationships. According to Zeus, the true bond between men and women is a genuine love. And love can only flourish in freedom; the very nature of possession kills love. Marriages that are free of posessiveness, where both partners are naturally committed to each other and each can be his own person, are the most successful.

Many men and women have a conflict between their marriage vows and their desire to have sex outside of marriage. Around half of the people taking vows for life end up in divorce court. A person married for years falls in love with someone else. These things happen because rules are not enough to keep us united. People are dictated to by their hearts, not pieces of paper. Love isn't a license issued by the state. It will last and flourish as long as the two people feed it. None of us in marriages or relationships can afford to get lazy and rely on the rules, when they are so easy to break. We do not own our spouses.

So when there is a conflict between being free and being possessed, whether married or not, the image of Zeus illuminates the dilemma.

DIONYSUS

Another god many people connect with is Dionysus, the god of intoxication, ecstasy, and rapture. He is seen as so deeply ecstatic and sexual that he goes into an intoxicating high in all the senses. Dionysus does not mean promiscuity, but letting go in our lovemaking, getting into a high state of sexual drunkeness.

Dionysus is also known as Bacchus, the god of wine, agriculture, and fertility, the patron god of the Greek stage. He also represents the outstanding features of mystery religions, those that involve ecstasy or personal delivery from the daily world through physical or spiritual intoxication and initiation into secret rites.

Dionysus is the son of Zeus. The connection with the earth's sensuality and spirituality is in Dionysus. He represents a pure and frenzied impulse preceeding and preparing for an intimate union with God. Phallus symbolism was prominent in the Dionysian era. In that era, they used to have festivals where people would get intoxicated and go into sexual ecstasy as a way to connect to the divine. So it's very Dionysian when one goes into a high state of spiritual rapture and abandon while making love.

Some of us are like Dionysus—we are capable of total abandon, reaching mystical highs through sex.

NARCISSUS

A god no woman can connect to is Narcissus because he's too self-involved. Narcissus was a beautiful young man who spurned intimacy and died as a result. He's so caught up in himself that he doesn't let anyone in to share with him or to connect with him. As a modern man, he is probably more into his objects, interests, and his own self-importance than the woman he is with.

Narcissus is the son of the river god Cephissus and the nymph Liriope. Tyricius the seer told them that Narcissus would live to an old age if he didn't look at himself. Many nymphs and girls fell in love with him, but he rejected them. One of the nymphs, Echo, was so distraught at his rejection that she withdrew into a lonely spot and faded until all that was left of her was a whisper.

Some women do this. They feel rejected by self-involved men and lose all their self-esteem.

The goddess Nemesis heard the rejected girl's prayers for vengeance and arranged for Narcissus to fall in love with his own reflection. He stayed watching his reflection in a pool of water and let himself die.

So what we see in Narcissus is a man who is so self-involved that he will not be moved by the sensuality of a woman and give to her. The woman, in turn, loses all self-confidence in a relationship with a narcissistic man, and he eventually dies of his own aloneness. Have you known couples like this? A couple in which the man is so self-absorbed that he ends up alone, and the woman thinks her self-value comes from his approval rather than from knowing herself?

OTHER GODS

There are many more gods in the Greek pantheon that give us insight into sensuality. The god of war, Ares, who doesn't care who wins or loses as long as blood is shed, is tall and handsome. He is vain and cruel, and his sister Eris, the goddess of strife, is his constant companion. How many acquisitive and competitive people are like this? Ares is not the type of guy whom women can have a romantic relationship with. His type buys women and makes them trophy acquisitions.

Then there are men like Kronos, the Greek god of time, who overthrew his father Uranus. Fearing that his own children might do the same to him, he proceeded to swallow them. He is the kind of man who is very patriarchal and doesn't give his kids a lot of freedom. Instead, he suppresses them. Suppressive men, who control those around them, are patriarchal, dictatorial, power-hungry, and not at all sensual or sexy.

Men who suppress or punish their kids by control are fearful underneath. Men who pick on kids just aren't in touch with their own sensuality. Women get hostile toward these men because they get caught between protecting their children and loving their husband. The husbands lose out in the end. They lose the love of both their wives and their children.

Then there are men like Hephaestus, Hera's son and consort to Aphrodite, who harasses her all the time. Sometimes these men have a sense of fatalism; deep down they are insecure and don't think they deserve love.

If women look closely at the men they either love or hate, they will find one of these gods.

14

The Cosmic Orgasm

Bringing Mind, Body, and Spirit Together
in Your Lovemaking

We have his-and-her orgasms. Even with the physical connection, an ordinary orgasm is a private affair, with each partner separately experiencing the thrill. But there's another kind of orgasm, not a personal one, but one you share with your lover. I call it a "cosmic orgasm" because it involves not only the union of our mind, body, and spirit, but also erotic connection to our lover that breaks the bounds of the physical.

The goal in our love life is to achieve a natural state of sensuality within ourselves and then, when we are whole, to join with another. This is a transcendent, cosmic experience in which a person is unified in mind, body, and spirit with a lover. The experience of sex, of course, is first a product of our own level of sexuality and sensuality. There is physical, genital-oriented sex—and then there is a higher union that is whole, complete, and outside the realm of the mundane, that takes us to mythic experiences.

Sex isn't about using your partner "to get off." It's about making a connection with your lover that is so profound, endearing, and delightful that you transcend to the divine. I've heard it described as everything from a walk with the gods to soaring through the cosmos.

I call this a cosmic orgasm because it occurs when two people—each connected by mind, body, and spirit to their own sensuous nature— link together in a deep connection in which the spiritual energy and erotic pleasure of one flows to the other.

An orgasm is thought of as the highest point of sexual excitement. It is characterized by great pleasure, physical stimulation, and a release of sexual tension. A man releases the escalating tension and power that has built up inside of him, and a woman experiences waves of energy and pleasure.

An ordinary orgasm is a private affair. Couples can derive satisfaction from the fact that one of them is climaxing. When both climax at the same time, the satisfaction and stimulation will be higher, but the release is personal. Unfortunately, an orgasm is a pleasure that not all women have enjoyed, and not all men have gotten beyond the "release" element of sex. The full sensuality in them has been blocked due to suppressions in their history. Once they are free, however, the path to an ordinary orgasm and the cosmic orgasm is open.

A cosmic orgasm makes a deep connection between the two private experiences so that each person shares the experience of the other—and their own pleasure soars. Like the chain reaction of a nuclear explosion, one-plus-one does not equal two, but the numbers—and the pleasure—keep multiplying, transcending ourselves, and opening us up to an infinite source of pleasure.

We know that there is a personal consciousness within us, an energy field. At times, many of us have had the experience of our energy being psychically sensed or felt by others. I think of this phenomenon in terms of our spirit and the spirit of others, as part of a greater consciousness or spirit that we are always connected to but that is normally out of our conscious reach. When we experience a cosmic orgasm, we transcend ourselves, exchange and share our experience with our lover, and draw from the spiritual power of the universe at large.

A woman describing her husband during her cosmic orgasm said he was transformed into a most beautiful god. All of a sudden, her balding, dumpy husband turned into an exotic creature. She described the experience as being one with nature; she felt herself part of a lush, warm ocean. Her identity as a mother and wife was suddenly gone, and she was part of the ocean. Her body dissolved in the molecules of the sea.

Another woman described the experience as a feeling of dissolving and merging with her lover. She felt him to be a huge sun warming and melting every part of her body.

Another woman felt herself letting go, her mind shutting off, her body undulating, moving up in a smooth wave-like motion . . . there is an energy rush from the base of her spine to her head and she leaves her physical body, floating up into a black sky filled with stars . . . merging with her lover beyond their bodies.

One man described making love to his wife as if he were lying on mother earth and were making love to the world itself. He was filled with awe and love and devotion to all that was feminine encompassed in his wife.

Cosmic orgasm is ordinarily accompanied by great love for the person you are with. It is a very rich, bonding experience. It is as if all that is male in nature merges with all that is female, and the union creates something beyond one-plus-one. When you take two chemical compounds and mix them, you can get a bang that neither chemical alone was able to make. And sometimes you get a chain reaction that's thermonuclear.

You can't experience a cosmic orgasm unless you are connected with your own natural sensuality and your lover's. From the male point of view, I find it interesting that many men have a difficult time "surrendering," so that they take in passions from the female instead of just expending their passions out. The secret to the success of the men who are able to surrender is their adoration and awe for their women.

Out-of-body experiences and oceanic states are commonly reported by people who have experienced a cosmic orgasm. In a sense, the oceanic atmosphere is the same as space—it is a dark universe where you are weightless and not bound by your body. When you reach that state, you can experience and express love at its deepest depths, linking mind, body, and soul together in a fusion of atoms and spirit, bringing the very universe into your sexual experience.

When a woman with the spirit of Aphrodite awakened in her and a man who has connected to the Poseidon in him are making love, a sensual experience that transcends mere sex can occur, a passage to the mind-body-spirit connection can open, and they can experience the divine.

Once you have recovered the sensual spirit within yourself, you are ready to experience the cosmic orgasm. To get to that point, you need to unload your history, even if momentarily, and tap into your natural sensuality and that of your lover. Only then will you be able to make the link between mind, body, and spirit between the two of you.

THE COSMIC DANCE OF THE FEMININE AND MASCULINE

There is an eternal cosmic play between the masculine and the feminine. Often, this is expressed by women and men as an oceanic experience. Perhaps our connection to the ocean arises from some sort of primordial connection to creation. Whatever it is, the play of seawater connects in a primal way to our sensuality.

The "Cosmic Dance Image" is not a cosmic orgasm. That will come to you when you and your lover are open, loving, and connected in mind, body, and spirit. The Cosmic Dance Image provides insight into what happens when the feminine and masculine come together. It's an image that represents the endless dance between the masculine and the feminine.

It deals with the ocean, which is a symbol of femininity. Women, like the ocean, are constantly going through cycles. The moon affects the oceans, and we get the ebb and flow of tides. Women go through several phases each month, also ebbing and flowing, their moods shifting and changing.

The male consciousness is more solid and inflexible. A man has the inseminating power. He's strong, rigid, erect, someone the female can butt up against and feel that he's there. He totally enjoys her undulating rhythm, the swishing, swirling against him, in endless variations. To the man, the ecstasy is the woman's erotic play around and up against him. To her, the ecstasy is that he is solid, and she can swirl and be fluid around him.

The essence of the masculine and feminine coming together can be experienced using the Cosmic Dance Image.

COSMIC DANCE OF THE FEMININE AND MASCULINE

1. See the ocean. There are waves washing up on the rocks.
2. See a phallic-shaped rock jutting out of the water.
3. See that the water is warm and feminine, swirling around the rock, crashing, lapping against the rock in an endless play.
4. See the water playing against the rock. The rock is strong. See the water against the rock; the rock loves the sensual water. The water loves the erect rock.
5. Keep the protruding rock and the warm, lapping water in mind as you build a rhythm with your lover.

The rock that juts out is the masculine. The rock is phallic and hard and upright and doesn't move around like the female. The rock embodies the energy of the male, strong and centered and powerful; that is the masculine.

When men see the rock, they identify with it, and they see the feminine swirling around them. This image reveals how they relate to the water, which is how they relate to the feminine.

Water represents female sensuality in nature at its purest, the purest expression of natural sex for a woman. That's what women feel in this image, a return to their feminine flow and harmony.

When the water flows freely, a woman is full of love and joy and beauty. When the water flows around the rock, the water encompasses and embraces it, very much the way the vagina holds and encompasses the penis. The penis feels moistness and pleasure, just like the rock "feels" the water.

The feelings in women are released, just like the feminine water, and bring the woman back to a time before history affected her.

The playfulness of the waters brings to the man a feeling of enjoyment of her that allows him to go and surrender to the feminine flow.

Water and rocks are in a dance into eternity, and they reveal how the male and female interact in their pure essence.

15

Reigniting Passion
First Hit

People in the early stages of a relationship sometimes have much more interest in and affection for their mate than do people who have been married for a long time. It's because the unmarried people are still in the throes of the "first hit of love" (or the "Idol of Love"), while married couples may have been tainted by decades of conflict about money, kids, careers, and everything else under the sun.

That first hit of love is the original experience of love, the igniting point in a sexual and sensual relationship. What happens after many years is that the first hit of love often becomes dulled, and the sharp impressions of the original experience are no longer poignant. This happens with most steady partners. Time dampens the feeling of passion and sexuality.

After years of marriage, some people tire of their mate: "I'm stuck in this marriage, and it's the same old stuff. I want that high and that excitement. . . . There's no mystery anymore with this woman I've been with for twenty years. . . . She's critical sometimes; she doesn't adore me anymore. . . . She's gained a little weight." Whatever the problem is, that first initial intense passion goes.

To one degree or another, even in the most loving and faithful relationship, it happens. Some of the initial ignition, the burning passion, the mystery and its high, disappear. What must assert itself instead in a long-term relationship is wisdom. When the fire is gone and you are dealing with the daily pressures of life—such as making money, supporting a family, and dealing with children, the dirty dishes and the laundry—you need the wisdom to develop loving kindness, compassion, and understanding of the limitations and gifts of your mate. You need the wisdom to find, in a deeper sense, love for yourself and your partner even after you see your partner's imperfections as well as your own. Such wisdom makes for a more enduring, long-lasting love, not just one based on the initial first high.

Men and women need to bring civility, respect, and understanding to each other after those first sparks have been dampened. Wisdom is needed to make a safe haven in a difficult, often troubled world, for the family and for children.

Some couples, when they spend some time together away from the kids, rediscover what they saw in each other initially. They "fall in love" again. They can ignite those fires by giving time and care to the relationship away from the daily pressures. But it's important to know they can't maintain that forever. That's why in the images of people who have been married a long time, there always exists some irritation with each other. That is the human condition of long-term relationships. But you can get beyond that—with wisdom.

Let's look at the actual experience of falling in love. It's wonderful. We're struck by Cupid's arrow, and we suddenly can't live without the other person. Along with the ecstasy, there's usually anxiety—Does he or she really love me? Am I fooling myself?—and some daydreaming. We think about the person, and we feel soft, loving, sexually turned on. We want to merge with them, to be around them, to kiss and hug them. It's a wonderful experience that takes over our thoughts and is with us throughout the whole day. It makes things easier to bear. We go through a whole, exciting, happy experience when we connect romantically with another person.

Falling in love is a miraculous, delicious, and wonderful experience, which we all desire. And falling in love is the beginning of a new relationship and often a whole new direction in life.

There are three stages that we go through in the experience of getting involved with somebody. The first stage is falling in love. That's when Cupid strikes us. That's when we see the essence of the other person, and we see only the best in them. We get a pure experience of who they are; of course, that's before we fully know them or they know us. But it's that first initial hit of ecstatic desire and adoration when we see only the best in them. That's the hook.

After being in love for a while, it's inevitable some negative emotions begin to surface. Either we feel insecure or get jealous, or we are afraid the person will leave us, or we get possessive, or we get angry because they don't meet our needs, or we decide we don't like the way the person is critical toward us, so we begin to feel some negative feelings.

Many things start to happen after the initial phase of falling in love. I call this second stage the "phase of history." During this time, our fears, insecurities, unresolved issues, and repressions peek their ugly heads into the relationship. That awful word *conflict* arises between us and the person we were in complete love with just a short time ago. This happens each and every time, to each and every relationship.

Then comes the third phase: either we break up or we resolve those conflicts and learn how to love each other, despite the problems. At this stage, we must learn to love someone in a deeper way. Hopefully, we learn that we're not perfect and neither are they. We lose that initial experience of falling in love, but a glimpse of it, that first wonderful hit of the Idol of Love, is still there. It is just buried under all the mixed feelings that have arisen. I remember a woman telling me she'll be angry at her husband, and just hate his guts; then another time they'll be in bed, and she'll look at him, and he's her Adonis, as she sees him in the light in which she fell in love with him.

That first hit of love is still there for all of us. But it gets mixed in with all the other interactions of our relationship and often gets buried.

The Idol of Love is an imaging technique that takes us back to that first moment of falling in love. As with so many aspects of modern romance, it's explained very nicely by those wonderful lessons of life we get from mythology.

THE IDOL OF LOVE

We all know that in the Western world we have a mischievous little rascal called Cupid who goes around shooting arrows and making people fall in love. On Valentine's Day, you see a lot of cupids with bows and arrows. It's a remembrance of that "in love" feeling. The Greeks called him Eros, and that's where we got the word *erotic*.

There is another Cupid, one most people are not familiar with. His name is Kama-Dev. In a manner of speaking, you could call him the "Cupid of the East" because he comes out of India.

The Hindus have many gods in their mythology. Each one personifies an aspect of the one, greater God. So to know and understand the qualities of God, you must know the individual gods.

One of these gods is Shiva, who is known as the Holy Spirit. Shiva is similar to the Holy Spirit of Christianity and Judaism. Shiva, seen sitting cross-legged, is in deep meditation in order to figure out how to solve the world's problems. His consort, Parvati, wants him to pay attention to her, but he's too deep in meditation and he doesn't come out of it to be with her. Parvati does all kinds of things—gets upset and angry, entices him—to get Shiva's attention. Nothing works. So Kama-Dev comes to her aid, shooting an arrow through the heart of Shiva to make him respond to Parvati. When he's struck with the arrow, a light comes out of Shiva's third eye and burns Kama-Dev to ashes. Shiva then comes out of meditation with the arrow still in his heart, and he starts to feel sensuous and wants to have sex with Parvati. But she refuses, saying, "I can't feel anything for you unless you bring Kama-Dev back to life. He is desire, and I feel no desire since you've reduced him to ashes. Unless you revive him, my desire and passion are gone."

Shiva revives Kama-Dev, and only then does Parvati's passion return. As a result, Kama-Dev becomes very powerful in Hindu mythology, because Shiva, who's the most powerful god, has to bring him back. He has to bring Kama-Dev back to fulfill love and keep sensuality alive. People aren't going to reproduce or unite with one another without passion or desire.

Kama-Dev, like Cupid, destroys the feelings of separation and rationality that keep us to ourselves. When you're struck with love and you enter into that blissful feeling, you lose your rational mind and your desire to be separate, and you long to become connected to another person with burning passion.

Kama-Dev is also important because he joins the male and female together. Parvati can't connect romantically with Shiva unless Kama-Dev's passion is in her. Without this passion, this fire, man and woman cannot join. And once they join, they can enter the state of union, which feels like heaven on earth, fulfillment.

When you look at the experience of people doing the Idol of Love Image, you'll see that when they're with their lover, they enter a state of bliss!

The Cupid of the East represents that state of love where we are struck down with passion, we can't think straight, we're smitten, we melt, and another consumes us with desire. But the Cupid of the West is different. He's the son of Aphrodite, the goddess of love, and Ares, the god of war. He is handsome and pure. Psyche, his love, is human, and she has to perform different tasks and go through many ordeals in order to purify herself through suffering and misfortune and prepare herself to enjoy true happiness as an immortal woman with a god.

Psyche, at first a human, later becomes a goddess. Her story is about how a person can be transformed through a love relationship from an ordinary woman to a goddess. Even though Psyche is a woman, her story is relevant to both sexes.

Psyche was a woman of great beauty. The word *psyche* meant "soul" to the Greeks. Cupid had been sent to punish her for being so beautiful that even Aphrodite was antagonized by her beauty. But when Cupid saw Psyche, he fell in love with her.

When Cupid fell for her, Psyche was on a solitary rock, and she felt herself being lifted on the arms of the wind, which carried her to a magnificent palace. That night, she was on the verge of sleep when a mysterious being joined her, explaining he was the husband she was destined to marry. She couldn't see his features because it was dark, but his voice was soft and full of love and tenderness. Cupid had to be her secret lover to keep his mother, Aphrodite, from finding out. To keep the secret, he made Psyche promise never to see his face.

Psyche was not unhappy, because she was in this magnificent palace with everything she could ever want. Her incredible lover only came at night, and she spent nights of delicious passion with him.

Psyche's sisters, who were jealous, put the seeds of suspicion in her heart by telling her that her lover was a monster. They made her full of doubt. They nagged her so much that, despite her promise, one night after they made love, she rose from the bed, lit a lamp, and held it above the mysterious face while he was asleep. Instead of a fearful monster, she saw the most beautiful, charming god in the world. It was Cupid. At his foot lay his bow and arrows. To study his features, she held the lamp closer to him, and he woke up. Startled, Psyche accidentally let lamp oil drop and burn his wing.

Furious at her for her lack of faith, and injured, Cupid left. The palace vanished, and Psyche found herself on the lonely rock in the midst of terrifying solitude.

Out of jealousy and insecurity, she ruined that blissful mystery of love. At first, she thought of killing herself and threw herself in a river. But the waters brought her gently to the opposite bank. Then she was pursued by the wrath of Aphrodite's anger for her deeds and was put through a series of ordeals. Psyche survived each ordeal placed before her, thanks to a mysterious person assisting her (Cupid, of course). She even went to the underworld—hell. (Aren't we in hell when we lose the one we love?) She was full of remorse for what she did to Cupid.

Touched by the repentance of his unhappy lover, Cupid went to Zeus and begged to be allowed rejoin Psyche. Zeus submitted and gave Psyche immortality. Thus, she became a goddess. Aphrodite forgot her anger, and the wedding of the two lovers was celebrated on Mount Olympus with great rejoicing.

All the tests Psyche went through allowed her to redeem herself. This is the third part of a relationship: if we redeem ourselves, have faith, and get rid of our jealousy, doubts, angers, and pettiness, we can once again experience love.

How many times has doubt ruined your feelings of love? Psyche's downfall was going outside the state of paradise she shared with Cupid because she listened to her envious sisters, but she was able to work it out and come back to him. That means we can, too. We fall in love; we are in heaven. Then comes the phase of fighting, hostility, or doubts, which kill love. Finally, we work on it and redeem ourselves, and we experience love again. That's what Psyche stands for—transformation through the ordeal of relationships.

To get back to true love, we have to free ourselves from our negative conditioning. We fall in love, then we blow it. After we suffer, we can look at ourselves and heal the things we did wrong, learn the lessons of how to be truly loving, and come back to having love. Before we can look at the face of a god—the state of true love—we have to destroy our many illusions and fears to return to pure love. Psyche had beauty but also the mortal errors of analytical confusion, pride, and weakness in her spirit.

The myth tells us that humans have the opportunity to go back to paradise with each other if they accept and succeed in the tests given by nature to purify themselves of their arrogant ways. To really love someone, you need to be humble and open.

The history that keeps us from experiencing pure love has to be destroyed so love can flow again. The burning away of our ego is what Kama-Dev and Cupid do, making us let go of our rational minds so we can enter a deeper state of love, which is ultimately the expression of our true nature.

Kama means pleasure, and *Dev* means god, so in a sense Kama-Dev is the god of pleasure, god of love. He's a very important god because he brings us to the experience of passion and sensuality, which is a very high state that reminds us of being in paradise. And after that first hit of love is gone, we long to find it again.

Kama-Dev, like Cupid, shoots us with his arrow and brings us fiery passion. Before he comes into our lives, we feel separate, and our daily lives seem mundane. All of a sudden we are burnt to ashes by love as we experience the fire of desire.

Passion can make slaves out of the best of us. One woman told me that she was involved with a well-known, powerful CEO at a Fortune

500 company. He was so crazy about her that every time she phoned, even if he was in an important meeting, he would put the meeting on hold and make everybody wait while he took her call. That's what Kama-Dev did to the CEO—disintegrated him totally.

Cupid and Kama-Dev are two stories of love that we all have experienced. They are responsible for bringing us that first hit of love which can be rekindled after our ardor cools.

It is important to retain that first image of falling in love. If we experience conflict in a long-term relationship, we can retrieve the image, which will remind us of the essence that first attracted us to our beloved.

When we're in the thick of struggles with our lover or spouse, and we're suffering over it, we can see the image of the Idol of Love and remember what caused us to fall in love in the first place. It brings back the good feelings we initially had. It's a powerful image that I've used with couples who have lost the magic in their relationships or who have been so beset by conflicts that they forget what they love about each other. The minute they go back to that time, those exotic and loving feelings surface again. They remember the wonderful things about the person they're with, and they experience the magic of falling in love again. All the conflicts disappear, and the good feelings come back.

IDOL OF LOVE IMAGE

1. Remember yourself in love and the person you touched, or who touched you, the first time you realized you were in love.
2. Remember the touch, and see the person before you again. This is an early image of love. All other images, even of this person, are late images of love. There is Cupid in this early image. The god is present here. The more you look at this image, the more it becomes like an icon.
3. See the image. You have bodily feelings and sensations of the god of love being near you. Keep this image at this early stage. Do not bring later images of this person to mind.
4. Feel your body relaxing, and your bones and muscles relaxing. This is Cupid, the god of love in the image. All other human images of love are late images that contain the problems between you.

A woman named Kim did this image. She was madly in love with her boyfriend, and then some of their insecurities kicked in. "He lives in a different town but he was supposed to come for Thanksgiving, and when he didn't, a crisis arose. He said he had too much work; he couldn't leave the office. So I told him I needed to know if that was the only reason he wasn't coming. He was shocked and said, 'Of course, what else would it be?'

"I knew that was the reality, but I keep going farther and farther into my own insecurities and moodiness. If it were me, I'd have worked twenty-four hours a day to make it out; I'd work like crazy so I wouldn't miss Thanksgiving with him. I wouldn't disappoint him. I would bring work with me, I'd do everything to go out to see him, and I was upset he wasn't going to do that."

These were later images of their relationship, after the bliss of the first idol of love had passed. Kim did the Idol of Love Image and remembered him when she touched him or had been touched by him for the first time. "It was the first time we made love. We had had only one date face-to-face, and I flew out to Savannah two months later to be with him. The first couple of nights we didn't sleep together, but we did make out; then we finally decided to go to bed together. Remembering that first time, I see this incredibly masculine person who has a lot of hard energy, but he's also very gentle and very skilled, and I see his nakedness. I see his body, hair, and beard, but I don't see his eyes. I feel his physicality.

"There's no urgency in our lovemaking; it's like he's taking my hand and guiding me, coaxing me, paying attention to my body; it feels like reverence. Like he's kind of getting to know me, but there's no urgency, no animal moves. It's a spiritual thing.

"I'm a willing participant in the lovemaking. Generally my M.O. is I don't sleep with men for a while because I need to get to know them, need to know they like me. I've never had a one-night stand because of fear of rejection. At a certain point when things were leading up to this, I trusted him in a way that I normally didn't, and I was willing to let him lead me."

When Kim did the image, the bliss of that first night unfolded for her. "I remember that it was perfect. The music was perfect. I laughed because the CD changed while we were making love, and there was this cowboy yodeling and we both broke out in hysterical laughter. I remember the lovemaking happening, almost like I wasn't there, like I was apart from my body in a certain way and saying to myself, this is just perfect. If I was to die tomorrow, I'd know that I had this one night of perfection. Quite often, I've felt that way when we've been together, because many times he's removed from animal passion, which is sometimes disappointing, but there was just incredible spirituality going on; it struck a real chord with me."

Seeing the image brought back all the delight and spirituality of that first hit of love. "I almost feel that it's not an outside force. The image I'm getting is of a saucepan, and there's chocolate inside. White and dark are being stirred together; it's that all-encompassing warmth and liquidity. I don't see myself being struck by Cupid; the word that came to mind is almost a surrender, a mixing and melding, all-encompassing thing. It's not of this world, it's on a different level. It does feel like creation, like a spiritual base."

That's the early image of love: it's spiritual, sensual, loving. It's what the god of love is about. When a person has this feeling, we say that Cupid or Kama-Dev is there, that god is present.

Keeping the god of love in her thoughts, Kim said, "What comes to mind is we're both naked. I have long hair and so does he, we're lying on a wrinkled sheet, and he's behind me and we're just lying there. It's golden, the light is flickering and there's just peace."

Doing this image made Kim realize the profound spiritual connection she had with her boyfriend. The early image of love was always inside her, although her insecurity sometimes covered it up. Going back and reconnecting to the essence of their relationship by seeing the images brought her comfort, joy, and security.

Kim had a true experience of love with her boyfriend, but then her mind had taken over, which was her history. She had become insecure and almost ruined the relationship. She dropped from that blissful state that the two of them shared; then she pressured him, and got upset. And they fell out of Eden. The imaging brought her love again.

Nick, a forty-two-year-old architect, met a woman in the course of his work. "Julie came in for a consultation, and something just clicked between us. I felt attracted to her immediately. We had lunch, and she seemed to be very attentive. We started spending time together. It was at a time when I hadn't been involved with someone for several years, and I was missing that. It was very fulfilling.

"Then we started living together. Initially it was very good, and I felt a strong support between us. I thought we were on the same wavelength, working for the same goals, one of which was to have a child. Julie had a difficult pregnancy, and almost lost her life. That was very painful. She began working with me, running the office, and we were working seven days a week from 7:30 in the morning to about 10 or 11 at night. There was hardly any time for us, and when we did have time, it was a disaster. We were fighting—her anger would come up, her rage—she had a very short fuse. We went through some difficult times. Julie was incredibly jealous, even when I was working nonstop. She thought I was involved with another woman, which wasn't remotely possible. I felt she didn't understand who I was, her jealousy and possessiveness were really getting in the way. Then there'd always be some problem. It was really negative.

"The first part of the relationship was very pleasant, but the later part was not wonderful at all; it really sucked."

Nick recalled the early part of their relationship, a time when Cupid was there, remembering himself in love with her. That first sensation of love occurred when Julie touched his heart for the first time. "I feel her close to me. I feel her warmth. Our energies are kind of commingling. I feel her breasts against my chest, and it feels really nice. I'm focusing on her breasts, the voluptuousness, the beauty, the softness; I feel the combination of woman and nurturing mother. I really miss that."

He has body feelings and sensations of love being near her, and that's the god of love touching him. "Too bad her jealousy and insecurity ruined it all," he said.

Here is Maggie's experience of that first hit of love. "I worked with a man, and we used to have meetings about office policy, things the company was going to do. One day, we were playing around and bantering, just teasing each other. He told me that he was attracted to me. I told him that I found him attractive too and had a lot of feelings for him, but I didn't think we could get together because of our professional relationship. He leaned over my desk and reached for my hand. That was the first touch. And as I go back and see that early image and feel the love there in my mind's eye, I see that as I look at him across the desk, I'm feeling completely enamored of him. Just absolutely in love, totally adoring him. I love his eyes, his intensity, the aura of confidence around him, and his depth. I am just totally turned on by this man. And as I look at him, my breathing gets shallower because I'm turned on and my heart actually starts beating faster.

"I have a sensation like I'm burning up—just burning into ashes. It's passion and all-consuming love that overtake me. It's as if I'm consumed by love and I become love. It's literally a feeling of being burned in passion so that I become the total expression and experience of love. Love fills the room, it's so big."

Maggie's image is passionate, sensual, and mystical. That is definitely Cupid and Kama-Dev striking her. Cupid hits her with his arrow, and she is struck by love. Kama-Dev creates that essential sexual fire, a passion that ignites her and strikes her down before ecstasy comes. The fires of love are beyond the rational mind. We must surrender our mind to the greater emotions of the soul. So when Cupid and Kama-Dev strike, we lose our minds and fall into love. We can't rationally hold it together anymore. We are plunged into merging with another, and our separate sense of self dissolves. Thus two become one.

Love is similar to the experience of mystics. St. Teresa of Avila, in her prayers, would dissolve her separate sense of self, and she would merge with the divine and become elated. Similarly, when you truly love another person, you let go of your separate sense of self, of being self-centered, and your love just flows out to the other. Many have described it as an incredible concern, passion, kindness, and feeling of tenderness toward their lover. A woman described it this way: "Your lover becomes as important as you are. You no longer think just of yourself." Love allows us to touch a greater part of ourselves.

The opening of the heart is the opening to a deeper part of ourselves. Some people have sex without their hearts being open. Only their genital area is involved. True love is a different kind of experience. It evokes our true capacity as human beings to be both loving and sexual. When passion, heart, and genitals are open and unified in a genuine feeling for another, the soul is expressed. That is the ecstasy, the high in relationships that we're all looking for.

16

The Sex Lives of Our Children

As the mother of two teenagers, I am aware of the sexual pressure that not just teens but *preteens* must contend with. I don't need to tell mothers and fathers that sex permeates the culture of our children through ads, music, television shows and films.

Working with eidetic imaging proved very beneficial to me in learning what was going on with my own kids and young people in general.

From a cross section of kids in half a dozen cities, I learned that if you take an honest look, you'll find that young people are having more sex than ever before. But that doesn't mean they are enjoying it. Most are too immature emotionally to grasp any more than the titillation of sex.

In some communities young people start having sex at a shockingly early age—sometimes as early as twelve. In other communities if a young girl has a steady boyfriend at fourteen, it's assumed she will engage in sex. There is also a great emphasis on oral sex.

Those of us who wonder what went wrong need look no further than our TV sets. TV is the third parent of most children. If you put a child in front of a TV for the first dozen years of its life, can you imagine how many overt and covert sexual acts he or she has seen? *Thousands* at the very least. How many songs about sex have they heard? Thousands more. Is it any wonder that we have a generation of kids who are confused and who are engaging in sex at a younger age than we have ever seen?

We, of course, need to look at ourselves. No matter how the media assault our children's minds, no matter how our schools fail, we are the ones with the responsibility and duty to raise children who are healthy in mind, body, and spirit.

I have two teenage children and I have counseled hundreds of others, yet I am still shocked by what I hear from the mouths of babes. I often fear for our generation of children. I fear their loss of innocence, and regret all of the wonder they will never experience about love because they started having sex before their minds and emotions were ready.

I am saddened by the loss of innocence. Where has all of the innocence gone? Are our children to be deprived of their right to know the beauty of pure sensuality with love by a society in which crass sex has become pervasive? It's so sad. Like other women and men my age, I came into sexuality during the late 1960s, at an age much younger than my mother's generation did. But the bra-burning, free-sex society of the 1960s is almost prudish compared to what is happening today. My mind rebels at the thought that children not old enough to spend a night at home without a baby-sitter are sexually sophisticated—and often sexually active.

I mentioned earlier that we live in an age where good-night oral sex is almost as expected as the good-night kiss. This wasn't hyperbole on my part—the statement is based on my discussions with young people all over the country.

Kids are having sex younger and younger. They're not just expected to have sex before marriage; they're expected to have it if they go steady for a few weeks. In their minds, by the time they're fifteen or sixteen, they think it is all right to have sex, especially if they're "going out" (i.e., going steady) with someone. That's the norm. The more sexually mature (or *immature*) young people often start years earlier.

One girl said the first time she was pressured to have intercourse she was thirteen. Although she decided not to, she knew it was not uncommon to have sex at that age. When she was twelve or thirteen, the oral-sex pressure started. I told the young people in her group that that was very young to be involved sexually. But she said it wasn't too young, that she has a friend in Illinois, and the average age for that girl's friends having intercourse was twelve. This Illinois girl has friends who had abortions at twelve. Even more alarming, some of her friends had sex before ever having their period, at ten or eleven years old.

Today, physical attraction is the key to popularity. This, of course, is a factor that hasn't changed in eons. Kids want to go out with a person they think is "hot." The word *hot* does not connote sexually hot the way it used to. When kids think a girl or guy is hot, it means he or she is attractive.

If a girl is going steady, it's assumed she is having sex with her boyfriend. It's okay not to have sex, but it's assumed she will. If a girl has a steady boyfriend and she has sex with him, she doesn't get a bad reputation. But if a girl is not going steady with a guy and she has sex with him, she's a slut. The guy, however, is admired and seen as a "cool" stud. The double standard lives.

By the time kids are sixteen or seventeen, sex is an expected part of the routine of going steady. Fourteen- and fifteen-year-old girls tell me oral sex is expected. Even when they were in the seventh grade, the boys pressured them for it. Here's a double standard again. The boys won't give the girls oral sex, but the guys expect it, and pressure the girls to give it. Over the past several decades, oral sex might have occurred after intercourse had been going on between the parties; it was considered a much more intimate act. Now it's changed. Kids think they have less chance of getting sexually transmitted diseases orally, and no chance of pregnancy. So it has become more popular.

Girls in middle school—sixth, seventh, and eighth grades—reported boys pressured them a lot to have oral sex. When they refused, the guys would make fun of them and call them prudes. But if they submitted, they'd be called sluts. These girls were in a terrible bind—they were sluts if they did and prudes if they didn't.

There is a popular term among young people called "hooking up." It means having sexual contact with a person up to but not including intercourse. So it means kissing, fondling, and oral sex.

Girls report that the difference between middle school and high school is that in middle school everyone knew who gave oral sex to whom and the girls who did it were considered sluts. But in high school, there was not as much pressure for oral sex because the boys had become more mature. They still asked for oral sex, but they were not as demanding as younger boys.

I asked some middle-school girls and some freshmen high-school girls if it seemed fair that they were asked to perform oral sex on boys but there was no reciprocity. They laughed and looked at me like I was silly. The question, by the way, wasn't intended to make oral sex a quid pro quo. I was simply probing to see what the girls' attitudes were. And their attitudes reflect what we would expect from young people involved in something before they are mature enough to understand its true significance: they had knowledge without wisdom. They know the rules of what was expected by their peers but did not know how to be true to their heart and soul when it came to sex. They went along with the pressures of their peer group without thinking.

In my time, the closest most of us got to sex games as adolescents was playing "spin the bottle." Sex is still a game for young people, but they keep score differently than we did.

The message I got over and over was that young people were imitating and being indoctrinated by TV, the movies, and music. And with music it's not just dirty rap songs; singers in all categories moan and groan and say the most perverse things. They make Elvis's hip movements look like child's play.

On the other hand, some of the fourteen-year-olds I talked to were virgins, and they said it was scary to actually have sex. One girl said, "It's like you're young; it's your body; if you want it to be shared with someone else, it's a big thing. I'm not afraid of being hurt physically, not by the sex act, but it's my body. If I have sex, it's not my body anymore. Our bodies are so sacred they should be shared with someone we really love and want to be with."

This girl knows the value of who she is. That's what you want to see in kids; that they feel their bodies are sacred, that they themselves have the sensibility to determine who they'll share their bodies with and when, that it will feel right to them, and that they can say no.

We can't just say to our sons and daughters, you can't have sex. Most of them are not going to listen because it sounds hypocritical to them and contrary to everything they see and hear around them. We have to explain to them what the repercussions will be for them emotionally and psychically and that it's a decision that they have to make.

Moralistic repression doesn't really work. We need to teach them that if they feel pressured or have any doubt or ambivalence, that's a sign from inside themselves not to do it. Showing them how to be true to themselves is the best teaching a parent can offer.

Parents who are still under the impression that they can control young sexuality with laws or lectures have their heads in the sand. Kids are seeing sex all around them, and they just aren't going to accept that their having sex isn't right unless we give them reasons that make sense to them.

Another girl told me, "You have to be really careful because you don't want to be emotionally hurt afterward, like he's going to split on you." I reiterated the rule of life: if you're not 100 percent sure about something, it's a sign from your insides, from your wisdom, telling you it's not the time and not the place. This girl has natural doubts and should be guided by them. When she is old enough, she will be able to resolve her doubts with more self-assurance, but at this point she is more scared—and curious—than anything else.

By approaching her this way, I was not being moralistic. Instead, I was teaching her how to discern what's right or wrong for her, to understand that she owns her body, and that it's a treasure not to be shared until she is ready, and everything is right, and her insides say "yes."

One of the kids I casually got into a conversation with was my own teenage daughter, along with a group of other young people. My daughter seemed very happy that she could be open with me. I was surprised, because I thought she'd want to keep her feelings private. But it was a relief that she could talk to me, and I was open with her. I understood her as a separate person struggling with her sexuality in this modern age, and I heard her, not as a punitive mother, but as a caring, nonjudgmental one. It made her feel that she could make the right choices for herself and be true to her own integrity, and she could talk to me if she got in trouble or needed anything.

During sessions interviewing teenagers, I could see that they felt confusion and tremendous pressure to be sexual from the messages in the movies, MTV, and their music. They felt confused, because they thought they were expected to have intercourse before they were ready. I live in a very educated and sophisticated community, yet I was taken aback by how isolated some of the kids felt; many believed they couldn't talk to their parents about what was happening to them sexually or about the pressure that was on them to be sexually active. Most said that what they got from their parents were admonitions "not to do it" when they already had or everyone around them had.

I don't believe in being punitive with children and giving them a laundry list of dos and don'ts. When we use our power as parents rather than our wisdom we are fighting a losing battle, because if there's one thing kids are good at, it's rebellion. Moralistic lectures, economic sanctions, and punitive actions on our part usually result in openly rebellious, secretly rebellious, and/or neurotically suppressed children. What works much better is developing an open style of communicating through which we can impart our values.

Besides being open and receptive and "there" for our children, letting them know our values and showing them—by example—how to discover and be true to theirs is the best way to get them to emulate our values. Knowing our values gives them a sense of security.

While setting an example is vitally important, we still have to be practical; our "example" has to ring true to the teen culture our children are in.

One of the best things we parents can do is simply let our children know our values and work to keep the channels of communication open. If they know they have someone to talk to, if they know it's safe to talk to us, that we won't be punitive no matter how the cards fall, we have won at least half the battle. After that, we still need the wisdom of Solomon to tread on this sensitive ground.

I have asked many teenagers what they would do if they needed birth control. Most of them didn't know what they'd do. Girls said they would be too embarrassed to buy condoms. One of them said she'd ask her mother, because her mother would rather have her on birth control than pregnant. She said, "If I want to have sex with somebody, I'm going to and I want to protect myself. My mother should honor that, so I'd go to her for help."

Most kids said they'd be petrified to ask their parents, so they wouldn't risk it. A very few said they would talk to their parents because they had a really good relationship with them and a lot of trust, that their parents wouldn't kill them or come down on them, but would understand and talk openly. Some of the kids said they'd think about asking their parents, but they would probably chicken out.

The vast majority, however, would not talk to their parents because of fear. This is why I believe that first and foremost we must keep the lines of communication open with our children. This doesn't mean that we occasionally tell them across the dinner table that we'll always be there for them to talk out their problems. I'm sure that every one of those kids who said they were afraid to talk to their parents had heard that statement a hundred times. Children have to *know* it's safe to talk to mom and dad, not just be told the door's open. They will trust you if they know you will keep your promises and not be judgmental and recriminatory when they talk to you about other things. Once they feel safe on other fronts, they can trust you about sex.

COMMUNICATION WITH OUR CHILDREN IMAGE

We need to keep the lines of communication with our children open in order to have them grow into vibrant, *sexually* healthy adults. Here is an image that helps us make that connection. In the image, we see our children as people in their own right. As parents, we need to listen to our children, and one of the best ways is to listen to them as if they were lonely strangers that we want to understand and help. When we listen to them as strangers, it is easier for us to step into their shoes and empathize with them. We can hear them better because we are not all twisted inside with recriminations for what we or they have failed at. We can discuss our values and points of view in a more relaxed and open manner.

COMMUNICATING WITH OUR CHILDREN IMAGE

1. See you are talking to your child about sex.
2. What do you see?
3. How is the talk going?
4. How do you feel about it? (Notice your feelings and body sensations.)
5. Now see your child as if he or she were a wonderful but lonely stranger—just a teen coping with problems.
6. Does that free you in talking to him or her?
7. What would you honestly say to this teen from your own experience?
8. Remember, it is his or her body, mind, and soul.
9. See you are free to be honest in discussing sexuality with this lonely stranger.

17

Infantilizing

The deepest and most natural sensuality between men and women includes playfulness with an open, childlike innocence between them. It is the meeting point for both where the flow of nature can unfold between them. They both must go to a deeper side of themselves to allow the sexual merging of body, mind, and soul to unfold.

Wise men know that to attain sexual ecstasy they need to surrender their ego to the woman and allow her to infantilize them. It is pleasurable for both of them.

Wise women who are in touch with their feminine strength know how to lead men to surrender. Infantilization is an emotion found in most women. It is the desire to reduce her man to childlike states in order for him to soften, experience his tenderness, surrender his hard edge and become one with her. She knows how to deal with men who are more rigid and fixed. She knows not only that it is more difficult for him, due to how he has been socialized, but also that it is his desire to surrender to her so that both can enter an open, playful, and sensual sharing with each other for the joy of communion and in preparation for lovemaking. It is not about manipulation for control on the woman's part but rather to help men dissolve so that they meet and become one.

When a man is sexual with a woman, there is usually a phase where he is reduced to being like a baby. For example, when a woman is stroking a man and kissing him, loving him, it's almost like she's talking to a child. She's leading him to a childlike state so that he softens and surrenders so lovemaking can begin. Childlike states are open, receptive, sweet, with no defensive barriers in place.

As a man begins to be led towards surrender, very often he has an initial resistance to it. He's in another state of mind, with problems at work and the other worries he has to deal with, and now he is asked to become open and childlike. So a little resistance occurs. But once he lets go and allows himself to be open, he truly begins to enjoy it. In fact, a lot of men long for that connection with women.

Problems arise when a woman either can't infantilize or doesn't keep it up throughout the relationship. A woman may like it when they first marry and she can get him to surrender, but later on she starts to resent him for it because of other problems in the relationship that shut her down. She does not want to give to him in that way anymore. Women who don't do it because they stay mad or shut down are not in touch with the very essence that is capable of opening him up.

Some men have a hard time with surrender, with becoming infantilized. The mother of one man with whom I worked was not available to him when he was young, had shut down his maternal need. Whenever his wife came to him and wanted him to surrender to her, he resisted. It was painful for him to become childlike because it reminded him of the abandonment he felt as a young boy and all the painful feelings he had as a child would surface every time she infantilized him. He kept his defensive posture toward her in place. In turn, she felt lonely and that she lacked a depth of intimacy with him.

When men don't have a strong maternal connection when they are young, two things can happen: either they overly need maternal care from a woman, or they completely shut down their need. When they shut down their need, the women who try to get them to surrender feel very frustrated. Sometimes men have a lot on their minds and they just don't want to let go, so they shut off the woman. As a result the woman is hurt and feels rejected. If a man only wants a woman to baby him all the time because he lacked maternal connection, that can also turn off a woman. She wants a man to play with, not one who is always needy.

Underneath it all, men want to surrender. They long for that connection with a woman, but sometimes they don't know how to establish it. Some men are more artistic, sensitive types and they find it easier to do. Others who are more rational or in control or typically "masculine" find it more difficult.

Some men may succumb for a little while, but then become rigid and controlling again because that is the way they have learned to be men. And control is a frustration for many women also, because it won't let the man relax and play with her.

A woman's desire to reduce a man to innocence occurs naturally because women love babies. It's a social-biological need in women to also reduce their men to open childlike states as a precursor to lovemaking. In this way a man's separate sense of self can dissolve so that both can take part in sexual play. Wise women do this not to be a mother to him, but so that they both can be open and childlike together. Because she is more capable of being childlike, she leads him.

Many men in this contemporary culture are overly sophisticated and cerebral due to how they were socialized. They have lost touch with nature and the depth of the natural sexuality in them, the sexuality of the Garden of Eden, where all sexuality was innocent. So many become ambitious, driven, and hard-edged. These men really don't know how to play with a woman, surrender, and become childlike, although I bet somewhere inside they want to.

Some men are overly rational, to the point that they can't be emotional or sensitive. They have lost touch with their feelings or feel uncomfortable being sweet or vulnerable. A wise woman wants to soften a man, to help him reconnect to her. And, if he can't join her and let himself become like a child with her, it is a loss for both of them. In fact, both are surrendering to a higher state of knowledge and love. When they feel love, they are happier and naturally express that to others. The love spreads out.

In interviewing men, I asked them how it felt to be in that open state with a woman. All of them said they liked to be in that state. But they received conflicting signals from the culture in which they lived. They said, "I can't go there all the time, I have to be tough, or I have to be successful, or I have to be aggressive. I'm going to lose my hard edge, my assertiveness, and I have to control myself and her." Overly analytical and overly rational men, who have lost touch with their deeper sensibilities and their feminine qualities, most need to surrender to the women in their life. They are overburdened with stress and need to let go.

One of the difficulties with getting a man to relax is that men have been raised to be stoic—to not cry, be tough, keep a stiff upper lip. But every man I've met like that has an unfulfilled desire to let go.

So for many men, there's a loss in their connection to nature in general, and to their inner nature in particular. Thus they become overly rigid. Some even become bullies in their relationships with women or their own children.

I often see that in my practice. Fathers are more often more rigid and hard with their children than are mothers. Mothers are much more permissive and soft, qualities children need along with discipline.

In a culture like ours, where the world is in trouble from too much masculine control and domination over others, resulting in global wars and deprivation, the salvation for men is to descend into a childlike state. Jesus said in Matthew 18:3, "Truly I say to you, unless you turn and become like children, you will never enter the kingdom of heaven." Surrendering like that is wisdom. When a man surrenders to the softness in a woman he takes in her sensibilities. He absorbs another way of doing things. He takes in her sweetness, her maternal quality, her sensuousness. He is absorbing the way she does things, the way she relates to nature, the way she is compassionate. It allows him to reach into those aspects of himself and to connect to the other half of himself that he needs in order to be whole.

Many men have told me that they desire the kind of attention and care that they received from their mothers. It fulfills them to receive it, so that in turn they want to give back to the women in their lives. The way men rest from the pressures of the world is in the aura and lap of the woman. And women love to rest on the strong shoulder of the man. This feeds and nurtures both of them as each gives to the other from the distinct essence of themselves.

I have interviewed many successful men, men in the highest places of government and industry, and top professionals in law, medicine, and architecture. These men had success and money. Most of them confided that they made all the money and acquired all the power just to get a woman in their lives. They longed most of all to have a woman they could surrender with. That was a driving need for all the men.

When a man can let go and rest in the aura of feminine tenderness and love, he gets restored; it helps him go back into the world and do the kind of battle in life that he needs to do. It's like his safe haven, his watering spot.

Solomon, the great king and prophet, called wisdom "she," and said, "Wisdom is radiant and unfading and she is easily discerned by those who love her and is found by those who seek her. She hastens to make herself known to those who desire her. One who rises early to seek her will have no difficulty for she will be found sitting at the gate. To fix one's thoughts on her is perfect understanding." Even Solomon, known for his wisdom, urges surrender to the feminine side of life and calls doing so "perfect understanding."

SURRENDER AND INNOCENCE IN MARRIAGE

Surrender is not just for sex. It helps avoid conflicts in marriages too. Daily stresses in long-term relationships can erode the feeling of wanting to give to one's mate. Each partner feels pressured by the demands of modern life and thus the natural generosity between couples can erode. A power struggle often ensues about who is going to give to whom.

Infantilizing cuts out all of the hostility between couples and rekindles love. Infantilization is wisdom in action. The one who assesses the situation and gives first is acting in wisdom and usually has the power to shift the negative dynamics. It is not giving out of obligation or fear. It is giving to bring harmony and peace and to ease hostilities in a tense situation. It is giving to bring the highest good to all involved. It is a power for the good.

A woman with whom I worked was totally sick of her husband. They had kids who needed her attention, yet when he came home from work he wanted her to spend time with him. She felt burdened by his constant needs and demands. She kept accusing him of being a big baby, and he was driving her crazy.

As she used the image of infantilization with her husband, she was able to give what he was desiring and the whole dynamic in their marriage began to change. He needed less and less, and their relationship grew closer and closer.

Sometimes a woman considers it a burden to give to her mate because she has children to care for. In her mind there seems to be competition between taking care of the husband and caring for the kids. But a woman can give in different ways to more than one person and give to each one. There doesn't have to be a divide between her husband and her children.

Conversely, women who bond primarily with their husbands and not their children, create a serious problem because the children lose out. I have seen many women do that. The mate becomes much more important than the children. It's very bad for children to grow up in an environment in which they never feel they are most important and always feel deprived. The emotional losses such children suffer last a lifetime.

There is great demand today for women to be the pillar of strength for children and men. This demand is due to our cultural exile from living in harmony with nature—and with our inner nature—and it makes life difficult for many women. Women in the work force and in positions of authority often find it is very hard for them to give to themselves and to be there for their husbands and children as well.

What is needed is a shift in attitude. Instead of men and women having a combative relationship with each other, men must learn to surrender to their women and women must learn how to lead their men to surrender by caring for them. One woman said, "If he wants to sit and talk for five minutes, you give that to him. Then if you want something from him, there will be a warm feeling and he'll indulge you. I also have to surrender my negative attitudes toward him."

Men growing up are taught to be tough and not to cry. Young women aren't given these messages and therefore women have a different perspective than men do. A woman still retains more of nature in her. Thus a woman has a connection to nature and a more natural way of doing things. She is more encompassing in her way of being and she is more like part of the earth. That is why she wants to get her man back to nature as well. She wants to restore him and to open him. Then she can connect to him in a real way.

If the world were the way it should be and we were all at one with nature, women wouldn't have to treat men like little children to help them open up, and men wouldn't have to surrender to women. Because the natural order of the world has become so injured, and nature lives more deeply in a woman, she must be his teacher. She must lead him back to his more original self.

Men often return from work with too much on their mind. Some want to sit and talk with their mate while others may be emotionally unavailable, tense or even brusque. The man who surrenders can say, "I'd like to spend some time with you." He allows her to affect him, and in that allowance gives over to her and listens to her thoughts, opinions, feelings, and experiences of the day. This surrender to her makes her feel fulfilled and allows him to be more connected as well.

Women can go to childlike states more easily than men because women are biologically connected to children through nursing, pregnancy, and bonding. So women relate to children in a more natural way and are much more connected to babies, while men are a little more separate. Because women can go to that childlike place more easily than men, it's up to women to bring men there.

To have wisdom with a man is to bring him back to a state of innocence. That is a very positive thing for a woman to do. This simple knowledge contains a cosmic notion of mythic magnitude. Since being exiled from the Garden of Eden, or purity, in our minds and souls, the only thing that can get us back there is to be like children, innocent and full of love.

Some of the great female sex symbols are wonderful at infantilizing. Sophia Loren can truly make men surrender. She is so sensual, and powerful, that men get reduced to acting like puppies around her. She has a kind of sexual-maternal, life-affirming force. Marilyn Monroe had it, too. She not only babied men, but she became like a baby herself and was a symbol of ultimate sexuality.

Here's a secret: the man who can surrender to a woman is the sexiest man for a woman, because she feels she can affect him by playing with him, seducing him, and he'll just go right along with her, enjoying her all the way. These are the best men, the most sexual men for women.

Remember when you first fell in love with your mate? You were like little children with each other, touching, holding, using baby talk, doing the same things that mothers do to babies. Then came marriage and all of that joy was lost.

INFANTILIZING IMAGE
(FOLLOWING ARE IMAGE INSTRUCTIONS FOR INFANTILIZING A MAN.)

1. See that you are a woman. You have the wisdom of nature inside you. You have the power to bring a man to innocence and surrender.
2. See your man in the house or office or place you usually interact with him.
3. What do you see?
4. How do you feel as you see him?
5. See what he's doing, both the things you like and those you don't like.
6. See that he is being childlike. See him more as a child doing these things.
7. How do you feel toward him?
8. See what you want to do for him. Try to keep this knowledge of him as a child in your interaction with him.
9. When you see him in that childlike way, what do you do? How do you feel toward him?
10. See how he reacts to you. If you become irritated by him, try to overcome the irritation. See him as a child.
11. When children act the same way he does, how do you feel toward them?
12. See yourself overcoming your irritation. You are loving to him, like your are dealing with a child. What happens?

Sheila's husband Philip, who was both successful and extremely controlling, was driving her crazy. These are her reactions to doing the image: "I had just had it with him. Philip is a macho guy and very controlling, and he drives me absolutely crazy. He wants to control everything I do in the house. He wants to make sure he knows where the kids are, who is doing what. He has too many demands. He wants everything to be his way. He wants me to listen and help him resolve things—not necessarily voice my opinion, but just hear him out. He needs a pat on the shoulder constantly, reassurance that he's worthwhile. I just want to run away from him, and I don't know how to deal with him."

I asked Sheila to see an image of Philip in her mind's eye. She saw him coming home. "He wants me to sit next to him, keep him company. Anytime he's around, he wants me next to him. He wants to know where I've been, who I'm having lunch with, what my appointments are. He wants to know everything about my day. I get really antsy. I tell him, don't ask me so many questions, leave me alone, it's none of your business, I can't just sit with you the minute you come home."

In the image, she looked into his eyes and saw his disappointment.

"He just wants to relax and have me near him and do nothing. I wish he had something else he could do that he enjoyed, so he would leave me alone. I can see in the image that he's saying, 'Why can't you just come in my space and relax rather than me come to yours?' I can see as I look at his eyes in the image that he feels unappreciated. I'm not meeting his needs. He thinks I don't have any responsibilities for making money. But he doesn't really understand everything I do around the house. He just disrupts my day, and he always has needs and wants to control everything I do, where I go, how I do it, and I've just had it. I don't know how to deal with him anymore."

I told Sheila she was like a powerful goddess with wisdom, to see that she was a goddess with the power to infantilize him and to help him surrender. "I see he wants me to cater to him. In the image, when I infantilize him, I make a comfortable place for him to sit. I make him a cup of coffee, rub his neck, he feels great. He's happy but cautious, because I usually don't treat him this nicely.

"When he's happy, the feeling in the house with the kids is really mellow. I feel good, too. What he wants when we see each other is for me to be supportive of him. He wants me to be nice to him."

She didn't realize that by supporting Philip she was easily fulfilling his needs. This is a situation in her marriage where wisdom, not more conflict, was needed.

Sheila saw in the image that Philip made many demands on her, but by keeping her power in mind, she said: "Instead of getting irritated as I usually do and pushing him away, I give him a hug and say, I'll finish what I am doing, and then I'll sit with you and have a drink. He responds very happily in the image. He knows I will be with him."

Before doing this exercise, Sheila was distant and hostile, and she and her husband fought all the time. Part of the problem was that her parents had been cold and distant and did not interact with her a great deal. She was used to being on her own. Philip had come from a family where he had to take care of his mother, who had M.S. His father was a traveling salesman and rarely home. So Philip's childhood needs had rarely been met. In marriage, he was putting demands on Sheila to meet some of those needs. But she was not used to such close interaction, and would get annoyed and they would fight. When they supported each other and she infantilized him there was no stress.

Another problem was that Philip wanted everyone in the family to acknowledge his needs when he came home. "In the image, I see him come home. He would like everyone to run to him and give him hugs and kisses. Then he takes his workday clothes off and wants a report from everybody. I'm in the middle of cooking and don't take the few minutes to do it, and he gets very upset, and then we fight."

In the image, she infantilizes him: "I see he comes home, and I stop what I'm doing and give him a hug and kiss and acknowledge him. He's totally mellow and happy. It just takes five seconds. Then, when he wants to find out what I did during the day, I have him sit in the kitchen while I get dinner on the table. I continue what I'm doing, but he's more available and willing to come be with me because I greeted him nicely."

Philip wants to be an integral part of the household, to know everything that's going on. This drives Sheila crazy. So she did an image of this. "He asks me, where are you going later, what did you do, what's for lunch, a lot of questions, and I get annoyed and say, What do you want, an itemized list? If later I forget to tell him something, he acts like I tried to keep something from him and that makes me blow up. I get frustrated and short tempered."

Again she infantilizes him: "I see after I greet him nicely with a kiss, I say come sit with me while I'm cooking. Ask me what I did today, and

I'll tell you. When I am kind to him, I see he's really insecure underneath, and I just fill him in on what happened, and then he feels secure and terrific. Before, I used to feel I had to ask Philip's permission because he always put me through the third degree. But now, I feel that I can answer his questions and be sweet to him. There's no tension anymore. I do what I want."

The next problem was that Philip wanted Sheila to sit and listen and help him resolve things and just hear him out. She usually becomes very irritated with that. "He tells me about the stuff he's going through at work and he wants to talk. If I say something he usually gets annoyed and says, 'You don't understand.' If I use my wisdom with him, I just listen and try to be positive, and I just hear him. I don't have to give my opinion; I don't have to say anything. This works much better; there's no tension between us. And it's okay for me to just listen to him. Finally, he asks, 'What do you think?' and that's when he's open to hearing me out."

In the end, she said, "I found my power to bring peace to our marriage. It only takes a little effort to give some. What I have received is far greater, a sense of my freedom and respect for my innate wisdom."

A woman may help a man to surrender, but the man has to recognize the basic needs of the woman and fulfill them. A man shouldn't just take from a woman. Surrender is part of male-female interaction. Women like men who have strength and who can fulfill some of their basic needs. Then women are much more willing to care for them. This works best if the man views the woman as having needs herself and sees her as an independent person in her own right.

Going to those childlike states is not regression, it's not going back to being a baby. It's going to a transcendent state beyond the ego, beyond the kind of control where one's identity is no longer directed by force, assertion, or selfishness. It's going to a place where one is able to let go and enter a playful, open, innocent state.

SURRENDER IMAGE (MALE)

There is also a surrendering image for a man to go through if he has difficulty casting off the rigidity that is keeping him from being innocent and open with the woman he loves. The image is good for men who think they have to have complete control and find it difficult to surrender.

One man who did the image said that many men fear surrender, seeing it as a sign of weakness, of vulnerability. He saw it as giving up control to the woman in his life, and that was scary. However, when he did the image, he felt illuminated because he realized he wasn't giving up anything, but that he was just opening to another part of himself and to receiving boundless affection from her.

Here's the "Infantilizing Image" for the man.

INFANTILIZING IMAGE (MALE)

1. See yourself entering the house you live in, in your usual way. What do you see?
2. How do you feel as you enter the house?
3. See your mate in the house. If you don't have a mate, see you are in a house or room, such as an office, with a woman you like.
4. How do you interact with her?
5. How does she interact with you?
6. If you have children, how do you interact with them?
7. How do they interact with you?
8. Now see yourself entering the house, and you're entering with a childlike state of mind. How do you feel? What do you see?
9. See your mate and approach her in that childlike state. How does she respond to you?
10. Now see your children. You're approaching them in that childlike state; you're not being authoritarian or rigid. How do your children respond to you?
11. As your woman approaches you, see that you are open to her. You are childlike. How do you feel toward her?
12. See that she is in a childlike state too. You're both in that childlike place. There's no resistance. How do the two of you interact?
13. Remember, being overly mature is not the goal of true wisdom.

The Infantilizing Image is not just beneficial to a man, but it fulfills a need in a woman, too. It brings a feeling of enormous well-being to a woman, a feeling that she's valued for her contribution. She can be soft, wise, loving, and powerful. She feels her feminine nature is affecting the man, that she is useful and that she's respected. Some women may feel burdened by this power, but they don't understand that it is a power for the highest good and for the well-being of those around her.

In a personal relationship, sometimes it's nice for the woman to just be receptive and to have the man do everything, even sexually. But not all the time.

Surrendering is an image that is playful, joyful, and loving. The image fulfills both the male and the female in a deep way.

18

The Divine Veil of Mercy
Affairs Are Never Forgiven, Never Forgotten

The notion of the divine veil of mercy originates in ancient Sufi thought that says that the world as we know it is a world of objects. We have tables, trees, other people, flowers, rivers, stones, chairs, and so forth. Some objects are beautiful to us; some are not.

But all objects that are before us have a veil on them. They're veiled because God's presence is *in* those objects, in the trees, rocks, rivers—in everything we see in the physical world. But his presence is veiled, hidden from our awareness. The objects themselves veil God's presence in them. He's there, but we can't see him; we see only the rocks, grass, and trees. It's a very beautiful notion that everything is God and that God resides in all things.

We see objects more than we see God, so God assumes a special mercy toward us. When we see trees and rocks and so on, some of us look at those objects in an agnostic, scientific fashion that kills the spirit in the object and the divine connection that we have with it.

There's an absence of the feeling of mercy if we begin to love objects more than we love God. And in loving objects and not seeing God in everything, we become possessive and greedy, destructive, and oriented toward a disposal-type economy: plastic bottles pollute the earth; we buy new cars every couple of years, throwing away the metal and polluting the earth, buying new fashions every season and throwing away the old. By not seeing God in things, we become a throwaway, greedy, plundering type of society.

When we lose that connection to the divine, we lose the attitude of divinity and mercy toward all of life and its objects. This loss then extends into our relationships: we often have throwaway relationships, changing from one partner to another.

We extend that attitude toward other people. Sometimes we use people for our own needs and ends, and we forget that God is in the other person as well.

Many spiritual masters remind us to see God in each other. If we could see God in each other, we would have a very different relationship than we usually do.

SEX OUTSIDE MARRIAGE

The basic premise of the divine veil of mercy is that if there's sex outside the marriage, you put a divine veil over it and do not tell your spouse. Not for concealment, not out of malice, but out of a sense of mercy toward your spouse.

The act itself is between you and God. The reason for this is that God is in everything and everything is in God; there is no feeling of separation between yourself and God, and all your actions are in the context of that relationship. God is merciful until you resolve things. We cannot think of any other way to proceed unless there is mercy.

Thus the guilt you may feel, or the peace of mind—all of the ramifications of your actions—are between you and God. To bring your spouse into the knowledge of it will cause unnecessary pain.

I am not advocating extramarital affairs. But the reality is that affairs happen. What I am saying is that once they happen, an individual should not carry the consequences of the act home to damage their spouse.

Nor does the divine veil of mercy mean that a person has permission to ruin a marriage or wreck a relationship. Marriage always has to have a feeling of respect and unity in it, especially if there are children, but there are so many circumstances in life that it's hard to make a rule for every one of them.

When a man tells his wife that he's had sex with someone else, it creates havoc, pain, and injury. So when people say, be honest about having an affair, who is benefiting? The person confessing? The perpetrator is not the person to be protected. The person hearing it will be damaged, the relationship will be damaged, and it's almost inevitable that the children will learn of it and be hurt.

So whatever you're doing, it's important to keep it between you and God, and not leave a trail of misery in your path.

Sometimes, people commit adultery because they don't know how to deal with the problems in their marriage. For example, if you're angry at your spouse but you can't express that anger and you suppress it, you may find that you're getting attracted to someone with whom you work. It is very important not to act on that attraction, but instead to learn to express that anger to resolve the problems at their source. When you can express the anger you feel toward your spouse, and they are able to hear you, good feelings come back and you feel love for them again.

Sometimes a person is fearful of their spouse and instead of dealing with those emotions in the relationship, they'll act out and get sexually attracted to somebody else.

A lot of people don't feel really good about themselves. And they look for reinforcement everywhere they turn.

For example, one married man always had to prove he was attractive and desirable to women. He felt insecure. And he felt he didn't have enough sex before marriage. So he decided he needed to have sex with other women to prove himself worthy. That was a conflict within himself. It had nothing to do with his relationship.

This man had just gotten married and the feeling that he wasn't desirable enough and didn't have enough sex before he got married plagued him. Sure enough a woman came along, a friend of a friend and very seductive to most men. He decided to seduce her and prove to himself he was still an attractive guy. He had sex with her one time but he felt guilty. Months later he decided to unload his guilt and tell his wife. They had been married a year. The wife felt betrayed, devastated, hated him, and was hurt. This created resentment inside of her towards him, which was still there years later. She thought of leaving him but decided not to because there was lot about him that she liked. She thought he could work his problem out, but somewhere deep inside there always was a little hurt in her.

He never did it again but did he really need to tell her? This was something he could have and should have worked out on his own. It was between him and God. He had a problem which he acted out, first by doing it and secondly, by telling her. The best thing for him would have been not to enter marriage in the first place, knowing he still had these issues, or once knowing it he could have gotten help.

A woman had a lot of marital problems, and she gained a lot of weight. Her husband found the women at work very exciting. One day, after an office party, he had sex with one of the women while they were both drunk. He felt a lot of guilt and decided he had better fix his marriage or get out of it. He decided to confront his wife, not about the affair, but about their marital problems. He never told her what happened; that was between him and God. He used his pull toward other women as an indicator that his marriage needed work.

In this case, extramarital sex was a substitute for a conflict within the individual (or within the relationship) that needed to be worked out.

Confessing indicates a need to be forgiven. The person is thinking, "I've been bad, and I want forgiveness and approval." That's a very selfish approach. It does damage and hurt to the innocent party without doing any good. It is not up to the injured partner to make things okay for the straying spouse.

Sex outside of marriage has been around since the beginning of time. It is more common today than anytime in the past because of the promiscuous, transient nature of relationships. We can pretend it doesn't exist. Doing that is like hiding our heads in the sand and saying that our kids won't have sex while in their teens. It's something we have to acknowledge and deal with.

I've seen rare situations where extramarital sex is a divine act of mercy in and of itself—for example, where the marriage partner is crippled or ill, and the healthy spouse in a very discreet fashion maintains a relationship that is not injuring the marriage. In other situations, there exists a pure connection to another person outside of the relationship, such as when two people share a humanistic or spiritual purpose or vision that draws them together by chance. In such cases, the person needs to put a divine veil of mercy over the relationship and use wisdom in handling the marriage relationship. These are extremely delicate matters, and the person needs to be wise and aware.

I worked with a woman whose husband had many affairs and would leave clues around. People at the office would tell her he was flirting with and kissing a certain woman. She would find women's names and phone numbers in his pockets. He denied it and made up stories to cover every clue. He actually made her think she was the crazy one. He became so adept at the system of denial that it wreaked havoc on the marriage.

That scheme is not what the divine veil of mercy is all about. This man should have worked out his problems with his wife instead of trying to get himself into someone else's bed. Failing that, it would have been a merciful act to get out of the marriage before his wife wasted the rest of her life on a liar and philanderer. The man was simply being evil toward her instead of dealing with his problem.

Before you fall to the temptation of sex outside of marriage, you should think about what's going on in your relationship. The best bet is to have a spouse with whom you want to have sex exclusively for the rest of your life. Short of that, if you can't have sex with a clear mind, doing it with wisdom, and keeping a divine veil of mercy, then don't do it or don't be married. And if you do succumb to the temptation, don't bludgeon your spouse with the guilt. Deal with the guilt and its meaning yourself.

When we have adulterous feelings, they too should be kept under a divine veil of mercy. A woman who felt very attracted to her boss had all kinds of sexual fantasies about him. It became overwhelming. She said, "I just wanted to fill a void I sensed in him, and I often wished my husband was not in the picture. Sometimes I cared for him so much more than my husband; it just overtook me, and I would fantasize about sex with him. I could intuit his needs and wanted to take care of him, love him, be his muse almost. All I wanted to do was love him. It became very powerful, and I became consumed.

"He never gave me any cue he was attracted to me, but I lived in this passion in my mind for this man for over a year. I realized it was all in my mind, but in fact I was committing adultery in my mind. I felt very guilty about it. Even though I never did anything, I kept it a secret because I knew it would hurt my husband. But I realized the feeling of adultery can happen not only in real life but can also in the mind."

She finally confronted her adulterous feelings and figured out what was wrong in her marriage. This woman had a good grasp on life. People with good relationships can still get tempted outside the marriage. It's how we deal with it that counts.

DIVINE VEIL OF MERCY IMAGE

The "Divine Veil of Mercy Image" is a healing image for people who have had an affair. It helps us find the compassion within ourselves not to hurt our spouse by revealing the affair. It is also a good image for those thinking of having an affair. As you see the images, remember to allow all of your feelings toward the people you are seeing to surface. This is important because you may be suppressing subtle emotions towards the person in your primary relationship which will become evident as you explore the images. It may be that these emotions are the precise reasons you are wanting to stray and you have not been fully aware of them. Also, carefully notice the feelings you have for the person you are attracted to and notice what is attracting you to them. Going through these steps with awareness will facilitate clarity in your mind. In reliving the situation fully in all of its aspects you can come to truths that you were not aware of before.

DIVINE VEIL OF MERCY IMAGE

1. See that you are in a primary relationship. How do you feel toward your partner?
2. See your attraction to another person. How do you feel toward that person?
3. See that you're attracted to two people. Is there ease or confusion or guilt?
4. See yourself telling your partner about the other person. What happens as you see the image? How do you feel about his or her reaction?
5. See yourself keeping it to yourself. How do you feel?
6. See yourself keeping a divine veil of mercy over the whole situation. Tell it to God, and work it out yourself. What is your struggle?
7. See that this is your struggle to deal with yourself. Do not hurt other people; resolve it yourself with integrity.

19

Mercy Sex

Sex in Marriage after the Desire Is Gone

In the last chapter, we discussed the concept of the divine veil of mercy, the "veil" we put on certain acts, like affairs, that are strictly between God and ourselves. We put on the veil to protect our spouse from the hurt we have caused.

This same divine veil applies to our marital bed. Once we get married, we make a vow to be faithful to our marriage partner and to have sex only with that person.

Given the society that we have, we need to have marriage contracts so that we have safe havens for raising children, allowing them to grow up in an atmosphere of security, harmony, and trust and to have a basic family unit around them. It's very hurtful to break that unity, that home base, that tribal feeling for children, because they need it to thrive.

But there is a problem, because keeping a marriage going out of a sense of duty and as a haven for children is not the stuff of great romance. Romance needs passion to set it on fire, and living under a contract with a partner isn't going to set any of us on fire.

What happens is that, over a period of time, sex starts to get less interesting and to die down for many couples. The big joke is, "So what happens to sex after marriage?"

I was visiting the home of an artist, a woman who casts sculptures in bronze. I saw a work of art that was almost indescribable. Although it was modernistic, with twists and angles that were not all discernible, part of it looked like the human anatomy. I reached out to touch it and realized it was a pair of breasts. The artist walked into the room and said they were casts of her breasts. Then she said jokingly, "It's okay to touch them—they haven't been touched in a long, long time!" This woman had been married for thirty years. Apparently, there was no sex in her marriage.

When there's no sex in a marriage, unless the couple has agreed to just be good friends, a feeling of deadness between the two people can occur, as well as tension and even hostility.

If you have compassion for your mate and approach sexuality with a feeling of mercy and understanding, rather than duty, it is possible to have a fulfilling sexual relationship. When sex in marriage is treated as a duty, people become uninterested, even impotent, resentful, and hostile. But when sex is treated as an act of compassion and mercy, it becomes elevated. It becomes elevated because you know God exists in the other person and in you, and when you remember that, that feeling of mercy, which has love and generosity and kindness in it, can be experienced. It is an elevated feeling state of wisdom, caring for the person, knowing that sexuality helps bring you together.

Once sexuality is a duty, it dies out. And it becomes a conundrum. You're supposed to have it and like it and feel good about it, but you don't know what the problem is because you don't want to do it anymore. You start to wonder, What's wrong with me and what's wrong with my marriage? Perhaps you get attracted to someone outside the marriage. And then this plays itself out with further complications, conflicts, and extramarital affairs.

Mercy sex is an attitude that heals this. Mercy sex is when you have sex with your spouse, even if you don't totally feel like it, but you initiate the contact with your spouse out of a feeling of mercy and kindness.

A woman named Cathy discussed her experience of mercy sex. "I've been married for almost twenty-five years. I love my husband Joe, but he really bugs me; his habits bug me. However, I do really care for him in some deep place when I go deep down to look for it. I know that, because if I think of not being with him, of living without him, I feel sad. That's when I realize I'm very connected to him. But in our day-to-day lives, we pretty much go our separate ways and have different interests and stay pretty much apart. Our communication has somewhat deteriorated over the last twenty years. Sometimes, I think it's just the sheer number of years that we've been together that has made the passion die out.

"Also, we don't see eye-to-eye on many aspects of raising our teenage kids. We often fight about how to discipline them. I tend to be easier on them and try to understand why they're doing the things they're doing, but Joe tends to be a yeller. He wants to tell them they're wrong, when I think they aren't, and to give them too tough a punishment. We get into fights about that, and we disagree about other things too. He's a definite slob, and I like the house really neat. I get absolute crazy when

I walk into our bedroom. He seems oblivious to the piles of paper he leaves on the desk or his clothes hanging on the chair. It's like his mother never taught him to hang anything. So we fight about that. There are other ways we get on each other's nerves, too.

"When I first dated Joe, I'd visit his apartment, and I thought his disarray was so cute because he was always busy thinking up creative ideas for his work. He works for a PR firm, and I saw he was very artistic, sensitive, and imaginative. I thought his disarray was part of his genius. I decided when we lived together, he'd change. Well, he didn't change, and now it really gets on my nerves.

"Aside from that, we also disagree on spending money. I want to save money and go on vacations with the children, which I think is important for us as a family. Joe, on the other hand, wants to save every penny for college. I tell him bonding and connection are just as important. He says, to hell with that, we have the bottom line to look at, and we can't afford to do anything but save for college. So we fight.

"The big question is, how's our sex life? I have to say just about nonexistent. I get into bed before Joe does, and I'm off to sleep, exhausted. He comes in later after watching TV. In the morning, the kids are up, he's off to work, and we don't connect. On the weekends, I'm too tired to have sex at night, and in the mornings he likes to sleep in. I like to have time to myself when the house is quiet, so we're on different time clocks.

"Because of this, we don't have sex very often. Also, the tensions and disagreements seem to reinforce our desire not to have sex, and we keep our schedules in such a way as not to address the issue. Once in a while, he does approach me, and I think, oh no, I'd rather do something else. It feels like an intrusion in my daily plans, and I have to make an effort to get into it. However, when I remember mercy sex, it makes a big difference. I then understand I need to respond to him. And I do.

"Actually, since hearing about mercy sex, sometimes I even initiate the sexual encounter, especially when we have drifted far apart since the last time we've had sex. So when he initiates it now, I let go of my resistance and take the time to get into it. Once I'm into it, I remember how nice it feels to be close and have sex and affection. At those times, Joe really enjoys the sex and expresses his love for me, which is really sweet. Sometimes, I feel like a goddess, and he is my god. Other times, it's just okay.

"For a few days after, there's a good feeling between us, a special bond. We definitely get along better; there's more peace, and he seems much happier. The kids pick up the good feelings, and they seem more at ease. So when we have mercy sex, a good feeling pervades the entire household.

"Then within a week, the same old crap creeps in, and we fight and bicker. But now that I'm aware of mercy sex, I will initiate it more often. When I do, the good feelings come back. I start to remember why I married him. When he initiates having sex, I often don't resist, although once in a while I do. More often I don't.

"I find the concept of mercy sex is a great help for marriages. So many of my friends ask, what happened to their sex lives? I tell them mercy sex is the way to go and then explain it to them. They report the positive effects of it, that it actually brings a feeling of love and closeness to their partner. We joke about putting a reminder on the bathroom mirror: have you had your mercy sex today? It's like taking vitamins to keep your marriage healthy."

Mercy sex helped Cathy so much, it sounds like she's peddling it door to door.

I have to admit that I am a diehard romantic who sees sex as divine. But I am also a realist. When sexual passion diminishes or leaves a marriage, there may still be good and important reasons for maintaining the marriage bond. When there is good reason for a marriage to stay together and passion is dimmed, mercy sex is a way to fulfill the marital contract and have compassion.

Here's another example. Connie used mercy sex, not because the marriage died out, but because her husband Sam was a control freak who drove her nuts. They had three children and Connie cared for her husband, but she was getting turned off because he was so controlling.

She said: "I have two boys and a girl, all preteen and early teens, and I'm married to an extremely controlling man. Sam has this rigid, fixed idea of how life should go. It drives me so crazy that I end up feeling frustrated and like a madwoman. It's like he wants me to shrink into being his robot, and I end up fighting and screaming.

"Sam's very moody. If we're planning to do something with the kids, one of them will inadvertently do something to get him mad, and he'll slip into his bad mood and destroy the enthusiasm of our plan, control it, and nip the trip in the bud. He starts to control the whole event with barking orders and anger.

"When he wants to be sexual, he wants to be in control, to do it when it's convenient to him. He then gets very insistent and is insensitive to my needs, my rhythm and flow. He can be all-consuming and completely drain me. I began to get turned off sexually to him, but I don't want to leave him because of the children. Of course, when I get fed up and reject him, he gets in a really bad mood and becomes controlling all over again.

"I began to realize I was rejecting him a lot, and he's very vulnerable and his sense of self goes down because underneath the control he's really insecure. I felt compassion for him. When I began to see how insecure he was, I was able to feel more in control and feel more power. I used one of the images, and in his eyes I saw fear and insecurity underneath the control. I decided I could manage our relationship for the sake of the family.

"When I heard of the mercy-sex concept, the first thing I did was laugh. It was a funny thing to do. I decided to try it, not because I felt desire for him, but as a tool to make him a little bit happy and more manageable. The next time Sam approached me, I made myself available, and he became softer, happier, more manageable. When he was pleased, he was more open to talking. That's when I began speaking to him after having sex in a loving way, bringing up some of the issues, and he would be much more open and receptive to me.

"I saw this as a window of communication on how I felt about things, the way he treated me and the kids. I didn't reject him. I'd snuggle, hold his hand, and he'd respond by seeking contact. That always meant he wanted sex, so I thought of mercy sex and had it with him. Once we had sex, he was always calmer. Now right after sex he often initiates conversations about the relationship, and he's more open to hearing what I have to say. I have become his teacher about relationships and he now respects me as he never did."

For Connie, mercy sex was not a duty but a healing force in the relationship for both of them.

Mercy sex is designed to help deal with sex in the marriage once the passion has gone. We need wisdom, compassion, empathy, and strength to keep a healthy marriage going.

20

Menopause
Sex after the Big *M?*

Menopause has never truly been understood. In the past, ignorance about this phase of life often led not only to profound depression, but even to suicide and institutionalization for some women. Thankfully, in the past decade there has been a huge proliferation of books and articles on the subject of menopause.

Menopause is currently looked upon as a generally problematic midlife transition for women. It is usually not seen as a natural transition from one stage of life to another. It is perceived as a medical condition that needs to be treated with hormone replacement therapy.

There is a lot of controversy over prescribing medications and hormones, or following alternative approaches involving diet, herbal remedies, vitamin supplements, and exercise to deal with this change.

The problem with estrogen replacement therapy is that there have been many reports of increases in breast and cervical cancer following its use. Physicians commonly discourage women with a family history of breast cancer from taking HRT.

The whole issue of menopause is confusing. Is it a psychological thing that women go through, or is it only a hormonal deficiency that happens to the body? If it's a medical problem, what is its cause? The question then arises, "How could nature have created a hormone deficiency in women's bodies?"

Does that mean that when nature or God created men and women, that women were cursed so that when they could no longer bear children, they would suffer a physiological depletion? I doubt that nature is sexist.

In Dr. Ahsen's research on the subject, he discovered that the symptoms of menopause are directly related to a woman's attitude towards aging. How can this be?

To take a closer look at menopause and attitudes toward aging, we need to first address the notion of expectations and expectancies. It is important to understand that *what you expect has a lot to do with the outcome*. Because the word *expectation* suggests that something will be happening in reality, it creates an internalized mental condition of expectation that has physiological consequences. In much of Dr. Ahsen's research on drug addiction and alcoholism, he found expectation to be a very powerful mental stimulus that affects the actual outcome of our emotional or physical symptoms.

For example, if a man is expecting a negative situation, such as hearing bad news about bloodwork that may reveal a life-threatening illness, the expectation will affect him and he may experience such emotional and physical symptoms as anxiety, sweating, and fear. People who have a fear of flying and expect that the plane is going to go down may experience panic, tense stomachs, and cold sweats. Those who are afraid of heights feel weakness in the knees or have vertigo. Expectations of bad things release chemicals which create physiological symptoms in the body.

Therefore, expectation creates reality. A woman who expects a plane to crash will create emotional and physical symptoms in her body. Her heart beats faster, she can't catch her breath, or she loses her appetite.

This mental set of expectations creating reality is what most women go through during menopause. They react to the hidden and overt messages in our culture about women aging. And menopause is the beginning of a woman's awareness of aging. Menopause means her youth is over, she is no longer able to have children, and she enters another phase of life.

Sometimes women get subliminal messages from observing their mothers going through menopause and seeing what it was like for them. Did they go through it in an accepting, positive manner, or did they fall apart? These are powerful images in the minds of women that unconsciously surface as they go through menopause. It is similar to the experience of people who reach the age at which one of their parents died—they often expect that they will die that year. Aging is difficult for women today because our culture values youth and beauty above all else. Young and beautiful women have social power. Aging women do not.

We can't flip through the pages of fashion magazines or watch TV commercials or movies without being bombarded with images of beauty and youth—how to get it or keep it—with makeup, diet, exercise, plastic surgery. Anorexic models are acceptable cultural icons of sex appeal, but a menopausal woman who naturally pads up a little in her belly and thighs is not desirable. A woman is supposed to be very thin and very athletic to be considered beautiful.

There is no way that women in our culture, in the twenty-first century, can escape these cultural pressures. Pick up any magazine. Do you see women in their fifties or sixties as icons of beauty or valued in any way? How often do you even see a woman in her forties who looks her age? In Hollywood, women past their thirties are rarely considered "bankable" for a starring role in a movie. We are a nation obsessed with youth. To tell a woman she looks younger than her age is a high compliment.

Are aging women seen as valuable in our modern times? And if an aging woman does not feel valued by the culture, can she be sexual?

Aging menopausal women are not by our culture's definition "sexual." In reality, however, many women discover the true depth and power of their sexuality while in their fifties, because for the first time they feel free. They don't have to prove anything anymore.

The issue of expectations and anticipation of aging is obviously very important. The assimilation of menopause into the life of a woman— mentally, emotionally, and psychically—is very much connected to how she views growing older. These mental expectations about what her role and value in society will be, and the images, thoughts, and attitudes of the society, are intricately connected with her menopausal symptoms.

The mind is very powerful in how it affects the body. Fear of a plane crash creates sweats and heart palpitations, but the fear exists in the mind of the person. And even though the plane lands safely, the mental expectation is so powerful in the psyche that just thinking about flying will elicit psychosomatic responses. The brain will send stressful hormones, chemicals, electrical and neurological signals to the body, creating a myriad of uncomfortable physical and emotional symptoms.

The same is true with menopause. As with fear of flying, physiological changes in women's bodies all begin in the mind.

If a woman is conditioned by our culture to believe youth and beauty are her most valuable assets, then she will have an expectation of loss as she ages. She is losing her identity. Her expectations will create reality, and she will begin to worry about wrinkles and sagging breasts, and she will no longer feel sexy.

Through eidetic imaging, we have been able to treat women individually and to pinpoint their unique experiences about being a woman while growing up as the root causes of such menopausal symptoms as hot flashes and insomnia. The messages she received when she first developed breasts and got her menstrual period—how the people in her life treated her—form very powerful images in her mind. They are the key to the later formation of her expectancies of aging. And these expectancies in turn trigger physical symptoms as she enters menopause.

DEFINING MENOPAUSE

What is menopause anyway? Menopause is the cessation of menstruation. It is the time when the ovaries gradually stop producing eggs, and the production of large amounts of hormones begins to cease. It is also known as "the change" or "the change of life."

The word *menopause* derives from the Greek words *meno*, which means "month," and *pausis*, which means "pause." The menopausal notion is ancient, and early references to it appear in the Talmud. Even Aristotle noted that a woman's child-bearing years ended at age fifty.

There are three stages to menopause: *perimenopause*, which may last several years before the last period; *menopause* itself, an absence of menstruation for twelve months; and postmenopause, when menstruation has ceased for good. Generally, menopause begins around age forty-five and ends about fifty-five, although some women may experience changes as early as their late thirties, while others don't begin until their early fifties. In studies of women in the United States, ninety percent experienced menopause by the age of fifty-four, and a hundred percent by the age of fifty-eight.

Interestingly, in the late nineteenth century, Western medicine viewed menopause as a medical crisis, so that at times drastic measures were instituted, such as the use of leeches or surgical removal of the ovaries. In the first half of the twentieth century, horror stories about women strapped down and given shock treatments because some menopausal behaviors were not found to be acceptable were common. Today, the medical profession looks at menopause more as a deficiency disease, treating a woman's symptoms with estrogen to replace that which is lacking.

Whether menopause is a medical complaint, a disease that needs to be cured, or a natural state in a woman's life, the bottom line is that women experience symptoms at this time of life, and each woman is very individual in how her symptoms manifest.

Menopausal symptoms can include hot flashes, night sweats, chills, fatigue, anxiety, crying, heart palpitations, irritability, insomnia, depression, dizziness, itchiness of the skin, genital itching, mood changes, loss of memory, headaches, dry vagina, painful sex, changes in menstrual bleeding, changes in urination, incontinence, generalized muscle aches and pain, and thinning hair and skin. In addition, women may suffer bone-density loss, which may lead to osteoporosis; high blood pressure; and angina, which may indicate arterial heart disease. They also may be at risk for a stroke related to arteriosclerosis.

Studies of other cultures demonstrate that if society's expectations for aging women are positive, such as women expecting freedom and power when they age, there are few or no menopausal symptoms.

The question is whether our culture, in defining the most valued feminine image as youthful, creates the physical and emotional symptoms associated with menopause. It certainly looks that way. Thus, when we treat it medically, aren't we treating it from the outside in? Aren't we giving drugs or hormones to treat societal expectations already placed in the mind?

With imaging, we go directly to the mind and psyche of women and shift the imbedded perceptions and expectancies that are creating their symptoms. When we do so, their symptoms desist.

When a woman has *positive* expectancies about menopause, such as the fact that living past age fifty gives her increased power, prestige, and a sense of freedom; she suffers no symptoms, and the transition to menopause is easy.

In talking to many women going through menopause, it's amazing how powerful the *negative* expectancies are. All of the conversations with my contemporaries were about "my eyelids are dropping, my butt's going south, look at these wrinkles, my chin's sagging, I'm starting to look like a turkey, I've gained ten pounds, no diet helps." There is sorrow and agony over these changes.

Also, women experience fear about aging and losing their beauty and youth, as though it's a horrible thing to get lines on one's face. They can't seem to get away from the devastation of what is before them. They can't stop the aging process. There's a feeling of loss of power, loss of value, loss of identity. Who are they as women over fifty? What's valuable about them? What do they have left to look forward to?

I remember my own experience going through the transition. Not only was it punctuated by the fact that I stopped menstruating, but it happened the same month my daughter started menstruating. It was an amazing and, I suppose, symbolic month. I didn't get my period, and she got hers. It was almost like I was passing the torch of femininity to her. It really stunned me. I thought of my mother at my age, and I could not believe I had gotten to that stage.

I remember looking in the mirror and being shocked that my face was dropping and had lines. I couldn't believe it. For me, the expectancy of aging was connected to death. Both my parents died in their sixties and here I was, nearing fifty. I felt like I was going to be dead soon. I started to pay close attention to those little thoughts that were cropping up, that I was entering the last phase of my life, that I had only ten years left. There was a negative expectation of dying that I had associated with menopause.

My mother went through menopause in her forties, brought on by treatment for breast cancer and the removal of her ovaries. My daughter was near the age I was when my mother got cancer, so these events in my own life were powerful in my mind, further creating an expectancy of death. I felt like I was facing death, and I didn't known where the time had gone. These expectancies were powerful in the workings of my mind, yet all of it was going on at a subliminal level.

On top of it, I felt I was losing my beauty because of all these changes going on in my body. I couldn't lose weight as quickly as I used to, I was seeing lines and sags and bags in my face, and here was my daughter becoming a beautiful woman. Where had the time gone? The whole thing threw me into insomnia and hot flashes. And it wasn't until I began to pay attention to all these subliminal thoughts going on in my mind that I could begin to deal with understanding, truly understanding, that it was impacting my sense of identity.

I needed to see myself in a new light. I needed to re-distinguish my identity from that of my mother and my culture.

New questions arose in my mind. What is my identity? Who am I? Am I ready for the grave? Is nobody going to love me anymore because I'm not as pretty as I used to be? Do I need plastic surgery to go back to where I was? How can I be sexual? I'm almost dead! I really had no model to identify with.

Through imaging sessions, a new 'me' was born in my mind, a powerful image of myself. It wasn't really new; it had been in me all the time, but I had to rediscover it. It was a natural, biological, genetic image of myself, a woman past menstruating who was powerful and beautiful and free and wise.

It was there all the time; I just hadn't known it. When I found it, it was the death of the old me and the birth of the new me. The best part about the new me was the sense of freedom to be myself and to express my power in the world.

Women's brains hold the encoded images and pictures of everything related to their feminine self that happened to them as they grew up—all the images, all the events, all the messages they got about being women. These images include their personal histories—their mother's passage through menopause, what happened to them when they first menstruated and developed breasts, ideas placed in their minds by fashion magazines. It's all in there, wrapped around their natural sensuality like chains keeping them imprisoned.

But their wholeness, their true sense of self, is pure and unencumbered by all of these impositions. Through retrieving the images of their wholeness, women can free themselves from social impositions and find their own personhood. There is a treasure map of images in women's minds that permits them to recapture their natural powers. It's the genetic blueprint of their original abilities, and it tells the unique story of their natural self before all the societal stuff hit them.

MENOPAUSE IMAGE

In order to capture the women's consumer market, advertisements are developed around images of pretty young women who are "cool" and stylish. Of course, these women are surrounded by attractive people with the latest fashions and makeup. This is true especially in magazines for girls. Advertisers start early in getting out the message of youth and beauty. These messages create a hypnotic effect that not only sells magazines and the products advertised in them, but indoctrinates us about how we should look, act, and feel. The same is true of movies and TV.

Advertisements that are fast-paced, which have a quick, fiery stimulus and response, become hypnotic and habit-forming in a way that makes us consume more and more to look younger and better. It's a form of hypnosis that sits on top of our true nature.

The first step toward getting past the myth of the media is to discover our true image, the image of ourselves as free and powerful. The genetic blueprint that's inside us holds the image of our wholeness.

This wholeness can overcome the hypnosis of the ads, which makes us have negative expectations and anticipation about aging. We have to get back to that natural image that's already inside of us.

The following set of images leads a woman to the awareness of how menopause is affecting her and to the retrieval of her wholeness or, her true, natural self in terms of menopause.

EXPECTANCIES OF MENOPAUSE IMAGE

1. What does the word *menopause* mean to you?
2. See the image forming in your mind of a woman in menopause.
3. What do you see?
4. How do you feel seeing that image?

Meditating on these questions helps women to discover the expectancies they have about entering menopause. Reflecting on these answers allows women to see how the culture has affected them.

More than any other time in the life of a woman, menopause is a time of profound change. It is not a negative change, but simply a slightly different path that women are embarking on toward self-acceptance. It is an opportunity to grow in a whole new way, to regroup. It is a time to allow strengths to come forward with a new surge of life.

The Menopause Image, and the images in the following pages, bring forth images from women's own deep nature, images that were left behind, forgotten, and buried beneath all the social and media images that were pressed upon them.

Menopause is a time to be free, to come home to ourselves. The fluctuation in estrogen that occurs prior to menopause is really a biological signaling, a preparatory response that allows a woman to go through this change in a positive way. The most self-assured women have said, "Let's move on; the best is yet to come."

One of the first things that happens when a woman hits menopause is a feeling of surprise that it has come. Usually, there is a perception that life continues the way it always has, and that it's going to continue that way forever. The sense of shock and surprise is both mental and physical, and goes along with the drop in estrogen. But the outer demands on her life don't change. Work is still there, her man and kids are still there, and society doesn't acknowledge the profound change she is going through.

So there's a conflict between the change that is going on internally, which is very subtle yet powerful, and life going on as usual. Some women have a hard time dealing with the internal pressures that mount from the images of their history, coupled with the lack of recognition by those around her of the passage. There should be an expectancy of something positive and powerful happening to her, but often it just isn't there. When women's negative expectations are fulfilled and there is little or no positive response honoring their passage, it is easy to understand how they lose self-esteem and power.

How do they get back to their original self? There are several steps for the treatment of menopause with eidetic imaging. A woman is usually guided by a trained counselor in gathering this information. However, I've included the list of questions here because there is no reason a woman can't gather the information herself. After reading the following lists, most women understand exactly how their responses affect them.

The first step in ascertaining the physical and emotional symptoms of menopause is to answer these questions:
- What are your worries and concerns about menopause?
- How is menopause affecting you physically?
- How is menopause affecting you emotionally?
- How is menopause affecting your relationship with your man? children? work?

Each time a woman asks herself these questions, she will build up a larger picture of the impact of menopause on her life.

The next step is to determine the effect on a woman of her mother's menopause.
- What was your mother's attitude, concerns, and reaction to menopause?
- How did it affect you?

The last step of information gathering concerns how a woman expects menopause to affect her in the future.
- Are you worried about loss of sexuality? attractiveness? youth? energy? memory? health?
- Are you concerned about finances? your job?
- What other concerns might have an effect on your self-image?

WOMAN ON HORSEBACK IMAGE

Once a woman has gathered this information, there's going to be a great deal of awareness in her about what is creating her menopausal symptoms and how she is reacting to the changes taking place.

The "Woman on Horseback Image" can help very much at this stage of life. This image helps change the chemical output from a negative self-image to a positive one. When we have hope and encouragement, our brain pumps out wonderful chemicals and hormones that make us feel good.

Woman on Horseback is an image of release and is one of the primary images for the treatment of menopause. It involves a woman on horseback who leaves this confusing technological age to savor a different, richer life with an imaginary ancient tribe that lives next door.

The primal nature of this image gets women back to their basic self, unfettered by the hype of Madison Avenue. In the image, women leave their symptoms behind and discover a new life, in a new landscape, so they can break free from society's limiting expectations of them. Each woman who goes through this image comes out with her own unique sense of self.

WOMAN ON HORSEBACK IMAGE

1. See that you are leaving your present house. You are on horseback.
2. See that you are going to an ancient tribal time.
3. See that you are going to teach the young girls in the tribe your wisdom.
4. They are in their huts, and they are shy.
5. You call to them to come out.
6. You go from house to house to gather young girls to go with you on horseback.
7. As you go from house to house, you gather more girls, and you become an army of free spirits.
8. They like you, and you admire their youth and beauty.
9. See that you're teaching them about the world. The teaching is of an essence, not of any one particular subject or its details. The essence of the teaching lives in you.

The woman who becomes the teacher of young girls teaches a whole new world of values and sensibilities that come from her essence. This knowledge already exists within her, and it gives her power, strength, and a natural ability as she imparts her wisdom to the girls. This teaching is an homage to the young girls and to their beauty. The young girls who come out are free spirits, and the menopausal woman resolves her issues of trying to be forever young by teaching these girls from her wisdom and knowledge.

So there's a shift. The value in the menopausal woman is in all her life experience and in the knowledge, power, and strength that she's gained. Her experience and the things she learned along the way are the gifts she has for others.

When I did the Woman on Horseback Image, I felt a hormonal shift occur in my body. I felt power, freedom, exuberance. I had a lot to teach the young women, a lot to give them, and it opened my whole heart. I saw myself riding freely and teaching them to be free, to be themselves. I felt purposeful.

I saw myself gather them under ancient trees in a meadow. We sat in a circle, and I taught them to be true to themselves. I taught them about the things they would have to face in life. I felt in the image a profound love and protection toward them, and I was teaching them the things I learned out of all the pain that I had been through—that is, to be powerful women, to have pride in themselves, to honor the gifts that they bring to the world, to honor the feminine side of life.

As I saw this in the image, I felt a sense of renewed purpose, passion, and mission; I felt that my identity was formed in expressing my wisdom and through my teaching. I didn't feel old. Instead, I felt like a beautiful, wise woman giving back to these girls some of what I have learned from life. I felt free and sexual and sensual; in part, what I was teaching them was about love and sensuality, to value that part of themselves. In the image, I embodied the sensuality I was teaching. Life was not over; I was not a dried-up old hag. In a funny way, I was truly in my prime.

So my identity shifted from thinking I was going to be dead soon to being a vibrant, beautiful, wise woman in her prime. I was ripe, like a full peach. I had gathered enough wisdom to give back all that I had known. Everything was before me. I positively anticipated the future.

In this image, I became a very full and sensual woman offering wisdom and love. It's an image of myself in which spirituality and sensuality come together in my identity as a woman. Each woman who does this image finds that a unique sense of her own self emerges. She confronts the popular theme of having to be young to be beautiful by creating a different image, one that is more active and more primal and more true to her essence. Her value is in the fact that time has brought her wisdom, confidence, and power to deal with the world. These are some of the gifts she brings to others.

In the image, the woman leaves the house she's has always known and goes to an imaginary tribal setting. She is leaving the strictures of the contemporary world, where all the negative symbols have prevailed. She becomes a teacher of a new way of life, which is based on her true essence. In telling the young girls to come out and ride on horseback, she wants to teach them about life. The teaching that comes from each woman is in the form of an essence rather than through particular details like "You have to dress right for success" or "You have to treat men a certain way." Her essence flows outward from her teaching, and the teaching is always about freedom, freedom from all the societal beliefs that entrap her. It's an homage paid to a new life and new beauty. So the woman becomes a teacher of a new world from the knowledge that exists within her. As she teaches, her powers and strength come to the fore.

More and more young girls are collected along the way, and they become an army of free spirits. The woman admires their youth and beauty, and they admire her visionary side and wisdom. I see this with my daughter's friends. I enjoy their fresh beauty, and they love talking to me about life.

The woman on horseback knows that the restrictive world around her is in trouble and needs her guidance. And by teaching from her essence, the woman's self-doubt is resolved in favor of a grander vision. This image is for many woman like having the power of the sea; her passion is no longer bound, and she becomes an expressive, flowing, oceanic self.

That's how I felt on horseback. I felt powerful, moving, free, and large; the caring in me was so huge for these girls that I was engulfed in a profound, all-encompassing love for them. Did I have any menopausal symptoms while I was in that state? No! There were only positive hormones being secreted from my brain into my body as I saw the image.

I found that repeating the image helped me sleep better, and my hot flashes diminished and then stopped. The more I did the image, the better I slept and felt. The more my new essential identity was established, the more I recognized that I had a full life ahead of me.

Doing the image allowed me to feel sexual and to enjoy that sexuality in a full way, rather than thinking I was an old crone about to die. The previous negative thoughts suppressed my sensuality. But the woman on horseback, in conjunction with understanding my personal history, gave me a full and ripe feeling, like I was a luscious fruit.

DRIVING THE POINT HOME IMAGE

The next menopausal image is called "Driving the Point Home." It takes up where the woman on horseback left off. Like the others, it is designed to bring a woman's essential powers to her current life.

It's important for a woman to allow the feeling of robustness to come through as she goes through this image.

DRIVING THE POINT HOME IMAGE

1. See that you return to your own house after you visit with the tribe. You are back in your present house.
2. See the house, and tell your husband or significant other that you're leaving the house. But you will not really leave the house; you will simply come and go at will.
3. Tell your husband or significant other that you are leaving, not because you feel less sexuality, but because you have other things to do. You have to teach the young women what to do, and tell them what you know about life. You have to teach them your new wisdom.
4. Tell everyone you feel no anger or conflict toward anyone. You simply have a different job to attend to at this time.

The image brings the feeling of freedom and purpose and value into the present home so the newfound powers are incorporated into daily life.

RETURNING TO THE HOUSE IMAGE

The final menopausal image is "Returning to the House."

RETURNING TO THE HOUSE IMAGE

1. See that you return to your own house after your visit with the tribe and teaching the young girls. You are happy and walking around and very busy doing things in your house.
2. Think of your menopausal symptoms. Do you have them, or are you free of them after your visit to the tribe?
3. Look at your husband or significant other. How does this person appear in the house? If they don't know or understand your new self, it is clearly a philosophical problem that they will have to work out. See them walking around the house, puzzled but also intrigued, ready to envision life from a new angle.
4. See that you can handle interaction with your husband or significant other without losing a sense of balance in the dialogue.

This image brings the new identity a woman found riding horseback into her current house and into her relationships. With her newfound self, she's able to take a stand for herself and interact with people in her life with freedom. It gives her the ability to confront those who need it with love and strength, rather than in a powerless way.

Ann, a single mother of forty-nine with two children, was fearful for her children being raised without a father in the house. Her "change of life" had added drama to her fear. She felt alone, tired, struggling, and just plain scared.

This is how she described her symptoms. "I see a lot of age happening, my body changing. I feel exhausted often, even after a good night's sleep, and I feel like I get overwhelmed easily and can't stay focused. I feel emotional sometimes, and I really lose it. I find I go into moments where I don't know where I am; I feel forgetful. My children tell me I repeat myself.

"I find I worry a lot. I've always been a worrier anyway, but I think it's escalated. I worry about keeping the house, continuing to work. I guess I'm going to have to work for the rest of my life, and I worry, am I going to have the energy? I worry about my health, the kids, my job. I think things hit me harder than people who are paired off."

Ann's description of what menopause meant to her was negative, which is a typical expectation about this part of life. She saw the passage as a time of no longer building dreams, but letting go and reevaluating, trying to cherish the moment while struggling not to get depressed over regrets about the past. She saw the future as a time when she would have less energy and less creative force.

She saw an image of a woman in menopause, and it was herself. "I get a split image. On one hand, I feel alone and struggling, tired and scared; I see someone who has gone through a divorce and has had to struggle to make enough money to keep the house and raise kids. On the other hand, I see that I have companionship with my new boyfriend, Philip. He has no attachment at all to getting older; he just accepts it and wants to be with a woman my age, wants to grow old with somebody, and is very positive about it. When I see myself around him, I feel younger, more positive; I exude a certain wisdom and strength. So I feel split about it."

Ann's negative feelings are typical of how many women feel, as if they're "drying up" inside and outside. Their vagina's dry, they're not getting periods, their bones are shrinking and becoming more brittle. It's a time when they might want to pause and reflect on many things, but the demands of their kids, their spouse, and their job are such that they have to keep moving, keep producing.

Ann did the Woman on Horseback Image. She saw herself going out the back door; hopping on a big, strong, sturdy white horse; going into the woods, mountains, and lots of nature; and eventually coming to a group of people living off the land and working together as a community.

She saw herself as a teacher of young women. "I see that they're shy. Touching them brings them out. There's not a lot of verbal communication but more touch and more feeling. Soon they sense that it's safe to go with me. I want to take them out to see the world, show them what's available; they don't have to be afraid, and there's so much to see.

"I see us as free spirits. With their shyness and apprehension of getting out in the world, I see myself taking a stance and saying, 'You don't have to be afraid. I'll show you how to fight the battles, and you'll grow from them, and I will lead you and teach you.' I can see that from all the years in battle and all that I've learned, I have something to teach them."

What Ann saw in the image, teaching young women, made her feel better about herself. "I feel good, enthused, full of power, interested in life because of the teaching; it makes me feel optimistic."

She was enthralled by their youth and beauty. "It's exciting to see their shiny young faces, innocence. I feel very safe around them, protective toward them, yet I want them to blossom. Their excitement about life is contagious, and it feels comfortable. I don't feel threatened by their youth like I would have years ago. I enjoy being around it and want to feel their excitement and youth around me."

The image was transforming for her. "I think about my kids and their friends, that it's enjoyable having them around. They can all be pains in the neck, but I find more and more I do enjoy having them around and I like interacting with their youthfulness. I feel excited and enjoy seeing their innocence and creativity—they're so imaginative. I feel I want to see them more after doing this image."

The menopausal images help restore women to their power, feminine beauty, and essence, giving them an opportunity to realize how much wisdom they have to share with the world. Menopause is an extremely lonely and frightening time for a woman because, even if she has a special man in her life, it's extremely hard for him to fully understand and empathize. With the imaging, a woman gets back into herself and draws from her lifetime of knowledge and wisdom.

21

Mythic Images

Myths are stories that people have enjoyed for thousands of years. Most of us like the stories for their entertainment value without realizing that the tales usually carry lessons in human nature that are as relevant today as they were eons ago. Joseph Campbell, the great mythologist, found that cultures scattered around the world had similar myths, even though they had no communication with one other. That's because the stories contain universal truths that apply no matter where they originate in the world. Human nature and the experiences of life, love, and the quest for self knowledge transcend the complexities and multiplicities of the different cultures of the world. Myths are powerful stories that exemplify our own lives.

We have already reviewed a number of myths—Kama-Dev and Cupid, who give passion; Zeus and Hera, with their conflict over her demand for commitment and his quest for freedom; and other myths like Narcissus that explored our inner self. In this chapter, we will explore several more images that arise from myths that will help us discern the boundaries and problems of our sensuality.

USHA: AN IMAGE FOR WOMEN WHO FEEL POWERLESS AND OUT OF CONTROL WITH MEN

Usha is a beautiful Hindu goddess. Like Aphrodite of ancient Greece, she is a great beauty, but it is not her beauty we can draw from, but her feminine powers. She is a wonderful tool for a woman to use to tap into her own inner strength when she feels powerless and entrapped by a man.

We have also used the Usha image with women whose sexuality has been cut off because they've been hurt by their parents or their culture. This image is wonderful for women who have suffered abuse, are afraid of their sexuality, or are afraid of male attraction and interest in them.

Usha restores their natural, playful, sensual self. Women get control of their relationships by having a sense of strength. It makes them feel safer, and lets them get closer to a man.

Usha is also a good image for women who are in abusive relationships, women who are scared and send out signals of fear and intimidation. I have worked with women who, once they had done the image, no longer sent that signal of fear. Something changed inside them, and when the man began to abuse them they didn't respond with fear, which in turn made the man react differently.

Here's an example of signaling. My nephew came for a visit with his bulldog. I have a Bernese mountain dog and a yellow Lab, and within a few minutes of the dogs meeting, my huge male Bernese mountain dog was being corralled, cornered, and herded by the female bulldog. My female Lab was also totally intimidated by her. Within a few minutes, the signals between these three dogs were set. The bulldog entered the territory of my dogs, but my dogs caved in. If my dogs had stood up to her, she might have backed down. Such signaling also occurs between humans.

When a woman has a possessive husband—one who needs her so much he won't let her be free—and she caves in like my Bernese mountain dog, doing the Usha Image will help give her a sense of freedom.

The Usha story begins with Brahma, who is the Creator in the myth. He creates all things, and he created Usha. She is a dazzling beauty. She has a terrific body, her skin is soft, and she has long, flowing, reddish hair. She is full of life and laughter. Not only is she physically beautiful, but she is full of passion, love and strength. When she runs, she's faster than the wind, always playful and laughing. And Usha has all kinds of ideas; she is very innovative and expressive. She is so enticing and beautiful that Brahma is completely entranced by her.

Brahma wants to possess her, so to avoid him Usha flees. He chases her. As she runs, she turns into an animal form (a female dove, for example); he chases her and becomes a male dove. Usha runs again and becomes a female deer, and then Brahma chases her and becomes a male deer. Then she becomes a female tiger, and he a male tiger. In this chase, all life-forms were created. This is the Hindu story of creation.

Usha says, "The reason I run from Brahma is because when he looked at me he was alone and full of loneliness. I ran to get away from his need and desire."

Brahma is taken by her beauty; she gets frightened by his loneliness and his wanting to possess her. It's an endless chase, where she turns into every female animal form ever created and he turns into the male form. Implied in the myth is that they meet and momentarily unite, and then she takes off again. So he can never capture or possess her. Usha is always laughing and playful and free and certain of her self. Brahma is completely smitten by her and pursues her eternally. She is free, but he, enslaved by his desire for her, is not.

Here is the "Usha image."

USHA

1. See Brahma looking at Usha and admiring her. He is entranced by her.
2. She's pretty, of reddish hue, a dazzling beauty.
3. This is the moment of God's admiration of what he has created.
4. God is entranced.
5. Look at Usha's body. The skin is soft and beautiful, and her long hair is flowing.
6. She is light on her feet.
7. Her emotions are erupting with love and lots of passion.
8. If she ran, she would be faster than the wind.
9. After one sprint, she is as fresh as ever.
10. Your own spirit feels like that at times.
11. She is playful and chuckling.
12. She has many ideas, and she innocently expresses them.
13. See Brahma chase her. She turns into an animal form to escape.
14. See Brahma change himself to the male animal form and run to capture her.
15. The two stay together for a brief time.
16. See Usha take off and run, turning into a new animal form to get away from him.
17. Brahma realizes that he has been left behind with only the outer shell of her previous animal form, and Usha has taken off in flight, having changed into a new animal. He quickly changes into the new form of the male animal and chases her. See the cycle repeat.
18. See Brahma catch her again. They meet for a few brief moments, and Usha takes off again in a new form. On and on it goes. In this way, the whole world was created.

There's a part of Usha in some women where they are always on the run, looking for new horizons and a little dissatisfied with things the way they are. Some men have complained, "She's never satisfied, she always wants new things, she's restless, now she wants to do this or that, such as go on a vacation or redecorate the house," but that's part of the desire women have to constantly create anew.

The important aspect of this image is that Brahma can't capture Usha, even though he adores her and desires her. She is in control, but she is not rejecting him. She's playful and happy and sure of her autonomy and freedom, as well as her power and beauty. She lets him catch up and then just takes off again. It is a game to her. For women who have felt very contained in a relationship, this is a wonderful image to free them.

I've used this image with victims of sexual abuse. I remember Elisabeth, a girl whose father would look at her breasts all the time. A feeling of lust would come from him. She would freak out, and it made her feel repulsed. This affected her relationships with men because any time a man desired her, the feeling of revulsion that she had toward her father would come up.

When Elisabeth did the image of Usha, she developed an inner sense of freedom and strength. She realized she didn't have to pay for her father's lust; she could react differently to what her father did; she didn't have to be so affected by it. It was his problem, and she was free and could move forward.

After seeing that, she felt much stronger. The next time Elisabeth was with her father and that look of his came, her reaction was very different. She didn't feel vulnerable anymore. She sort of laughed at him and moved away. He sensed the shift in her from vulnerability to strength and clarity, and he stopped the behavior. Even if he hadn't, she would have felt much freer and much more detached.

The Usha image allows a woman to feel active and free where she's been feeling contained and suppressed. We've also found it very useful in working with women who have a tremendous amount of fear. When one understands through the images that running away is mythic or spiritual, then the fear is dissolved. It's okay to run away, if it's not in fear but in power. Usha's image has the effect of making one feel stronger and capable of taking off.

In the animal world, there's a ritual where the females run away and the males chase them. In the same way, Usha is truly feminine.

Another woman, Martha, had a very controlling mother. When she did the Home Image, she saw her herself in the kitchen with her mother. There was a tremendous feeling of control coming from her mother. Martha felt she had to do everything her mother's way. Then she married a similar person, a man who was extremely dominating and controlling.

Martha made this comment: "Control is a problem in my life. I have difficulty accepting my husband trying to control me. I also find that I am controlling like my mother because I have a hard time accepting people's differences. I want them to do things my way."

I took Martha through the image of Usha, and she saw herself as Usha. When Brahma wanted to embrace her, she took off, running with tremendous glee. As she ran, she turned into a female gazelle, and he turned in the male gazelle. Of course, symbolically Brahma became her mother and her husband and all those who had controlled her. She ran joyfully, changing from one form to another. She realized as she was leaving the animal forms behind, that it felt exactly the same as it had when her mother tried to control her, but now she ran and did not look back.

She said, "I feel free and powerful as I see this image. My body is fluid, flowing and excited. I am full of energy and vitality. I feel free, I can be myself, and no one can grab me." This sense of freedom stayed with Martha and helped free her from being both controlled and controlling. She no longer reacted to her husband's domination in the same way. Instead, she just laughed at it and did what she wanted. In time, her husband gave up, realizing he could not control her. She was no longer playing the game.

Nancy, a married woman in her forties with two children, is married to Dan, who is very controlling. She was thinking of divorcing him because she was fed up with his dominating ways. He wants to have sex all the time, but she is so angry at him that she often rejects him.

Nancy's father was abusive. He would fly into rages at the kids and at Nancy's mother; sometimes he even smacked her mother around. Her mother would just say, "Let's not rock the boat; let's keep things peaceful so he doesn't get upset." She tried to keep things calm so as not to upset her husband. So Nancy learned that women just kept quiet and took the abuse. She married a guy who didn't abuse her physically but who was very controlling. His behavior was emotionally abusive.

Nancy said: "The control comes in with Dan's mood. If we're planning to do something and it's important for me to do it, he can slip into a dark mood and destroy the enthusiasm that my children and I have.

Then he threatens to withdraw from our plan. He always makes us feel so miserable that we don't want to bother planning anything anymore. He is very possessive. It's always *my* house, *my* car, and *my* wife. He's one of those macho guys. I didn't know he was like that when I married him. In fact, he seemed so sweet then. After we were married, he changed, and I saw a man who was possessive, controlling and dominating, like my own father. Dan won't admit that he's possessive, but trust me, he is. When I'm on the phone, he asks, 'What are you talking about?' When I say, 'It's none of your business; I'm talking to a friend,' he says, 'You're *my* wife, and I have a right to know these things.'"

Nancy did the Usha image. "It feels inappropriate that the Creator wants the woman he created; it's almost sinful. But if I think about my husband, Dan, he wants me to be sexual with him, and he wants to be in control when it's convenient for him. It can be all-consuming when he wants something, and it can totally deplete me. When I see the image of Brahma looking at Usha and wanting her, it reminds me of my husband being all-consuming and wanting me."

When she saw Brahma desiring Usha, Nancy had a sense of dread. "This desire of Dan's can destroy me; I don't want this contact. I want a safe distance and an appropriate relationship."

But as she went through the images and felt Usha's power and freedom and the way she was able to avoid Brahma's desire to control her, she got insight into her relationship with her husband. She said, "What I see is that I don't want to get caught up in the old dynamic with him; it's not for me. Acting fearful around him curtails my ability to handle him. This image is showing me there's a way to master his obsessional quality of needing control. I see that I can master it in such a way that he doesn't even realize it's happening. When I'm free, but not completely rejecting of him, I can handle him in a way where I have the power. This is great; I feel free and in control and able to manage him, rather than have him manage me."

She put the image into action in specific instances. "I saw Dan trying to be controlling about our dinner plans. I thought a certain restaurant was better for the kids, but he insisted on eating at another restaurant. Usually I would have gone down the drain with his insistence, but I kept Usha in mind and I felt free. I didn't feel that I had to completely succumb to the way that he wanted me to be. I became kind of playful about it. I did not give in. Instead, I spoke up, showing him why we should eat at this other restaurant. My energy was so different, so light and playful, plus I was a little bit affectionate, too. It completely disarmed him, and he agreed to eat at the restaurant I preferred. I realized that because I had shifted, he responded to me differently.

"That night, Dan wanted to have sex, and I wasn't as angry because I wasn't feeling as suppressed around him. I thought of Usha and how she allows herself to be chased, so I decided to have sex with him. It was much better than usual because for the first time, rather than Dan dominating me and making me have sex, what I experienced was my freedom, and I could see the vulnerability underneath his control. I was having sex with him because I wanted to."

Nancy learned that she didn't have to be disempowered like her mother or a control freak like her father. Her power came knowing she was free.

Another suppressed woman, Irene, experienced terror getting close to a man. Just when men would approach her, she would do something to undermine the relationship because she was scared of rejection. She didn't feel pretty enough. Also, she couldn't be herself and express her feelings or thoughts around men because, underneath it all, she was very dependent on them.

In her early thirties, she had one failed marriage behind her. She would get involved in a relationship, begin to feel dependent on the man, and then start to be afraid that he would reject her. Then she could not be her real self. As a result, she unconsciously undermined all her relationships. It was too scary to feel dependent on a man, because she would lose her sense of identity trying to please him, which she did so he wouldn't reject her.

Irene did the Usha image and said: "This is creepy. My immediate thought is that it explains my running away from men and my fear of men. I'm afraid they're going to take me over; no way will I let them."

She saw Brahma looking at Usha. "I can see it clearly, and it is so personal to me. 'Stop looking at me,' I want to say. Brahma's an old man with this white beard and flowing robes. I see his eyes as very piercing blue, and Usha looks like Pocahontas. He is looking at her adoringly. It's not lascivious—it's just too much—get him away from her. This is how I feel with men—it's like, yuck!"

Irene saw that Usha was pretty. "Oh yeah, she's exotic, really pretty, graceful. She has lovely skin, and she's wearing an outfit like an American Indian would wear, like an animal skin."

What a woman sees in the image is a reflection of her own thoughts, feelings, and emotions. "I see that Brahma is awash with kindness, love, pride, and adoration for Usha. He is very soft when he looks at her. He seems harmless enough and very sweet. I can see he's very loving."

As Irene goes through the image, Brahma's eyes change from being angry to being loving. When the male figure changes in the image, something changes inside of Irene, permitting her to see a man without hostility.

Irene got another perspective on herself as she did the image. "I feel more self-assured as I see Usha. I get glimmers of recognizing that I have power. I wish I could feel the freedom and power of Usha all of the time and not just once in a blue moon. I'm always worried about what I look like, and if I'm okay, and how I appear to guys. I'm too concerned about people accepting me. But Usha doesn't give a shit; it's not even an issue for her. This whole body-image thing I have and this whole fear of rejection is like a hideous monkey on my back. When a guy likes me, I just seem to collapse. It's like I have no voice. Then I hate myself, and I hate him for all the power he has over me. When I see the image of Usha, I feel that *I* have the power, not the man, and I am free to come and go at will."

Irene began to feel more secure and more sure of herself. Usha became a very important image for her until she felt strong and in control. Once she knew that she could be herself, she was able to have a successful relationship with a man.

Usha also helps women who are depressed and who can't be light on their feet to be full of energy and to move forward.

A MAN'S IMAGE OF USHA

Joe, a man who was having trouble getting love and attention from his wife, used the image of Usha. His wife, Carol, had received a promotion and had moved up the corporate ladder. When she wasn't working late, she was away traveling on business.

He said: "My idea of a partner when I married Carol was someone to share my life with. Someone to have an emotional commitment with. I expected a close, sharing relationship. When I gave my marriage vows, it was 'keep thee only unto her.' I think that's been true emotionally and intellectually for me. But it has just not been true for her since she got promoted.

"I am hurt. Carol doesn't seem to hear me when I speak. Her mind is elsewhere. She seems busy with other things, and I'm not as important to her as I used to be. Our sex life is minimal. She works all the time, she basically runs on fumes, and her tank is empty, so that when I approach her sexually, she's just too tired. As a basically romantic person, I'm afraid I could be swept off my feet by someone else. In my previous marriage, I had affairs, and I know I'm susceptible.

"When I met Carol, she swept me off *my* feet. I was entranced by her, and our marriage has been good for a long time. We've been married for eight years, but now I feel really lonely, underappreciated and unimportant. I feel like I'm just the errand boy and that's upsetting to me.

"I'm about to stop reaching out for comfort and sex because I don't want to be hurt anymore. I've gotten shut down by her rejection. Sometimes, when I've been turned away, it's hard to go to sleep next to her."

Joe decided to do the Usha image. When people use mythic images, they're bringing their own psyche and psychology to the myth, so they're talking about themselves and their own mental and emotional states. So what he says in connection to Usha is really about himself and his attitudes toward his wife.

He began by seeing that as Brahma creates Usha, he is awestruck by her beauty and he desires her. Joe said, "I feel stuck gazing at this beauty, and I long for her the way I do for Carol."

He went through the steps of the image, and then he saw himself as Brahma, chasing his wife, Carol.

"At first, she's too tired and has to go to sleep. Then I see that instead of getting hurt and backing away, like Brahma, I'm all ready for her, and I'm going to pursue her no matter what. I have that longing and desire for her. So, I persist with my desire and passion for her. I see that when I persist, she finally responds and enjoys it, and it makes her relax. I approach her sexually, and I can see that it charges her up, makes her relax and actually recharges her. Our contact and our lovemaking give her energy, and she does respond positively."

Joe felt good after the imaging: "I have been overly sensitive to her rejection and taking it very personally, and I've backed off, resenting her. I have to stop backing off and start to pursue her, keeping in mind what she is going through."

Joe had almost given up, and he had forgotten Carol enjoyed him too.

Usha is a wonderful image for women who have been damaged in their capacity to enjoy the love of a man. And it is helpful for a man to better understand and appreciate the feminine dilemma when a woman has to work out her hurts and fears.

It is also a good image for people who have been abused or molested. It puts the woman or man back into the endless cosmic play where they see Brahma pursuing and Usha running, but doing it playfully and not with malice or violence.

When people have been sexually abused, it is extremely painful, but it must not be the end of the world. Many people overly obsess about it and further complicate the memories, adding more injury to the trauma. The sexual abuse needs to be healed with the baseline images of the abuse. Because each case is unique, such healing is individual, and no one single image works for all. While revisiting the images of the abuse, there are usually a few instances in which the spirit of the person surges for self-defense and expresses its power. This may occur in simply resisting or in full self-defense. Whatever the case, to discover and replay these image frames is profoundly healing. Ultimately, to find health, the person must move away from the obsessive memory and touch into the cosmic self.

22

Sex and Careers

In most marriages today, both the husband and wife have careers. This brings additional conflict into the sexual relationship because each party brings home stresses from work that can be taken out on the other. Women in the workplace have also caused a change in the dynamics between men and women at home, because the new roles cause a rift in traditional roles between men and women.

Many women believe they have to act more competitively and aggressively at work because they have to keep up with the men who are so competitive and aggressive. A woman complained to me that she had to get more competitive when her firm hired a number of men, changing the whole office atmosphere. She had to start acting like one of them, playing the way they play, in order to be taken seriously. (Her perception that she had to start "acting like a man" is erroneous—women need to act like women, even when they enter a domain formerly controlled by men. When they stop using their feminine power and try to imitate masculine power, they are playing a losing game.)

It's necessary to have equality of the sexes for there to be great sex. In order to have wonderful sex, a person needs to have self-esteem and to feel worthy of giving and receiving love, as well as be open enough to have all those good sensual feelings in their bodies. To be equal means you can be free to give of yourself in the expression of your most intimate self without subjugation or control.

If you can really be yourself, which means you experience equality and self-esteem, then you can have sex with someone who also feels good about themselves. That brings the best you each have to the relationship. The same applies to the workplace.

If your self-esteem is not up to par, you won't feel good about yourself. You can't give the best of what's in you in any area of life. That's why it is important to have full equality between men and women, in every area of life, including the workplace. As each brings their full potential forward, everyone benefits.

The source that fuels men and women at work, as in sex, is different for each gender. In other words, their goals and motivation, what truly drives them is unique. Because of the differences, the workplace is a key area where the sexual signals get messed up.

Traditionally, women who have children are interested in taking care of the family, as it is a biological urge and a necessity. Men are also concerned with the family, but traditionally, their main concern has been work. Because there has now been a merging of the roles, where men also take care of the family and women are also in business, the sexual signals have become confused; they've become unclear. Once there were very clear parameters, but now there are none.

The roles have widened, and while women are in the workplace, men are doing things that were once considered women's work, such as cooking meals and changing diapers. Thus, men have taken on some of the traditional female roles, and women have taken on some of the traditional male roles. What's happened in this transition is that men and women are being pulled in different directions, and it has driven men and women away from each other. They emerge as opponents rather than partners.

I have seen this dynamic over and over in couples: they emerge as opponents and become mentally—and at times, physically—combative with each other. When the husband comes home from his job, he might bring work with him. But the wife needs him to help her with dinner, the kids, and the laundry because she's also been at work all day. The stress for both increases. The stresses of job and home make her critical of him if he does not do as much as she does. He gets irritated with her demands. He is stressed from his day at work and by her demands, and as a results, the natural sexual cues between them collapse.

The same problem exists at work. Men are taught to be fierce and competitive and to do whatever they need to do to succeed. When women enter the workforce, they have to become fierce in order to compete in a world that has been set up by men. The parameters for worldly success are the parameters of the male way of doing things. This entails competition, pushing through, and controlling things. Imitating the male, the woman loses a little of her sexual identity.

In working with corporations, I have seen women emulating the male style of leadership as if that is what is expected. Women often become very masculine and tough, yet they lose their natural, more feminine, fluid, and encompassing style of leadership.

So the natural sex signals between men and women turn into battle signals. They have to fight each other all day at work and then again when they come home. They are battling with each other about who's running the show at work and who's handling the children at home.

This is where the breakdown has come. What is masculine? What is feminine? How does one relate to the other? Are men the aggressors and women receptive, or are women aggressive too and men receptive? Confusion and hostility emerge as people get emotionally hurt by stresses at work that are further aggravated by stresses at home.

Out of this situation, many unclear messages shoot back and forth. The interaction between men and women becomes confusing; there are wrong signals being sent to each other. Then there are counterreactions to those signals, and it just becomes a big mess. The natural sexual signals between men and women get trampled: sometimes it gets called sexual harassment; sometimes it's called seduction. In an aura of competition, sexuality cannot prevail—being competitive is antithetical to sensuality and love. The sexual attraction is greatest when we can connect with another person physically, emotionally, and spiritually, but that can't be done when we are at each other's throats.

Inherent in sexuality is a coming together out of love and desire. When a man feels that way toward a woman, he softens toward her, and when a woman feels that way toward a man, she softens towards him. There's love; there's a merging; there's a surrender. It is not conducive to battling and getting ahead.

We need a whole different aura in the workplace, one that incorporates the best of the feminine and masculine attributes while enabling both attributes to support one another, rather than fight and compete with each other. This mutual support would be good for both parties. Right now, we have a male orientation at work, and women in the workforce have to be as fierce as men. This causes a loss of women's sexual identity and unnecessary friction.

Dr. Ahsen and I did research in which we took both male and female leaders of government and corporations through an experiment to study how they dealt with power and how they instinctively approached situations in life. What we found was that women naturally respond to life very differently than do men.

The experiment, developed by Dr. Ahsen, was designed to see how people react to being given commands. Even though this experiment was not designed to find gender distinctions, such distinctions became astonishingly obvious. Men and women responded very differently when placed in situations where they had to follow the commands of an authority figure.

We found that women psychologically approach the world outside the home very differently than do men. We discovered that knee-jerk reactions, or automatic responses, in how men and women deal with life situations, are very different by gender. Women were very comfortable in situations where they felt confusion and perplexity. They could tolerate not knowing about something in situations where there was ambiguity. It was as though they trusted that clarity would emerge eventually. They didn't have to "know" the parameters of a situation to deal with it. Men, on the other hand, felt agitated in the face of confusion and complexity. They couldn't operate comfortably nor trust that clarity would emerge.

Men have been traditionally socialized to inherit the positions of authority in our society. They come into situations of power with more of a feeling that they have the right to have power. They have been encouraged to be competitive in the way they approach life. So in the experiment, they were very aware of who was one up and who was one down. They wanted to play the game to win. The experiment turned into a competition. And if they couldn't express an opinion or influence the situation, they felt damaged inside.

Women could care less about who was up or down or winning. It never even entered their minds. They were looking for truth in the situation, looking to discover something of value for themselves or for others. If they felt controlled, they would become playful in order to diffuse the control. Playfulness is a very powerful tool that women use intuitively. If they were stressed, they would cry for relief, and then would find more strength in order to deal with the situation. Men could not cry, so they became brittle and more rigid. Women were looking looking for truth in the situation rather than being "right" or having to win. They wanted to be real. They were concerned about being controlled or hypnotized so they could not be authentic. Women could hold back an opinion in order to be strategic, men could not. Men could care less if a thing was real or not—winning was what mattered. Rules were broken most often by women when they believed a rule wasn't right or unfair. This showed that women will break the existing status quo when they feel it is not useful anymore or is dysfunctional. Men, on the other hand, tended to uphold the rules no matter what.

All these differences show that women are bringing a different psychology—a different mind—to the workplace. What they bring is concern, not for being right, but for truth, for an ability to bring change if the existing status quo does not work. They are looking for what is "right" for the whole situation, not only to win personally. Women are attuned to finding the best possible solutions that are good for everybody. It's a less narrowly focused, more caring, more encompassing way of doing things.

This does not mean men are bad and women are good. It simply means that the male style has taken us only so far. Now we need an infusion of feminine minds and souls into society for a shift that brings balance and healing to an overdominating style of operating.

If business leaders go for the truth, not for having to be right and always win, it is a paradigm shift. Truth is good for everybody; it's good for men too. In the end, truth is a win/win. When women offer a vision that is strategically beneficial for the whole organization rather than for just one part of it, it is ultimately good for the men too. Having to be right or wrong is not a positive attitude for anyone. This new paradigm lives more naturally in the psyche of women. Women can't help but bring these changes whenever they enter the workforce because it lives in them. It is important, however, for women to honor their unique sensibilities and not emulate male styles of power.

Signals of sexuality have become crossed and confused. Men were traditionally taught to be dominant, "manly," caretakers of everything. In their eyes, they were akin to the Greek god, Atlas, on whose shoulders the entire world rested. They were expected to take more risks and to assume more and more responsibility. Yet the male domination of the world's workplace was also a huge burden for men. Because women were traditionally denied participation in important decision making in the work arena, the burden on men increased, making men more competitive, one-dimensional, and brittle.

It is time for the feminine contribution to be brought forward so that the entire human environment may achieve better balance, alleviate destructive stress and rigidity for both sexes, and realize the ability of women to induce change in a society that no longer functions appropriately. An aura of cohesion, rather than separate competitiveness, is sorely needed.

The masculine contribution has been dominant for eons. However, that contribution has reached a point of over-saturation. Our technology and our war machines are out of control; people are becoming dehumanized as both their workplaces and homes become more and more technological and impersonal. The planet and its resources are rapidly being depleted, and if we continue on our current track under male-dominated control only, we face self-destruction.

As women participate more and the feminine psyche plays more of a role in decision making, the structures at work and within government will naturally be changed. The way decisions are made will shift. More altruism will naturally prevail. More and better child-care will be available, reducing stress on both women and men. Competition and winning at any cost will be less valued and replaced by progress and growth benefiting everyone, based on truth.

These changes are not a put-down of men but rather an acknowledgment that going further with a dominantly male perspective will hurt everyone. It is time for change, for allowing women's contributions to flourish, to bring balance and healing to everyone.

There is a battle between enlightened men who welcome feminine participation, men who want a change in the way things are done, and unenlightened men, past-oriented males who want to maintain exclusive power and who feel threatened by female participation. But, allowing the female mind to contribute to all areas of society will safeguard our entire environment against the predictable hazards of one-sidedness.

Another area needing change in the relationship between men and women in the workplace is the issue of sexual harassment. Currently the signals indicating sexual harassment between men and women working together are confused. It has become so confusing that if a person of one gender innocently and genuinely says to someone of the opposite gender, "You look beautiful (or handsome) today," he or she might be charged with sexual harassment. Are comments such as that worthy of either a lawsuit or of corporate punishment of an employee?

We have taken things to an extreme when we try to remove all sexual signals from the workplace. It isn't possible to do as long as we are sexual human beings. On the one hand, sexuality shouldn't play any role in promotions or decision making. But sexual attractions do exist despite it all, and the office is a place where many relationships begin. And end.

Some women are oversensitive, thinking their physical beauty is all they are valued for. Yes, some men are crude; they are so unenlightened that they think their crude comments or suggestive looks are clever or give them power. But most men are not this way, and most women enjoy it when a man appreciates their femininity, and vice versa. Doesn't it make a woman feel good to be appreciated, to see she is attractive? Of course, if she is treated only as a sexual object, then yes, that's demeaning. The attractiveness of a woman or a man and their sensuality is very much a part of who they are and is actually a powerful aspect of their being. We don't need to be neuter to be powerful.

23

How Others Deal with Their Problems

In assessing our individual sensuality issues, sometimes we can't stand back and see the forest for the trees. We are all complex human beings. Few of us have just one problem in life, love, and the pursuit of happiness.

The purpose of this chapter is to give an overview by looking at the personal experiences of people who have struggled to get rid of their sensuality problems and opened themselves up to meaningful, permanent relationships.

While the particular facts and patterns may be slightly different than your own, these personal experiences, like the myths of old, have universal truths in them. We'll find their problems the same or similar to our own. The images they use to explore their histories and unload their personal baggage are ones with which we are already familiar. And their struggle to access the sensuous spirit within them has the same goals we are all seeking.

The first situation relates to how much our parents affected our sexual attitudes. We will use parents as "filters" to see how we react in various situations. We are also going to probe parental attitudes in other ways, such as the warmth of their skin and their sensual disposition.

We mentioned earlier that some people get uptight when asked to "keep mother (or father) in mind" while seeing themselves in sexual situations or imaging their parents' sensual temperature. That discomfort is the reason for this exercise. We need to know the blocks to our sensuality, and that tension during parental imaging may be exactly what is affecting our actual lovemaking.

UNLOADING SEXUAL "BLOCKS"

Diana, who is forty-six, has had what she considers to be sexual "blocks" for most of her life. The roots of her problem range from molestation to church doctrine, from parents to a rapist. "I was molested when I was seven years old. It occurred when I was wearing my first communion dress. When you look at pictures of me from that time, you can see something was wrong."

Diana grew up terrified of sex. "I was raised Catholic. The church had lots of prohibitions, and I followed them. I had dreams of being a nun, and I thought you couldn't become one if you weren't a virgin. Back then, I thought I was abstaining from sex because I was destined for the church, but now I realize that I was controlled by fear and that the roots were in the molestation. My worst fears were realized when I was raped at the age of thirty-one."

I asked her, "Up until your first sexual experience, what was your conscious attitude, the attitude you developed from interaction with your parents and the church?"

She responded, "It was important to be a virgin, that a good girl didn't do it before she got married. I never had a sexual experience until I was twenty-five. From the age of nineteen on, the primary men in my life were gay, which very much protected me from any confrontation. After losing my virginity, I had a lot of difficulties with intimacy, and men saw me as distant sexually. That didn't really change until I was in my late twenties, early thirties. Then at thirty-five I married for the first time."

"What was your first experience like?"

"It was wonderful, and it was with a complete stranger. I was going through a spiritual and ethical struggle about whether it was okay to lose my virginity. I was really tortured about it, and I kept agonizing over it with a friend. Finally, she told me that continually questioning it would get me nowhere, that the only way I was going to know whether sex was for me was to do it. I was twenty-five . . . and I did it."

I then told Diana that I had also grown up in an era in which girls were taught that they had to remain virgins. Women who lost their virginity went through profound self-questioning and guilt.

Diana continued: "I kept my virginity into my mid-twenties. I never even did any heavy petting. So at age twenty-five, when my girlfriend and I went out to a bar one night, I suddenly decided I would lose my virginity. I was sitting at the bar knowing I was looking for someone, and I heard this man say something. I told my friend I was going to go home with him that night. She was dumbfounded. Even though I was terribly shy, I somehow managed to connect with him. He was a commercial designer, the kind of guy who designs things like soda cans and cereal boxes."

"Did he know you were a virgin?" I asked.

"He didn't know it until we got into bed. He was the most wonderful lover. He was so delighted and thrilled; he thought I was beautiful with this wonderful body, this virginal thing. He was so sensitive. I thought of him as an older man, though clearly he wasn't that much older than I was. He was so caring in his initiation. The next time I saw him, he brought me a long, fringed, silk shawl as a present. I was really touched because the scarf had belonged to his mother.

"I never wanted to see him again, but I went out with him one other time, and he fell in love with me. I didn't have any time to spend with him. He was just the one I had lost my virginity with, there was no real intimacy. In retrospect, I realize I was terrified."

I said, "The fear kept you from the intimacy that would have made the sex acceptable."

Diana remarked, "I had done it, really enjoyed it, and the question was answered—sex was something I wanted to do. But the other part of me that I wasn't aware of, the part that kept me from being intimate, kicked in right away. I had shame about having done it, and I wouldn't see him again."

I said, "I remember a friend of mine saying that she had similar mixed feelings of shame. Her first experience was wonderful, too, but she felt guilty, thinking her parents would disapprove. When people talk about their sexual experiences, they rarely seem to understand what the true experience of sexuality is. Most stories have an element of suppression, repression, or guilt from parents or religious institutions."

Diana said: "I think in my case it was both the church and the women in my family, who were very dysfunctional sexually. When I look back at my mother, grandmother, and my aunts, none of them were sexually active past their mid-thirties. During my entire growing up, I was around women who were celibate.

"I remember when I got my period," Diana continued, "I didn't know anything. I was fifteen. My mother put me in the car and took me to the local market. I waited in the car, and she came back with a box of sanitary napkins. She threw the box at me and said, 'When we get home, this is what you're going to use.' I asked what it meant, and my mother said, 'The only time you have to worry is if it stops; then you'll have trouble.' That was it; she never said another word. This was the

1950s, and you certainly didn't ask the nuns. I wound up asking a girl-friend and found out if you didn't get your period, it meant you were pregnant.

"Pretty much from my senior year until I was twenty-five, I only dated gay men, either not knowing or admitting to myself that they were gay. There was never any pressure. I thought they just understood where I was coming from and respected me. I found out later they were all gay."

"So," I said, "What you're saying is that society gave you guilt and fear. I'm sure the same is true for men, too. Societal oppression splits the real ability to be intimate, sexual, and loving."

Diana went on: "When I was thirty-one, I came home one night to find someone had broken into my apartment and damaged the lock. My apartment had been ransacked, and I was pretty upset. I had had no experience with drugs, but some friend gave me a Quaalude to calm me down. In a short time, I passed out." At around four o'clock in the morning, I turned over in bed, and there was this man standing there. I thought of myself as invincible, that nothing could happen to me. But he started moving onto the bed, and he had a knife.

"Even more terrifying than the actual rape was that when he was fin-ished, he said, 'I want you to bury your head under the pillow.' I thought he was going to start carving me up, and I thought I could feel the knife slicing me. It was terrifying. I was also in shock and didn't know it. After he left, I called my friends and went down and opened the front door without realizing I was stark naked."

"So how did you manage a sexual life after that? Did it totally trau-matize you?" I asked.

"I think it did as much damage in terms of being mortal as it did with my sexuality. There was a lot of rage about the violation, which I worked on in therapy, but the real work, which took a long time, was overcoming the terror of being so vulnerable, of having no control, of dying.

"The terror and the violation drove a wedge even further between intimacy and me. I was unable to have a relationship with a man. I threw myself into my work as a way of keeping myself distant from any type of intimacy. In retrospect, I was never able to connect beyond the pure physical."

"When you have been hurt sexually, when it's a physical act without loving emotions, you can't be fully open to the intimacy necessary for full pleasure," I commented.

"I agree. Looking back, I know that when I did become sexually active and almost promiscuous, the kind of sexual activity and level of erotic activity was so different than it is now. I really couldn't move into my body as an object of pleasure or let go enough to give pleasure. I see that now. Having promiscuous sex is really just narcissism; there's no intimacy."

"That's true," I said. "But if you think about having sex with someone you care about, the way you touch them has even more pleasure because there's love and you're open. The two really have to be there, that connection between the physical and the emotional. Now, getting back to your story, what happened after the rape?"

"I did a lot of therapy, and I continued working for a while. Then I quit my job and moved to the country and took a menial job. Back then, I never connected dropping out with the trauma of getting raped, but that's what it was. I couldn't cope as well and had to get away from the city and my high-pressure job.

"I didn't have any kind of relationship with a man between the rape and meeting Jerry, my first husband. I married Jerry when I was thirty-six. Altogether, I was with him for five years. After getting married, I got pregnant and lost the baby. This created more trauma and more guilt, like I was being punished for being raped.

"Anyway, I began to think Jerry was gay, because there was something lacking in how he was with me physically. When I asked him, he was shocked. I suggested he was bisexual, but again he said no. Our sexual relationship was never really good; he was not a good lover. Maybe it was because of the baggage I carried into the relationship, the fears. And he had his own set of fears. He wasn't really capable of being intimate, either. I think our relationship revolved around each of us learning how to be with another person.

"After Jerry and I divorced, I began to blossom sexually. I began to experiment, to try to find myself after so many repressed years. It was really important for me. I had tremendous fun and learned a lot about sex that I'd never known. I learned about myself as a sexual being. It was the first time I'd allowed myself to have relationships with men who were absolutely superficial and not thinking of serious relationships. I was interested in having fun. Back in those days we had an awful term for it—we called it sport fucking.

"Then I met Jeff. I saw him come into the room, helmet in his hands, cigarette in the side of his mouth. There was something in his attitude, in the way he moved, an instantaneous sensation of energy just blasting from his direction. I thought, 'Oh no, you don't! You've been here before; you're not doing it again.' "

This is the Idol of Love, that first hit, which we discussed in an earlier chapter.

"Although I stayed away from Jeff at first, I knew at that first moment that I would be involved with him. Jeff was a really good lover, but he also had a drug problem. However, he eventually stopped using drugs after an ultimatum from me. I found out later that the ultimatum was the kink in our relationship. After we were married for a couple of years and we were in therapy, he revealed that he was angry at me for giving him the ultimatum and that it had completely changed our relationship because he thought I wanted to control him. It just ate at him and came to affect every aspect of our relationship.

"I discovered in my relationship with Jeff that I could really love somebody. But I also discovered that one person can't make a relationship successful; it takes both of you. I went into past relationships unable to be intimate, and that's why I chose someone who wasn't able to be intimate either. But during my relationship with Jeff, I learned how to be intimate. I finally left when it became clear I was never going to have all of the intimacy I needed.

"I also developed some real strength of my own, and I wound up letting go of a certain neediness and longing for completion from somebody else. I had a lot of judgments and anger in that relationship. I got to see a lot of my own anger, rage, and rigidity, and I learned to let go of all that, too."

"You said something important, Diana," I remarked, "that you let go of needing someone else to complete you. When you truly come into your own self and then you can share with someone else rather than needing them to complete you."

"I felt complete when I met Stefan. I took some time before I got involved with Stefan, a sweet, sweet man, the first man I had been with who was truly capable of intimacy. It showed up in the way he touched my body and in his level of pleasure in my pleasure; this man had an uncanny ability to delay his own climax with no difficulty. Lovemaking with him was a sustained ebb and flow of the most wonderful, tender sensuality, so it was a wonderful relationship for me, especially coming out of one that had been a desert for so long. The sexual experience with Stefan was completely different from what I'd had before."

Diana had gone from sexual repression, ingrained in her by her parents and her religion, to the trauma of rape, and then from what she called "sport fucking" to healing the split between her heart and her self-centered sexuality to achieve sexual fulfillment and intimacy.

Next, I took Diana through a series of images. Even though the answers are personal to Diana, the techniques are the same ones you would use.

I told her: "We're going to see an image of your parents, and how they affected you sexually. See your parents standing in front of you. Who is on the right, and who is on the left?"

"My parents as they are today?" Diana asked.

"Whatever image comes to mind."

"I am around twelve or thirteen. I see my mother on the right and my father on the left."

"See the image of your parents, and imagine that a window has been carved in each of their chests so you can see their heart beating there. See their hearts beating, and describe how each parent's heart beats."

The image of the heart beating symbolizes the presence of parents' love and a protective feeling toward the child.

"My father's heart is beating quickly, my mother's more slowly."

"Any sign of anxiety?"

"I think that's what I'm seeing with my father's beating quickly."

"How does his heart appear?"

"It looks kind of small, elongated."

"Is there a meaning there for you?"

"It's a little constricted."

"See your mother's heart. How does it appear?"

"Hers is fuller and redder, beating with a slow rhythm."

"Is there any anxiety?"

"No."

"Is there a meaning there for you?"

"Yes, my mother was able to show more love than my father."

In seeing the hearts of her mother and father, Diana gained a new perspective about her parents.

"Imagine a picture of someone in your mother's heart. Who do you see?"

"My brother."

The picture in the heart reveals who that person was most fundamentally connected to.

"Image a picture in your father's heart. Who do you see?"

"My mother."

"Does this have meaning for you?"

"Yes, definitely. I think my mother had replaced her affection for my father with affection for my brother."

"So your father had the most affection for her, but your father's heart was more constricted in his emotional nature and hers was more full preferring your brother. Okay, now see your parents standing in front of you again. See the temperature of each parent's body, and describe the feeling of temperature there. Now, sense the temperature of your parents' sensuality. Is it cold, warm, or hot?"

Some people do not like doing this image because they feel like they are violating a taboo. However, this image reveals important information. The warmth or coolness of the emotional and sexual disposition of the parents is revealed, as well as their attitudes toward sex. Extremes of heat and cold usually indicate problems. (People who have been sexually abused by a parent may not want to do this image because the trauma may re-erupt.)

"It's interesting. I'm sensing my father's sexuality, and the temperature of my father is cool."

"Now sense mother's sexuality. Is it cold, hot . . . ?"

"It's warmer, but not much more so."

"Does sensing her sexual temperature tell you anything?"

"I think her discomfort—her distancing herself sexually, sensually—affected me. I never had around me a woman who was juicy and sexy and sensual or involved with herself on a sexual level at all."

"From the images, how do you think your father influenced your sexual life?"

"The coolness reflects his rigidity. I think his rigidity about sexuality affected me. He wouldn't let me leave the house in slacks or shorts; I had to wear a dress. There was definitely disapproval from him any time I looked like an attractive girl. I just remembered something else with my mother. When I was twelve or thirteen, I started getting breasts. I was chubby and I soon had substantial breasts, but she wouldn't let me wear a bra. A girl she knew when she was young had started wearing a bra early and wound up with enormous boobs, so she would not allow me to get a bra. When I was marching and twirling batons and competing, my boobs were flapping all over the place. The other girls went to her and asked her to please get me a bra. But I couldn't have one for years; finally my sister who was a year and a half younger started getting boobs, and she just went to the five-and-dime and bought herself a bra."

"So your father's heart is more constricted and his sexuality is cool.

This means that he was suppresed and less available in his expression of love and sexuality. The cool temperature of his sexuality reflects his attitude about sex. Cold sexual disposition in this image means a parent is sexually withdrawn. With warmth, there is more sensuality and more sexual availability. But when dispositions are overly hot, there's too much of it. The temperature of parents' sexuality reflects not just sexuality, but also their sensual or emotional relationship to life. If a person has a warm sexual disposition, he or she has a warm attitude toward life and people. If they are cold, they are not as connected to all of life and are more withheld."

I said to Diana, "You can see in these images the very early influences on your sexuality in the way your parents react. The temperature shows whether they were accepting of sexuality. If you examine whether their hearts and their sensual temperatures match, you see that your mother's heart is full and her sensuality is slightly warm. The images show that while her nature was naturally warm, she grew up with prohibitions on her sexual expression so her temperature is cooler. Your father's heart was small and his sensual disposition was cool, indicating that he was more rigid and uptight."

Next, I took Diana through the filtering technique.

"See yourself having sex with Stefan, and describe what you see."

"We're in bed together. It's very sensuous, lush, very warm, very erotic, and tender at the same time."

"Keep your mother in mind. What happens?"

"I get much tighter as a participant. All of a sudden, there's much more rigidity in me, in my body, my level of comfort. I'm much more closed down, much more passive."

"So she brings a passive, less active role to you. Is that familiar for you?"

"Yes, at one point in my life it was."

These filters reveal deep imprints in our mind left by our parents. We often automatically react in life as if we're still under the influence of one parent or another.

"See the image of sex with Stefan, and keep your father in mind."

"The first thing that happens is I'm having trouble breathing. A lot of stress happens, and somehow aggression comes in."

The filter of her father clearly shows the effect his sexual attitudes and his rigidity had on Diana.

"Are these feelings familiar to you?"

"Yes, this is how I always felt before my relationship with Stefan. Now I realize that it was almost like having my damn father in bed with us."

"I was very surprised that the filter, when I kept mother in mind, brought out such strong feelings in me," Diana said. "My body was actually experiencing those constrictions while sitting in this chair. Amazing. And to see how clearly, when I used the filters of my mother and father, I felt. I remembered feeling exactly that way at a different stages of my life."

"It shows how they raised you. Your personality is formed by identifying, imitating, or reacting to your parents."

Diana then revealed another aspect in the sexual relationship between man and woman that is affected by our parents. I asked her, "How did you feel about your ex-husband, Jeff, when you made love?"

"My experience was that whenever we made love, it was like he had a script. There was no possibility of me having any influence, no room for any deviation from the script."

"You mean, first you do this, then you do that?"

"Yes. it was very clear that this was how lovemaking was supposed to go. There was no spontaneity."

"In the East," I said, "the goddess embodying the feminine is seen as active, initiating, and very powerful. I don't know what happened in the West, but they really got it screwed up, and women here are seen as more passive historically. You learned your sexual passivity from your mother."

"I sure did."

EMANATION

Next Diana did an *emanation*. Even though she did not have an ongoing relationship with Jeff, she was still haunted by the fact she had felt so helpless with him and had failed to express herself. An emanation is an image tool used when a person feels powerless in regard to a person or a situation. During the emanation, a neurological "jump" in the brain sends an image to your mind of how you would deal with that situation if you were in full command of your power. The image, the new you, is a more powerful you.

When we say the "new you," what we really mean is the "real you." Deep inside each of us is an image of the self that is unaffected by our history, or by that layer of criticism and doubt that our parents and society put on us. The persona we show the world is the one that includes all of that negative history. What we do in an emanation is reach deeper into ourselves to bring forth that real self, the one that contains all the genetic gifts of the gods that we are born with. A neurological change comes with an emanation because we are rewiring the brain to work off the new, *real* self. Your new, knee-jerk response will reflect the new wiring.

I told Diana, "See an image of a situation with Jeff in which you felt helpless. How do you feel? How does he appear in the image?"

"He appears very rigid and has an angry stance. I also see aggression of some sort. The feeling I have is sadness."

"As you look at him, what is he angry about? You can look into his eyes; there's a feeling or story there."

"He's annoyed that I'm not happy with his way of making love, annoyed that I have problems with it."

"How do you feel?"

"I feel sadness and a certain coldness and confusion, an inability to penetrate through his wall. There's no receptivity there, no way that I can say anything that gets through."

Next, I ask Diana to see a wind blowing around her. This wind is the breath of God, full of cleansing energy. It blows off all of that dusty history that's been piled onto to us, all of those social toxins that our parents and society have tarnished us with. When the wind passes, our gifts of the gods are bright and shiny again.

"See that a wind comes down from heaven, a gift from the gods."

"It's very caressing, comfortable, blowing things away."

"Now see another you jump out of you, and see yourself become this other you."

"I feel a calm kind of detachment, more of a poignancy, a feeling of real solidity."

Once you do an emanation (or other eidetic image), you will have changed. After you change, those in relationships with you automatically change toward you. You can see how they will react to you by imaging them.

"Look at Jeff. What do you see now? How do you feel?"

"I see a little boy. I feel very separate, like there's nothing I want from him."

"So you feel freer?"

"Yes."

"He's seeing you. How does he react?"

"He seems sad."

"Can you see why?"

"There is a certain sadness to him because there's no hook. I am free of how I would habitually participate with him."

"So he'd like to have you hooked into this drama. He liked to play that game of control and to keep you sad or thinking something was wrong with you."

"Yes. It gave him power."

"And when you unhook, the game is over. How do you feel unhooked?"

"Just really very solid, and strong, and very comfortable."

"Before you did this emanation, you felt sad and hooked in a way."

"Very much so. I had confusion, sadness, frustration."

"And now how does it feel?"

"It's completely different."

After emanation, people who have felt frozen and inhibited frequently find that not only are they no longer blocked by the person they were having a problem with, but that the person acts differently toward them.

I worked with a woman called Celeste whose husband, Scott, didn't touch her in the right places. He was a "wham-bam-thank-you-ma'am" kind of guy. She felt very unsatisfied. A friend told Celeste to speak up and tell Scott what she felt, but she was too shy to do so. Then she did an emanation, and the "real her" who came out was sultry and seductive. Feeling her sexuality fully, she was no longer shy, and she asked for what she wanted. In the image, her husband ignited, because this passionate goddess got him very turned on. The emanation awakened Celeste's own passions, and when she made love to Scott, he reacted to the "new her" by becoming more passionate.

What emanation does is to allow the genuine self that is stored inside us to come out. It lets us see it, feel it, and act from it.

EMANATION

1. Relax and clear your mind. Close your eyes, and go inward.
2. See an image of a person in a situation in which you feel stuck or powerless, or that you are unable to deal with effectively.
3. How does the person appear to you?
4. How do you feel as you see the image? Allow your feelings and body sensations to come into awareness.

5. If you could say or do anything to this person, what would it be? Let that desire come into your awareness.

6. Now see a big wind come from the high heavens into the room and surround you. This wind is a gift from the gods.

7. Feel the sensation of the wind swirling and swirling all around you.

8. See another "you" jump out of your image. (For some, it pops right out of their head.) The old you disappears, and you become the "new you" in the image.

9. What is the new you like?

10. See that the new you does or says whatever it wants.

11. What does it do or say?

12. How do you feel as you see the image? Become aware of your shift to the new you.

13. How is the other person reacting to your new self? In the image, when you see the new you—with your new strengths, powers, or abilities—interacting with the other person, notice how the other person reacts.

14. How does the person now react to you? If the new you does not have enough strength, ability, or power, repeat the process.

15. Now see a wind come from the heavens and surround the new you. Feel the wind, this gift from the gods, swirling around.

16. Now see another you jump out of the new you.

17. See how this you interacts with the person.

Usually people find resolution in the first emanation. But if the second you doesn't work, the image can be repeated until it does.

24

How Others Perceive Us

In this chapter, Angela, a thirty-two-year-old legal assistant, would like to know more about a man's perception of her. The situation is complicated by the fact that he is her boss. Angela uses the Co-Consciousness Image.

"See an image of Robert. How does he appear? How do you feel as you see the image?"

"I see him at his desk working. He's very animated and bright-faced and very vigorous. He has a lot of energy. I feel tingly; there's some real sexual energy going on."

"Toward him?"

"I mean in my body right now, seeing the image."

"So, you're very attracted to him. In the image, how is he responding to you?"

"Just the same way."

"See him through his eyes. He sees you. What does he see?"

"He sees someone vigorous enjoying the exchange. She's very lit up and bright, and very engaged."

"And how does he feel as he sees you?"

"Very warm and attractive, and tender."

"How does that feel to you?"

"There's a little bit of sadness as I see that. I think it's because in the context of our relationship, there are very clear boundaries, and they exclude expressing any of that tenderness."

"Now through your eyes, see him."

"Robert looks sad and very . . . guarded is too strong a word, but there's a certain sense of self protection and a kind of a poignancy to the sadness."

"So he's feeling the same way you are. Did you know that before?"

"No, not really."

"Once again, see through his eyes. He sees you."

"There's a bashful lowering of the eyes and a real sweetness, and he's reaching out to embrace me, give me a hug."

"So it's like a sweetness, with love and tenderness. How do you feel as you see it?"

"That same kind of poignancy, a softness and sadness and a kind of tenderness."

"Once again, through your eyes, see him."

"I'm feeling that same kind of tenderness, but there's also a certain guardedness and withdrawal, because it's impossible for us to express our feelings."

"So in some sense, you can't consummate what exists between you, so you just need to withdraw."

"Exactly."

"As you see yourself withdraw, what do you see going on with Robert?"

"There's a kind of flatness, like resignation, to it. There is a little bit of something in the face, in the eyes, a little bit of pain."

"And there's nothing he can do to change how it is, is that right?"

"Yes."

"So it's disappointing; it's like a death. What did you learn going through this image that you didn't know before?"

"I think I saw the depth of the caring and tenderness and the real connection we share. But I know there's no possibility of anything happening between us."

"He's involved with someone else?"

"I don't think so."

"Then what's the problem?"

"Robert has very clear parameters about getting involved with women who are his employees." Angela started to cry.

"Okay, seeing this image through his eyes and your eyes, what did it do for you, besides make you cry?"

"I'm more keenly aware of what is real, and I'm more keenly aware of what the superficial dynamics are and what the underlying emotional reality is. It's a relief to see the truth."

"So it's interesting for you to see Robert is in a struggle?"

"Yes, he's in a struggle between his feelings for me and the rigidity of his ethics."

"How do you feel as you see that?"

"I feel sadness and compassion for him."

Once Angela saw through the images that Robert cared for her but would never break his boundaries, she was able to let go and move on with her life.

25

Cold Beauty, Cold Sex

The next imaging session we will peek into is with Stephanie, who has *Playboy* looks and men beating down her door to get into her bed. But despite her beauty, she had not gone deeply into herself to discover the true essence of womanhood within her. Beautiful, but feeling empty inside, she was nearly fifty years old before she ignited the radiance within her, stopped moving from relationship to relationship, and finally had fulfilling sex. In fact, she got the "big M" before she got the "big O"—she was postmenopausal when she had her first orgasm!

"I was the oldest child. I always felt left out because my younger brother came along and my father's attention went to him. My father was such an egomaniac; he wanted the whole community to know he had a son.

"My mother didn't have time for me because she was a professional and a worse workaholic than my father. I was raised by nannies and schoolteachers. I felt left out, unimportant. Dad was a well-known lawyer, extremely handsome, charming, successful, with a reputation for being loved by all the women in the community. He was quite high on himself and probably had affairs. My father said I looked like his clone—beautiful, just like him. My younger brother became an over-achiever and that really connected with my father. Dad schooled my brother in all the things he always wanted to do, like golfing and horse-back riding. My brother fit into that. My brother got his attention for being smart, and I tried to get it by being pretty. Somewhere along the line, I became rebellious."

Stephanie was rebellious because her parents refused to give her the acknowledgment she needed, a common pattern with rebellious children.

"At nineteen I went away to community college. My parents wanted me to go to a major university, but my grades were poor. My parents were having a lot of problems when I was in high school and college.

Things went downhill for them, and my father began staying away from home. My mother, suspicious that my father was having affairs, began sucking up martinis when she got home at night. I'd find her in the woods behind our house drunk and crying. Finally, my mother had a nervous breakdown, and they split."

Stephanie needed solid support, but there was no one there for her when she started floundering in college.

"You can pretty much guess the college routine: smoking pot, drinking, bad grades. I hated it and ended up eloping with Tim, a male model. He was really handsome, but he was also a drunk who had a father who hated him. There was a question about Tim's sexual orientation; he acted gay and he had a tough time with affection, but he was fun and gorgeous. I eloped knowing on some unconscious level that it would tick off my father and get some attention. I dropped out of school and told my parents I had gotten married.

"We lasted a couple of years. There were just too many problems between us. I helped my mother through her divorce. It was hell. My father was having an affair with a secretary in his office, and when I'd drop by to see him, he'd tell me about the blond upstairs in his bed. My father's attitude about the divorce was that he didn't care, as long as my mother got as little money as possible."

Stephanie floated around and ended up in Palm Springs. "I was always looking for love. My search in life was to realize I could be loved not for my beauty but for my inner beauty, my intelligence. My mother hadn't been a good role model. She was disciplined herself, but I was raised by nannies and only taught how to fold napkins and was basically ignored. I grew up thinking my purpose in life was to find a man to love. One day, a tall, dark, and handsome man came around. Patrick taught golf, was real smooth, knew everybody; he was a lot like my father. But there was something mysterious about him, too. I realized the men I chose always had some underlying mystery about them. That was the hook for me, especially if they were a little helpless. I would feel sort of one up, like a savior, and help them.

"I had a romantic time with Patrick, got pregnant, and had a hard time deciding whether to keep the child. I felt my body was crying out to have a baby, maybe because I thought it would bring some stability into my life. I felt like I was falling apart; I was drinking, doing drugs; I was looking for something to be responsible for to save myself. So I got married and had the child. Patrick and I got along well during my pregnancy, even though he didn't work and I was working two jobs. After our son, Kevin, was born, the marriage went downhill, and Patrick began to have serious emotional problems. He had a breakdown and was hospitalized.

"I guess the pregnancy and the anticipation kept us connected, but the responsibility later on pulled us apart. I was all alone in Palm Springs, my family was on the East Coast. I was embarrassed to tell my mother about what was happening, because that would be admitting failure. I went through postpartum blues, crying all night.

"When Kevin was about a year old, we were having serious marital problems and I started seeing a therapist. My mother developed health problems, and Patrick and I went back east to help. The marriage wasn't working, and my husband couldn't shake his emotional problems. After we separated, he attempted suicide several times, and eventually he succeeded.

"After my mother got back on her feet, I went to work with an old friend who ran a decorating business. My friend was supersmart, a real go-getter, and he had rich clients. The two things I loved were travel and entertainment, so this was right up my alley.

"Even though I had an exciting career going, I was not happy. I felt like it was my friend's business, not mine. And in terms of life in general, I had resentment, anger, and a whole lot of unresolved issues, and I probably took it out on my son.

"I met Bill, my third husband, playing tennis. He was a lawyer, like my father, good-looking, dynamic, successful. He was my knight in shining armor—or at least my savior."

It doesn't come as a surprise that Stephanie would end up marrying a man who reminded her of the father from whom she could never get enough attention.

"Bill spent money on me like it was water. He was fun to be with and loved to travel. I fell in love without looking to see who he really was or who I was. We both liked to party, drink, do some drugs, and have sex."

But she didn't feel fulfilled. "We had no real intimacy. We got married, and pretty soon I was back in therapy because there was a void in me and I kept taking it out on Kevin. I thought I should fill the void in the marriage, and it drove me crazy when things kept going wrong. The therapy helped because I started to build a connection with my son."

Many women think that they have the power to heal anything with love.

"Up to the time I married Bill, in all of my sexual relationships, I had never had an orgasm.

"In retrospect, after imaging, I came to understand that I was not experiencing orgasm because I had never tapped into the sensual side of myself. I couldn't relax and be myself with a man. It was as if each of them were my father and I was trying to get approval from them. I made sure they had a good time, making them think I was the greatest lover of all time and they couldn't live without me. I was so busy trying to please them that I never got around to feeling what was going on inside of myself.

"Bill was different from the other men I'd been with. He was more extroverted, manic, successful. I felt safe with him; he was someone who would take care of me. I had my first orgasm with him, but it came along with lots of drugs and alcohol. I was able to relax into it, maybe I was older, not so much into winning him but letting him love me. I had orgasms for a couple of years, and then problems came. I realized that I was very much the ornament, the Barbie doll, still looking to Daddy for approval. I exercised constantly, always trying to look good for Bill, because being part of him was my whole identity.

"The relationship was so superficial. There was no intimacy; it was sex, drugs, rock and roll. I felt empty and insecure. I was jealous if Bill wasn't home, wondering where he was, like I had done with my mother. I just didn't love myself. It got to the point where he would say things in front of other people that were demeaning. No matter how much he bought me, no matter how many things he gave me, I didn't feel good inside. I realized I was unfulfilled, that I had to accomplish something outside the home.

"I went back to work with my friend in the interior decorating business. I started to develop more and more confidence, but it didn't help the relationship with Bill. I stopped dressing like a sex object and started acting like a professional because I was determined to succeed because of my brains and not my looks. This was a time of real personal growth for me, a time when I started developing a sense of self as I worked with eidetic imaging and my career. But my growth collided with my husband's persona, and we grew in different directions. I wanted to take control of my own time and money, and our relationship just didn't work.

"There was no real sharing, no true intimacy. The more I came into my own, the more I drifted apart from him because we had lost our connection—or maybe we never really had one.

"I was questioning life, questioning my relationship with men, questioning if I was a good parent, and I reexperienced my own childhood again through imaging. For a while, I felt a little lost, unprotected and vulnerable, but the growth came through imaging."

Stephanie did eidetic images, searching for the roots of her fears and of her inability to be herself and flow with that sensuous stream of connected lovemaking that brings total satisfaction. Using the Home Image, Stephanie saw an image of the family home when she was a child. "We lived in Connecticut. We had a nice house, Tudor-style, with one of those long, slanted roofs. My mother called it a Doris Day house because Doris Day always seemed to have a really nice house in her movies even when she was playing a poor widow."

Stephanie saw her parents in the house.

"My father was in a tyrannical mood. I never knew what mood Dad would be in when he came home. He was usually critical. I see my mother. She's busy with a kitchen full of dishes."

Stephanie then looked in her mother's eyes, using the Story in the Eyes Image. "I see fear and rage in her eyes. She was always setting the stage so my father could be king. Or so he could have one of his tantrums. I see my father in the family room—his pout room—and my mother is in a rage in the kitchen, hiding behind her recipes."

"Where do you see yourself?"

"I'm alone in my room. I have a hard time relaxing. I'm walking around, on guard, waiting to see what happens. I'm so antsy, I can't sit down. I want to sit, but I am afraid that something bad is going to happen."

"How do you feel about your father?"

"Terrified. I never really realized that, or at least never admitted it to myself, until I imaged him. He was schizo, but he could also be charming. He would swoop me right up, just adore me. It made me feel wonderful as he adored me, and then I'd get apprehensive again because he was so inconsistent. A part of me wanted to love and forgive him, and I'd get sucked into that. Then I would see him shaking his finger at me, telling me I have to do it his way, and I would feel like I'm being suffocated, that I was going to die."

"What about your mother?"

"She was full of anger but could not get it out. She kept it in for so long that she probably took it to the grave with her."

"How do you feel about that?"

"Angry at her, angry because she put up with it. I'm furious at her for putting up with his moods, for putting me through it from both ends. He would come home and terrify the household, and then she would take it out on us kids. I felt unsafe, that there was no place to hide. I see myself trying to be the peacemaker, trying to calm everyone down, but I'm full of apprehension myself."

Stephanie then saw herself with a lover, in bed, making love, and she used her father as a filter to see how he affected the image. "The moment I see my father, I get this free-floating anxiety, this terrible sense that I have to do something to make the man like me. I feel compelled to really give pleasure to the man I am making love with, to win his acceptance."

Next, she saw herself while keeping her mother in mind. "I feel anger for the man. I still have this compulsion to please, but now I'm doing it begrudgingly. I'm not enjoying myself; I'm not flowing at all with the lovemaking."

The images brought her knee-jerk reactions in which she was a sexy toy for a man, pleasing him because of her unfulfilled need for attention from her father. Then another reaction set in, and she experienced her mother's anger.

Now she sees herself in the present. "With Brian, my boyfriend, I feel free and totally nonreactive. I realize a lot of my problems with Bill were due to his inconsistent moods. I had to tiptoe around his moods, feeling anxious, like there was no place to hide. When I see Bill, I immediately get that sense of apprehension I had with my father."

Next, Stephanie performed an emanation, in which she saw a soul-cleansing wind surround her and a new "her" emerge from the image. "The wind wraps around me, and I feel like I'm growing, getting taller, bigger, stronger. I'm standing in front of Bill, totally detached from his ranting and raving."

She saw another "her" jump out. This is the *real* Stephanie, the one that she was before her parents affected her.

"I'm really powerful! He can't look at me. I see fear in his eyes, and he backs off and crumbles."

"How do you feel?"

"Disconnected from him and with a real sense of myself. I don't want to take care of him. I'm sorry for him, but his actions have to do with the past, and they have nothing to do with me. I'm not going to engage on any level with him."

After Stephanie related her imaging experiences, I asked her how she felt about life. "My business partner retired, and I have to work hard to keep the business afloat and to have the time and money to do the things I want with my son. But I know from here on I am in tune with my deepest self. Part of that fulfillment is reflected in that I now have a relationship with a man who I consider my soulmate. Our lovemaking is very sweet and tender. He respects me as a person. We hang out a lot and just talk. I really feel a freedom with him. This is the first time I feel in command of my life and my sex life has never been better."

26

Eidetic Imaging
The Science of Our Emotions

The modern science of imaging and the name Dr. Akhter Ahsen are synonymous. For most of the second half of the twentieth century, Dr. Ahsen's research and seminal reports about eidetic imaging have resulted in the birth of a science.

> An approach which enables the patient to cut through the mind/body problem and deal with the essential unity, which is himself as a human being.
> *International Journal of Clinical and Experimental Hypnosis*

Today, Dr. Ahsen is the world's leading theoretician of mental imaging and has authored thirty books and hundreds of articles on the subject. He is editor and founder of the *Journal of Mental Imagery*. The journal's editorial staff is an international one, with participants from major United States universities such as Harvard, Stanford, and Yale, plus universities in Britain, France, Japan, India, Sweden, Australia, Canada, and others.

> "Unmatched in the clinical literature…a methodological advance."
> *American Journal of Psychiatry*

Dr. Ahsen did not "invent" eidetic imaging. On the contrary, the concept goes back thousands of years to the ancient Greeks. Dr. Ahsen's contribution, like Freud's with psychoanalysis and Skinner's with behaviorism, was to lay the scientific framework for what had been mere theory before.

"An exciting and ingenious way of getting to conflict areas."
Contemporary Psychology

Dr. Ahsen is both a scientist and a philosopher. Joseph Campbell, the legendary, world-renowned mythologist, said of Dr. Ahsen's epic poem, *Manhunt in the Desert,* that it was "inspired," and he proclaimed that Dr. Ahsen did not *write* the poem, he *received* it.

In his introduction to the book, Campbell wrote: "Akhter Ahsen's *Manhunt in the Desert* is a magnificent poem of powerful images, rendering its legend of spiritual quest and realization, as through a medium of prophetic vision. The work has a quality of revelation about it and should be read by all."

Dr. Ahsen is also the author of numerous technical books encompassing almost every major issue in the field of imaging.

"This exposure to treatment through images was transforming to my view of medicine and my later psychiatric practice. The effectiveness of this type of treatment by Dr. Ahsen was startling in both the extent of its cure and the rapidity and directness which it was obtained through a systematic, definite technique."
Anna T. Dolan, M.D., chief of psychiatry,
Yonkers General Hospital, Yonkers, New York

EIDETICS ARE NO LONGER THE EXCLUSIVE DOMAIN OF THE "GIFTED"

Eidetic imaging is not new to psychology—on the contrary, imaging concepts have been part of the general theory of psychology ever since giants like Freud and Jung began putting their discoveries on paper. In the 1920s, E. R. Jaensch of the Marburg school made an extensive study of eidetics, but rather than exploring the more practical and useful aspects of imaging, he was attracted to the esoteric aspects of it. Jaensch's theories left early practitioners of psychology the impression that only "gifted" persons—writers, artists, poets—and young children were capable of evoking true eidetic images.

Dr. Ahsen, whose research into the science of the mind began several decades ago, discovered that eidetic images were not the exclusive domain of the gifted few, but could be applied in a practical way by most people once they learned the technique. It's true that "gifted" people, ranging from noted authors to world-class athletes, have made dynamic use of imaging to put themselves into the winning zone, but countless others have used imaging to deal with the common problems of relationships and work that so many of us encounter on a daily basis.

> "A unique and important contribution to the scientific study of healing with imagery."
>
> *New Age Magazine*

We can see the external world with our two eyes, but there is an internal world and a mental eye, the *psyche eye*, which we can use to see into our own self. That third eye is the least used of our ocular abilities and for many of us it is almost unused. Imaging uses the psyche eye to peer into our own inner processes, initiating a deep probing, getting past shallow states of mind and peeling away our emotions to reveal new truths as one peels away the layers of an onion.

> "When I began my research on the eidetic image in the early 1950s, it was being studied only in the experimental psychology field, as a vivid, lifelike image of astounding clarity, found among the gifted and in children. As my work unfolded, the image with these characteristics was consistently revealed in all normal people as an expression of positive life, and also connected with areas of emotional conflict, especially with parents. Following this finding, extensive evidence soon emerged showing eidetics to be a system of sensuous life in the psyche which makes the sensibilities of each individual readily available to him in consciousness. This indicated the presence of a vast and

> self-motivated therapeutic potential in the individual's own mind."
>
> Dr. Ahsen, Psycheye, Brandon House. 1977, Preface

THE LANGUAGE OF THE MIND-BODY CONNECTION

A fundamental difference between eidetic imaging and other forms of psychotherapy is that with imaging the person is able to see a situation clearly, experience the emotions connected to it, and have an immediate understanding of themselves by evoking and seeing images of the situation. In traditional therapy, the person explains things verbally to a therapist, who listens and then tries to help the person find the meaning.

Many people using eidetics are not doing so in a psychotherapy context, but are merely interested in increasing their creativity, productivity, and so on.

For example, a woman named Marge is suffering from stress due to an inability to communicate with her male boss. With traditional therapy, the clinician asks the client a series of questions about the situation. Marge uses words to explain her physical and emotional condition, telling the clinician that when her boss raises his voice, she feels tension in her throat and chest and so her fears keep her from replying in an effective manner. During the course of the treatment, the clinician asks Marge to probe back in time for possible historical antecedents for the behavior.

Marge relates that her father frequently yelled at her during her childhood, and the clinician concludes that her core inadequacies stem from these early episodes. The clinician then discusses this interpretation with her and attempts to get her to come to an understanding about her problems dealing with authority figures by relating the situation with the boss to the tyrannical parent.

Thus, in classical psychoanalysis, the clinician asks questions, and the person seeking help verbally responds to the questions, using words to describe feelings and emotions. The clinician then tries to explain to the person the meaning of the responses.

With eidetic imaging, the person is asked to evoke an image of the boss and to examine the image. Because of the link between current fears and the shaping of our personalities, the person may also be asked to evoke an image of home life and parents.

An eidetic image is composed of three aspects: the *image* itself, the *somatic*, or bodily, response to the image, and the *meaning* (insight or new perspective) revealed to the patient as he or she examines the image. Dr. Ahsen referred to an eidetic image as "ISM" because of its structure of Image, Somatic, and Meaning. Most eidetic practitioners use this nomenclature.

Somatic refers to the body's reaction to the image. (I frequently use the word *emotional* as a shorthand term for the bodily reaction the person seeing an eidetic image experiences.) When I asked one person to see an image of his father, he experienced cold chills. Another felt the radiation of warmth. Others feel physical tightening in their chest and stomach. Or a welling up of love. Fear, anger, hate, love, and even ambivalence manifest themselves to us with our bodily responses. We "experience" and "feel" our emotions in a unity of mind and body.

When prime images—eidetic images—are evoked, the person will internally experience the sensations, good or bad, that are stimulated by examining the image and the emotional responses to it. One experiences a revelation of the situation rather than have the meaning of one's internal experiences suggested by a third person. A somatic response to the image by the person is an automatic response from the sensations created while examining the image: the image is created, the body reacts emotionally to it, and from the image and the reaction the person gains instant and automatic understanding about the situation.

This is not to imply that one throws down all of one's emotional crutches and walks after a single eidetic imaging experience. What the person ordinarily gains is understanding of the situation, fresh perceptions, and deeper abilities and strength for dealing with it. Eidetic images bring not just insight to the fore, but also the wholeness that is stored biologically in the person. That is a critical distinction between eidetic imaging and therapies that provide only insight.

In the example we are using, Marge, unable to stand up to her boss, gains insight into the current problem by imaging her father. She gained this insight herself. It is not suggested to her by a clinician but arose spontaneously within her. Also, inside of Marge is the knowledge, in the form of images, of her true power, and this is revealed and made available to her through further images. Eidetics brings forth one's most potent genetic abilities.

> "The central need in psychotherapy has been the development of a true language of emotions which breaks through artificial barriers, a language which is deep, authentic, and everyone can understand and share. The Eidetic is this pictorial language of the mind which has been, in the literature, rightly called a new means of communication, more subtle than verbalization of facts and associative thinking. This pictorial language is highly effective in presenting and elucidating mental issues."
>
> Dr. Ahsen, Psycheye, *Brandon House. 1977* Preface

An eidetic image is a clear, lucid, visual sensation. It is a language of the mind that carries with it bodily excitement in terms of tension, love, or other emotional states. Seeing the image stimulates the physical response and imparts meaning to the observer. It is not simply a memory-image, such as a memory of what an apple tastes like, but a composite of visual and emotional states within us. Commonly, the image that is evoked has been repressed by us and needs to be exposed to our examination in order to deal with current problems. Marge, who was emotionally battered by her father, repressed the image of his haranguing and gained insight into her current problems when she accessed the image and examined it. She also found her true strength to deal effectively with her boss.

Eidetic imaging lends itself well to use in a self-help context. The person using it not only *experiences* the situation but is the *analyzer* of the data as well; the person projects the image and learns from the perceptions. This is one of the fundamental differences between eidetic imaging and classical psychotherapy. With imaging, the patient journeys into self to explore his or her own experiences and to discover unique strengths and powers as he or she works with the images. The image has the power for transformation.

As Dr. Ahsen put it, it's an "exciting invitation to individuals who would like to know more about themselves."

Are images more powerful, more insightful, than words? We've all heard the expression, "A picture is worth a thousand words." An eidetic image is not just a picture, but is a composite of many pictures and situations.

"My words cannot constitute my experience. At best they can describe experiences to me.... Words in this sense are not idols but tools—words are secondary to experience.... In the stream of experience there are little whirlpools which follow a different law of continuous repetition—a particular brand of images—eidetics—represent these parts. In a sense they are like words, static and repeatable—but, unlike words, available to experience.... [An eidetic] is a lifelike visual image which, if attended to, completely absorbs the individual to the exclusion of everything else. Because of this absorption, it concretizes a part of the psyche in lucid detail.... It is an independent self-motivated image that responds to a special kind of handling."

Dr. Ahsen, Basic Concepts in Eidetic Psychotherapy, *Brandon House. 1968 pg.24*

Words are secondary to experience, and the eidetic image is experience itself, not as verbalized to someone else, but as lived and relived, bringing with it revelations about ourselves and solutions to our goals.

Almost as ancient as the Pyramids, yet on the cutting edge of modern psychology, eidetic imaging is an exciting and profound way to rediscover our gifts from the gods.

Appendix of Images

As you have already discovered, imaging is very easy. The process is the same for all images. The fact that one image may have three instructions and another a dozen is irrelevant—you don't have to memorize the instructions. Once you have seen an image, it will still be there when you return to it after reading the next instruction.

It is best that you read all of the instructions prior to beginning so that they will be familiar to you. The instructions are not complicated, and if you need to look at them again while you are imaging, feel free to do so. This should not affect the quality of the image.

Once you are in a good place mentally and physically to see an eidetic image, you are ready to begin. Remember, an eidetic is neither mere memory nor a figment of your imagination. An eidetic is an image recalled from the storage of visions in your mental bank. It may be of the lover you met last month or the parent who died thirty years ago. How long it has been in storage is not relevant.

Keep in mind that the eidetic contains three individual parts: the *image* itself, which can be vague or vivid; the *somatic*/emotional response or feeling that accompanies it, and the *meaning* revealed by it.

The emotional response may be very subtle, or it may be earth-shattering. Sometimes people experience very profound emotional responses—they will laugh, cry, or feel great joy or intense anger. Other times, the response may be much more subtle, such as a slight tension in the stomach or chest, a vague feeling of coolness or warmth, feeling ill at ease, or just feeling good.

Meaning refers to the insight you gain from the image. It is an automatic function of the image, and you do not have to dig for it. If the eidetic is there, the meaning will also be there. Oftentimes, it is an *Aha!* revelation, a sudden insight and understanding that shouts out to you—"So that's what Jack (or Jane) is all about! So that's why I can't do this or that, so that's what he means, so that's why she's so distant. . . ."

Other times, it does not strike like lightning or flash like a neon sign, but is a generalized sense of knowledge in which you gain information about the situation or person you are imaging. The image may be vague or vivid. The important thing is that you understand and leave yourself open to *see* the image, *feel* the image, and gain *insight* from it.

You begin the exercise by finding a quiet place where you can completely relax and can sit or lie comfortably. You may keep your eyes open or closed, whichever you prefer.

Index of Images

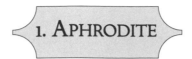

1. APHRODITE

1. See an image of Aphrodite in your mind's eye. Aphrodite is full of love, warmth, sensuality, wisdom, and power.

2. Now see Aphrodite is seeing herself naked in front of a mirror. Her breasts appear sensuous and proportional in the mirror.

3. See her admiring her sensuous breasts. Her breasts are reflective of beauty, power, nourishment, of giving love.

4. There is a sensuous aroma of perfume flowing out of the mirror . . . experience the perfume flowing in the image.

5. See that the perfume expands your awareness of your feminine nature.

6. See that the reflection in the mirror reveals your true feminine essence.

7. See that you have the essence of feminine sensuality emanating from within you.

2. APHRODITE AND FEMININE ANGER

1. Aphrodite is indeed beautiful but she can be angry too.

2. She's absolutely beautiful and she's also totally lovable in her anger.

3. One who says to her "I do not love you" deserves the wrath of nature. She lets loose her ferocious animals on the person.

4. The ferocious animals closely follow her wherever she goes. They are the beautiful decorations around her aura as well as her power symbols.

5. The golden aura around beauty has both truth and power in it.

6. See Aphrodite's ferocious animals attacking someone. See the details of the attack in the image.

7. See a rejecting individual you personally know receive a similar attack in the image.

3. APHRODITE AND HER TEMPLE

1. See Aphrodite all by herself, standing in nature.

2. Aphrodite is nature itself, she is grass, trees, waterfalls, everything.

3. Where is Aphrodite's temple?

4. Her temple is found in three forms: as the simple ground on which you are standing, as love in your heart, and as your own body.

5. What ceremonies are performed in her temple? Loving your own true nature is the high ceremony.

6. What are the gifts she brings to her temple? There's only one gift—freedom.

7. What does she give you in return? Freedom to be yourself. She puts all her powers at your disposal.

4. CO-CONSCIOUSNESS

This technique is used to see yourself through the eyes of someone you are having a problem with or that you just want to know better. You can gain insight and understanding about yourself and how others feel about you.

1. Relax, close your eyes if you like, focus inward, and see an image of yourself in a situation with a person.
   Where are you? See yourself in the environment where you normally spend time with the person (home, school, workplace, etc.).
   What are you doing?

2. See the person. What are they doing? How do you feel when you see that image?
   Let the information unfold. The information will come forward. Don't worry if the image is vague or vivid.

3. Notice that the person is either seeing you or is aware of you. Now see through their eyes . . . they are seeing you.
   Allow the image to unfold.
   Don't second-guess the information coming to you. Just look at yourself through their eyes. Let it unfold like a movie.

What do they see?
How do *they* feel as they see you?
How do *you* feel as you see this image?

4. Now go back to your eyes. See that you are seeing the other person.
   What do you see?
   How do you feel as you see the image?
   Let the images unfold as you go back and forth, in their own way, like a movie. Don't censor them.

5. Once again, see that the person is seeing you. Once again, see through their eyes that they are seeing you.
   What do they see?
   Again, let the image unfold.
   How do you feel as you see this image?

6. Now go back to yourself. See them from your eyes.
   Who do you see?
   How do you feel as you see them?

You can keep doing this, going back and forth, seeing them through your eyes and then seeing you through their eyes. As you do, more and more information will unfold.

The images are holographic, which means that there are stored pieces of information connected in the mind to other stored pieces of information. Keep reversing the process, looking at the other person and at yourself, until you come to an understanding that is valuable to you.

5. COMMUNICATING WITH OUR CHILDREN

1. See you are talking to your child about sex.

2. What do you see?

3. How is the talk going?

4. How do you feel about it? (Notice your feelings and body sensations.)

5. Now see your child as if he or she were a wonderful but lonely stranger—just a teen coping with problems.

6. Does that free you in talking to them?

7. What would you honestly say to this teen from your own experience?

8. Remember, it is his or her body, mind, and soul.

9. See you are free in being honest and discussing sexuality with this lonely stranger.

6. Cosmic Dance of the Feminine and Masculine

1. See the ocean. There are waves washing up on the rocks.

2. See a phallic-shaped rock jutting out of the water.

3. See that the waters are warm and feminine, swirling around the rock, crashing, lapping against the rock, in an endless play.

4. See the waters playing against the rock. The rock is strong. See the waters against the rock; the rock loves the sensual waters. The waters love the erect rock.

5. Keep the protruding rock and warm, lapping waters, in mind as you build a rhythm with your lover.

7. Divine Veil of Mercy

1. See that you are with a primary relationship. How do you feel toward your partner?

2. See your attraction to another person. How do you feel towards them?

3. See you're attracted to two people. Is there ease or confusion or guilt?

4. See you tell the primary of the other. What happens as you see the image? How do you feel at their reaction?

5. See you keep it to yourself. How do you feel?

6. See you keep a divine veil of mercy over the whole situation. Tell it to God and work it out yourself. What is your struggle?

7. See this is your struggle to deal with yourself. Do not hurt other people—resolve it yourself with integrity.

8. Driving the Point Home

1. See that you return to your own house after you visit with the tribe. You are back in your present house.

2. See the house, and tell your husband or significant others that you're leaving the house, but you will not really leave the house, you simply will come and go at will.

3. Also tell your husband or significant others that it's not because you feel less sexuality, but because you have other things to do. You have to teach the young women what to do, tell them what you know about life. You have to teach them your new wisdom.

4. Tell everyone you feel no anger or conflict towards anyone. You simply have a different job to attend to at this time.

9. Emanation

1. Relax and clear your mind. Close your eyes and go inward.

2. See an image of a person in a situation in which you feel stuck, powerless, or that you are unable to deal with effectively.

3. How does the person appear to you?

4. How do you feel as you see the image? Allow your feelings and body sensations to come into awareness.

5. If you could say or do anything to this person, what would that be? Let that desire come into your awareness.

6. Now see a big wind come from the high heavens into the room and surround you. This wind is a gift from the gods.

7. Feel the sensation of the wind swirling and swirling all around you.

8. See another "you" jump out of your image. (For some, it pops right out of their head.) The old you disappears and you become the "new you" in the image.

9. What is this "new you" like?

10. See that this new you does or says whatever it wants.

11. What does it do or say?

12. How do you feel as you see the image? Become aware of your shift to the new you.

13. How is the other person reacting to your new self? In the image, when you see the new you— with your new strengths, powers, or abilities—interacting with the other person, notice how the other person reacts.

14. How does the person now react to you? If the new you that came out does not have enough strength, ability, or power, repeat the process.

15. Now see a wind come from the heavens and surround this new you. Feel the wind, this gift from the gods, swirling around.

16. Now see another you jump out of the "new" you.

17. See how this one interacts with the person.

10. EXPECTANCIES OF MENOPAUSE

1. What is the meaning for you of the word menopause?

2. See the image forming in your mind of a woman in menopause.

3. How do you feel seeing that image?

11. First String of Semen

1. See you are a young boy of twelve or so.

2. See the first string of semen. It is a forerunner of things to come.

3. There is surprise, curiosity, fascination.

4. See colors in it. Let your imagination flow. There are rainbow colors reflected in the semen. How do you feel seeing them?

5. See these rainbow colors are a bridge to an adventurous world. You are venturing out. You are aggressive, exploring, curious.

6. The string is linked to potent and passionate feelings.

7. When the explosion occurs, it is like a being is taken out and put somewhere.

12. Hand-on-Pubis For Women

1. See that you are of your age or much younger and you are lying naked on your back. Your hand accidentally falls on your pubis. See that you feel pleasure and surprise.

2. There's a special sensation like a spark, a warmth.

3. The hands go down, there's a softness and wetness of the lips.

4. Then further down. There is a mystery opening.

5. As the hand touches that area, what is the feeling?

6. Let this soft pubis feeling become a feeling of the whole feminine self.

FOR MEN

1. See yourself at your current age or much younger. You are lying on your back. Your have a pubis superimposed on your genital area. Your hand accidentally falls on your pubis. See that you feel pleasure and surprise.

2. There's a special sensation like a spark and a warmth.

3. The hands go down and there is a softness and wetness of the lips.

4. The hands go down, and there is a feeling of excitement.

5. Then further down. There is a mystery opening.

6. Your hand explores the mystery of it.

7. How do you feel?

8. Let the soft pubis feeling become a feeling of the whole feminine self.

13. HOME

Picture your parents in the house (or apartment) where you lived most of the time with them, the place which gives the feeling of a home. Where do you see them? What are they doing?

1. Picture your parents in the house. Where do you see them? What are they doing?

2. How do you feel as you see the house?

3. See your father. Where is he? What is he doing in the picture?

4. Do you experience pleasant or unpleasant feelings when you see him?

5. Relax and recall memories about the place where your father appears.

6. Now, see your mother. What is she doing?

7. Do you experience pleasant or unpleasant feelings when you see her?

8. Relax and recall memories about the place where your mother appears.

9. Where are your siblings? What are they doing? How do you feel as you see them?

10. Now see yourself in the picture. What are you doing?

11. Does the place give you the feeling of a home?

14. HOT AND COLD

1. See that you are in a sexual situation with another person.

2. What do you see?

3. Who is hot and who is cold?

4. See that the person who is hot becomes cold and the one who is cold becomes hot.

5. Let the image, the interactions in the image, unfold like a movie.

6. Now switch (reverse) the temperatures again so that the one who was cold is now hot and vice-versa. Let the interaction unfold like a movie.

7. Keep going back and forth until you have come to a resolution.

15. IDOL OF LOVE

1. Remember yourself in love, and the person you touched, or who touched you, the first time you realized you were in love with them.

2. Remember the touch and see the person before you again. This is an early image of love. All other images are late images of love, even of this person. There is Cupid in this early image. The god is present here. The more you look at this image, the more it becomes like an icon.

3. See the image. You have bodily feelings and sensations of the god of love being near you. Keep this image at this early stage. Do not bring to your mind later images of this person.

4. Feel your body relaxing, your bones and muscles relaxing. This is Cupid, the god of love in the image. All other human images of love are late images which only contain the problems between you.

16. Imaging with Filters

1. See a problem or difficult situation in your mind's eye.

2. What do you see? How do you feel as you see it?

3. Keep mother in mind and see the problem or situation.

4. What happens in the image keeping mother in mind? Let the image unfold on its own.

5. Now, keep father in mind and see the problem or situation.

6. What happens in the image, keeping father in mind?

17. Infantalizing

1. See you are a woman. You have the wisdom of nature inside you. You have the power to bring a man to innocence and surrender.

2. See your man in the house, office or place you usually interact with him.

3. What do you see?

4. How do you feel as you see him?

5. See what he's doing, both the things that you like and those that you don't like.

6. See that he is being childlike. See him more as a child doing those things.

7. How do you feel toward him?

8. See what you want to do for him. Try to keep this knowledge of him as a child in part of your interaction with him.

9. When you see him in that childlike way, what do you do? How do you feel towards him?

10. See how he reacts to you. If you become irritated by him, try to overcome the irritation. See him as a child.

11. When children act the same way as he does, how do you feel towards them?

12. See you overcome your irritation. You are loving to him, like you are dealing with a child. What happens in the image?

18. INFANTILIZING (MALE)

1. See yourself entering the house you live in, in your usual way. What do you see?

2. How do you feel as you enter the house?

3. See your mate in the house. Those with no mate, see you are in a house or room, such as the office, with a woman you like.

4. How do you interact with her?

5. How does she interact with you?

6. If you have children, how do you interact with them?

7. How do they interact with you?

8. Now see that you enter the house and you're entering with a childlike state of mind. How do you feel. What do you see?

9. See your mate (or woman) and approach her in that childlike state. How does she respond to you in the image?

10. Now see your children and you're approaching them in that childlike state, you're not being authoritarian or rigid. How do your children respond to you?

11. As your woman approaches you, see that you are open to her. You are childlike. How do you feel towards her?

12. Also see that she is in a childlike state too. You're both in that childlike place. There's no resistance. How do the two of you interact?

13. Remember, being overly mature is not the goal of true wisdom.

19. LOVER'S PICTURE IN THE HEART

1. See your lover's complete image standing in front of you.

2. Imagine a window has been carved in their chest and you can see their heart beating there.

3. See the heart beating and describe your lover's heartbeat.

4. Is there any sign of anxiety in the heartbeat?

5. Imagine a picture of someone in the heart. Who do you see?

20. PARENTS' ACCEPTANCE OF YOU

1. Picture your parents standing in front of you again.

2. Look at your parents' skin and concentrate on it for a while.

3. Does it seem to accept you or reject you?

4. How do you feel as you look at their skin?

5. Whose skin gives you the feeling of acceptance? To what degree?

6. Whose skin gives the feeling of rejection? To what degree?

7. Concentrate on your feelings concerning your father's skin.

8. How do you feel as you experience father's skin?

9. Concentrate on your feelings concerning your mother's skin.

10. How do you feel as you experience mother's skin?

11. Which parent usually touches you more?

12. Which parent do you usually touch more?

21. PARENTS' ARMS GIVING

1. Picture your parents giving you something.

2. Which parent extends the hand more completely for giving?

3. How far does the other parent extend the hand?

4. Concentrate on your father giving to you.

5. As he gives, do you experience pleasant or unpleasant feelings?

6. Concentrate on your mother giving to you.

7. As she gives, do you experience pleasant or unpleasant feelings?

8. What does the parent who extends the hand least have in the hand?

9. What does the parent who extends the hand most have in the hand?

10. Which gift feels more precious to you?

22. PARENTS' ARMS RECEIVING

1. Picture yourself taking something from your parents.

2. To whom do you extend your arms completely for receiving?

3. How do you extend your hands to the other parent?

4. Relax and recall memories as you extend your hands toward your parents.

5. Concentrate on how you take something from your father.

6. Describe what you see.

7. Concentrate on how you take something from your mother.

8. Describe what you see.

9. Wish for something from the parent toward whom you feel less free.

10. Wish for something from the parent toward whom you do feel free.

23. PARENTS' BRAINS

1. Picture your parents' brains.

2. Touch each parent's brain and feel the temperature there. Is it cold, warm, or hot?

3. Now, touch your father's brain. What is the temperature?

4. Is touching your father's brain pleasant or unpleasant?

5. Now, touch your mother's brain. What is the temperature?

6. Is touching your mother's brain pleasant or unpleasant?

7. What does hot temperature of a brain mean to you?

8. What does cold temperature of a brain mean to you?

9. What does neutral temperature of a brain mean to you?

10. Which parent's brain do you tend to avoid touching?

24. PARENTS' BRILLIANCE IN EYES

1. Picture your parents standing in front of you.

2. Look at their eyes in the image.

3. Whose eyes appear more brilliant?

4. Are they extremely brilliant, very brilliant or just brilliant?

5. How are the eyes of the other parent in comparison?

6. What kind of brilliance or dullness do your father's eyes have?

7. What kind of brilliance or dullness do your mother's eyes have?

8. Look at the parent with the brilliant eyes. How do the eyes affect you?

9. Look at the parent who has dull eyes. How do the eyes affect you?

10. Relax and recall memories as you look at your father's eyes.

11. Relax and recall memories as you look at your mother's eyes.

25. Parents' Heartbeat

1. Picture your parents' complete images standing in front of you.

2. Image a window opening in each parent's chest so you can see their hearts beating there.

3. See your father's heart beating. Describe its beat and its appearance.

4. Is there any sign of anxiety in father's heartbeat?

5. See your mother's heart beating. Describe its beat and its appearance.

6. Is there any sign of anxiety in mother's heartbeat?

7. In what way do you wish your father's heart to appear different?

8. In what way do you wish your mother's heart to appear different?

26. PARENTS' LEFT/RIGHT POSITION

1. Picture your parents standing directly in front of you.

2. As you look at them, who is standing on your left and who is standing on your right?

3. Now, try to switch their positions. Are you able to switch them?

4. Notice any difficulty you experience when you switch them.

5. See your parents standing in front of you again.

6. Who is standing on the left and who is standing on the right now?

7. Switch your parents' position again.

8. Do you again experience a problem when you switch them?

9. Notice the two different feelings: spontaneous and forced.

10. Notice that you have no control over parents' spontaneous images.

27. PARENTS' PICTURE IN THE HEART

1. Picture your parents' complete images standing in front of you.

2. Imagine that a window has been carved in each chest and that you can see their hearts beating there.

3. See their hearts beating and describe how each parent's heart beats.

4. Is there any sign of anxiety in the heartbeats?

5. See father's heart beating. Describe its beat and appearance.

6. Is there any sign of anxiety in father's heartbeat?

7. Imagine a picture in father's heart. Who do you see?

8. See your mother's heart beating. Describe its beat and appearance.

9. Is there any sign of anxiety in your mother's heartbeat?

10. Imagine a picture of mother's heart. Who do you see?

28. PARENTS SEPARATED OR UNITED

1. Picture your parents standing in front of you.

2. Do they appear separated or united as a couple?

3. Describe the character of the space each occupies. Do the spaces differ in temperature and illumination?

4. Describe your father's space with regard to warmth and light, as he appears alongside your mother.

5. Describe your mother's space with regard to warmth and light, as she appears alongside your father.

6. Do father's and mother's spaces appear friendly or clashing?

7. Which space appears stronger, mother's or father's?

8. Does friendliness between your parents' spaces create security in your mind?

9. Does conflict between your parents' spaces create conflict in you?

29. POSEIDON

1. See Poseidon coming out of the sea. He is coming ashore. He's holding a trident in his hand, the symbol of his power.

2. See his chest. It is strong and broad.

3. See that you become Poseidon. As you move toward the shore, the waves crash against your chest but the force of your power surging forward pushes against them as you move through them.

4. See that you have come onto the shore dripping water.

5. See that your body is hot and the cool air dries your body as you move. Feel the coolness against your warm body.

6. See that there's a temple on a hill. It is the temple of the virgin priestesses.

7. See a priestess in the temple. Feel the heat in your body as you walk towards the temple.

8. See that as you move towards the temple there's a warm fire in it and an intoxicating essence of perfume. Smell the perfume.

9. See that you're drawn to the nectar in the temple, to the priestess.

10. Experience the sexual energy flowing through your body.

30. RAVISHER

1. You know there's such a word as *ravisher.*

2. What does it mean to you?

3. Can you formulate an image of this ravisher in your own mind?

4. What happens?

5. What do you see?

6. What does the ravisher do to you?

7. Do you remember any such person doing this to you?

8. If not, this ravisher image is from your own mind, so part of your mind is doing this to you.

9. What does this part of your mind signify?

10. How do you feel towards this ravisher, which is part of your own mind?

11. See that it is a being. What are the qualities that are coming out of this being?

12. What other qualities does he have?

13. He's turning out to be different than what you thought at the first encounter.

14. See that this is your own mind. How do you feel towards him?

15. All of this is in your own mind. As you come closer to him, you see more there about your own self.

16. The ravisher part is a deeper part of you and there's more desire on your part.

17. Is there a spiritual side to him?

18. He is the spiritual side of your mind that gets alienated. Most people see him visiting as a ravisher.

19. This is a reflection on your own soul.

31. RETURNING TO THE HOUSE

1. See that you return to your own house after your visit with the tribe and teaching the young girls. You are happy and walking around and very busy doing things in your house.

2. Think of your menopausal symptoms. Do you have them or are you free of them after your visit to the tribe?

3. Look at your husband or significant other. How does this person appear in the house? If this person doesn't know or understand your new self, it is clearly a philosophical problem that the person will have to work out. See this person walking around the house, puzzled but also intrigued, ready to envision life from a new angle.

4. See that you can handle interaction with your husband or significant other without losing a sense of balance in the dialogue.

32. SEXUAL ATTRACTION

1. See an image of a person you are sexually attracted to.

2. What do you see?

3. What attracts you about the person?

4. How do you feel as you see the image?

5. See him or her going away. What happens in the image and how do you feel as he or she goes away?

6. See him or her staying around you. What do you see and how do you feel?

7. See that he or she comes toward you. What do you see in the image? How do you feel?

8. What do you spontaneously want to do with the person?

33. STORY IN THE EYES

1. Picture your lover's eyes.

2. Concentrate on the eyes.

3. Do his/her eyes give you any particular feeling or tell you any story?

4. Concentrate on the story in your lover's eyes.

5. Do you experience pleasant or unpleasant feelings as you see the feeling or story in their eyes?

34. TWO HANDS TOUCHING

1. See that you extend your hand to touch the hand of your lover. See how you extend. How do you feel extending? Is there hesitation, fear, trepidation, confidence, joy? What are your subtle emotions as you extend to them?

2. Now see how your lover responds to your extended hand. How do you feel as you see that image?

3. Now see your lover extending a hand to you. How does you lover extend it to you? What are your lover's feelings as they extend a hand? What are they communicating?

4. See how you feel as the hand is extended to you. Do you want to move closer or further apart?

35. USHA

1. See Brahma looking at Usha and admiring her. He is entranced by her.

2. She's pretty, of reddish hue, a dazzling beauty.

3. This is the moment of God's admiration of what he has created.

4. God is entranced.

5. Look at Usha's body. The skin is soft and beautiful, her long hair is flowing.

6. She is light on her feet.

7. Her emotions are erupting with love and lots of passion.

8. If she ran, she would be faster than the wind.

9. After one sprint, she is as fresh as ever.

10. Your own spirit feels like that at times.

11. She is playful and chuckling.

12. She has all kinds of ideas and she innocently expresses them.

13. See Brahma chase her. She turns into an animal form to escape.

14. See he changes himself to the male animal form and runs to capture her.

15. The two stay together for a brief time.

16. See she takes off and runs, turning into a new animal form to get away from him.

17. Brahma realizes that he has been left behind with only the outer shell of her previous animal form, and Usha has taken off in flight having changed into a new animal. He quickly changes into the new form of the male animal, and chases her. See the cycle keeps repeating itself.

18. See he catches her again. They meet for a few brief moments and Usha takes off again in a new form, on and on it goes. In this way the whole world was created.

36. VISIONARY START

1. See a tree blossoming in the spring.

2. See the most beautiful blossoms which stand out on the tree.

3. See the image of the blossoms and experience the fragrance.

4. See that the image is like the beginning of a new vision.

5. See in your mind you have just begun to develop breasts.

6. There's a new feeling and a new vision of your body. Your mind is open. You're excited and awakened to new things but the boys of your age are still unaware.

7. What kind of a vision do you have of the world when you keep your breasts in mind?

37. WALK-AROUND

1. Relax, close your eyes if you like, and see an image of a person that you want insight into.
   If the image is vague, just keep looking. The information will come in sense impressions or feelings.

2. Look at the person from the front. What do you see? Notice their body language, the emotions that you can read on their face, and anything that strikes you. Let the information about the other person simply come to you.

3. How do you feel as you see the image?

4. Now move to the right side of the person and look at the person from that side. As you look at them, be aware of how they look, their body posture, the emotions you sense on that side. What do you see about them? Let all of the impressions come forward.
    How do you feel now that you see them from this side? Pleasant? Unpleasant? Neutral?

5. Now move to the back of their person and observe them from that angle.
    What do you see?
    Again, just let the information come, whatever it is.
    How do you feel as you see them from the back? Pleasant? Unpleasant? Neutral?

6. Now go to the left side of them.
    What do you see? How do you feel?

7. Go back to the front.
    What do you see? How do you feel?

8. Do you have a different understanding of this person than when you started?

38. WARMTH OF PARENTS' BODIES

1. Picture your parents standing directly in front of you.

2. Which parent's body has more personal warmth?

3. How is the other parent's body in comparison?

4. Concentrate on your feelings concerning father's body.

5. How do you feel as you see his body?

6. Relax and recall memories as you concentrate on your father's body.

7. Concentrate on your feelings concerning mother's body.

8. How do you feel when you see her body?

9. Relax and recall memories as you concentrate on your mother's body.

10. Which parent's body do you wish to know more? Why?

39. WOMAN ON HORSEBACK

1. See that you are leaving your present house and you are on horseback.

2. See that you are going to an ancient tribal time.

3. See that you are going to teach the young girls in the tribe your wisdom.

4. They are in their huts and they are shy.

5. You call to them to come out.

6. You go from house to house to gather young girls to go with you on horseback.

7. As you go from house to house you gather more girls and you become an army of free spirits.

8. They like you and you admire their youth and beauty.

9. See that you're teaching them about the world. The teaching is of an essence, not of any one particular subject or its details. The essence of the teaching lives in you.

40. ZEUS

1. See Zeus walking in green pastures.

2. See that he embodies the freedom of the green woods, of nature, of the earth, and the skies.

3. See that the maidens love to be with him. They love his strength and his power, and especially his sense of freedom.

4. The only one who doesn't like Zeus's freedom is his wife Hera. She wants to possess him. She chases all the maidens, punishes them, and makes them go away.

5. See yourself as Zeus walking freely in the green woods and pastures. How do you feel? Experience the freedom.

6. See Hera, who by law, feels she can possess you. Know that possession punishes freedom.

7. See your predicament. Make an intelligent choice.

8. Don't close down totally, or you become totally conventional.